WAR AND CHANGE
IN TWENTIETH-CENTURY
EUROPE

A note for the general reader

War, Peace and Social Change: Europe 1900–1955 is the latest honours-level history course to be produced by the Open University. War and Society has always been a subject of special interest and expertise in the Open University's History Department. The appeal for the general reader is that the five books in the series, taken together or singly, consist of authoritative, up-to-date discussions of the various aspects of war and society in the twentieth century.

The books provide insights into the modes of teaching and communication, including the use of audio-visual material, which have been pioneered at the Open University. Readers will find that they are encouraged to participate in a series of 'tutorials in print', an effective way to achieve a complete command of the material. As in any serious study of a historical topic, there are many suggestions for further reading, including references to a Course Reader, set book and to two collections of primary documents which accompany the series. It is possible to grasp the basic outlines of the topics discussed without turning to these books, but obviously serious students will wish to follow up what is, in effect, a very carefully designed course of guided reading, and discussion and analysis of that reading. The first unit in Book I sets out the aims and scope of the course.

Open University students are provided with supplementary material, including a *Course Guide* which gives information on student assignments, summer school, the use of video-cassettes, and so on.

A318 War, Peace and Social Change: Europe 1900–1955

Book I   *Europe on the Eve of War 1900–1914*
Book II   *World War I and Its Consequences*
Book III *Between Two Wars*
Book IV *World War II and Its Consequences*
Book V   *War and Change in Twentieth-Century Europe*

Prepared by the course team and published by the Open University Press, 1990

Other material associated with the course

Documents 1: 1900–1929, eds Arthur Marwick and Wendy Simpson, Open University Press, 1990

Documents 2: 1925–1959, eds Arthur Marwick and Wendy Simpson, Open University Press, 1990

War, Peace and Social Change in Twentieth-Century Europe, eds Clive Emsley, Arthur Marwick and Wendy Simpson, Open University Press, 1990 (Course Reader)

Europe 1880–1945, J. M. Roberts, Longman, 1989 (second edition) (set book)

If you are interested in studying the course, contact the Student Enquiries Office, The Open University, PO Box 71, Walton Hall, Milton Keynes MK7 6AG.

Cover illustration: British wartime poster, c.1940 (*Purnell's History of the Second World War*, London, Macdonald)

WAR, PEACE AND SOCIAL CHANGE: EUROPE 1900–1955
BOOK V

WAR AND CHANGE IN TWENTIETH-CENTURY EUROPE

*Arthur Marwick, Bernard Waites,
Clive Emsley and John Golby*

**OPEN
UNIVERSITY
PRESS**

Open University Press
in association with
The Open University

The Open
University

A318 Course team

Tony Aldgate *Author*
Kate Clements *Editor*
Charles Cooper *BBC Producer*
Henry Cowper *Author*
Ian Donnachie *Author*
Nigel Draper *Editor*
Clive Emsley *Author*
David Englander *Author*
John Golby *Author*
John Greenwood *Liaison Librarian*

Antony Lentin *Author*
Arthur Marwick *Author and*
                Course Team Chair
Ray Munns *Cartographer*
Bill Purdue *Author*
Wendy Simpson *Course Manager*
Tag Taylor *Designer*
Bernard Waites *Author*
Geoffrey Warner *Author*

Open University Press
Celtic Court
22 Ballmoor
Buckingham
MK18 1XW

and
1900 Frost Road, Suite 101
Bristol, PA 19007, USA

First published in 1990. Reprinted 1992, 1994

British Library Cataloguing in Publication Data
War, peace and social change: Europe 1900–1955.
  War and change in twentieth-century Europe
  1. Europe, history
  I. Marwick, Arthur, *1936–* II. Open University III. Open
  University, *A318 War, Peace and Social Change Course Team*
  ISBN 0-335-09313-2 ISBN 0-335-09312-4 (pbk)

Library of Congress Cataloging in Publication Data
War and change in twentieth-century Europe/Arthur Marwick . . . [et al.].
      p. cm.—(War, peace, and social change; bk. 5)
  Material for an honours-level history course produced by Open University
  ISBN 0-335-09313-2 ISBN 0-335-09312-4 (pbk)
  1. Europe—History—20th century. 2. Military history,
Modern—20th century. 3. Europe—Social conditions—20th century.
4. War and society. I. Marwick, Arthur, 1936–   II. Open
University. III. Series.
D424.W37 1990   940.5—dc20   90-7435 CIP

Designed by the Graphic Design Group of the Open University

This book is set in 10/12pt Palatino by Rowland Phototypesetting Ltd
Bury St Edmunds, Suffolk

Printed and bound in Great Britain by
Redwood Books, Trowbridge, Wiltshire
1.3

CONTENTS

Acknowledgements

Grateful acknowledgement is made to the following sources for permission to reproduce material in this book:

Tables 28.1 and 28.2: Winter, J. and Wall, R. (eds) (1988) *The Upheaval of War: Family, Work and Welfare in Europe 1914–1918*, Cambridge University Press; Table 29.2: Halsey, A. H. (1972) *Trends in British Society Since 1900*, Macmillan, London and Basingstoke/Routh, G. (1965) *Occupation and Pay in Great Britain 1906–1960*, Cambridge University Press; Table 29.3: Goldthorpe, J. (1980) *Social Mobility and Class Structure in Modern Britain*, Oxford University Press; Table 29.4: Halsey, A. H. (1972) *Trends in British Society Since 1900*, Macmillan, London and Basingstoke; Table 29.5: Glass, D. V. (1954) *Social Mobility in Britain*, Routledge; Table 29.6: Carr-Saunders, A., Caradog Jones, D. and Moser, C. (1958) *A Survey of Social Conditions in England and Wales*, Oxford University Press.

INTRODUCTION TO BOOK V

Arthur Marwick

This book, consisting of three units, offers to students and general readers alike an overview of some of the most important issues relating to war, peace and social change between 1900 and 1955: a summary and distillation of what has been contained in Books I–IV, with references to books published since those books were written. For students this book has the essential purpose of helping them to revise for their exam. But it should also be of interest to the general reader as a demonstration of how to start thinking about major historical topics.

The crucial point I want to make here is that historical study is concerned with *thinking* almost as much as it is concerned, inevitably, with the accumulation of information, ideas and interpretations. To students preparing for an exam, the advice is: don't try to cram in new information, but instead *refresh* your memory of what you have already learnt, and *reflect* on the sorts of problems and questions you are now expected to be able to address in an informed and intelligent way. I have long argued that whatever the reading, one concentrates more, and therefore retains more, with a number of questions in mind as one reads (good books, of course, will raise new questions of their own). This book contains a series of topics ('revision topics', you could call them, if that does not seem too limiting), all of which could be discussed on the basis of material and ideas already provided in the first four books of the course, though here some fresh perspectives will be opened up. (In fact, a very good way of revising is to look at 'old' material in a slightly 'new' way.) As in other academic subjects, knowledge in history is constantly being extended and refined: the true student of history looks out for new books in the fields in which he or she is interested (through reviews in *The Sunday Times* or *The Times Literary Supplement*, for instance). Earlier books in this course have stressed that many of the biggest issues are open to varying interpretations, so there is no question of our discussions suddenly becoming out-dated in the light of new publications. Still, students of war, peace and social change should want to know if some striking new contribution on the subject is published. (Open University students will be supplied with a regular *Newsletter* which will convey up-to-date bibliographical information.) In Book V the opportunity will be taken to relate striking new publications to issues which have already been very thoroughly discussed. Clive Emsley, for instance, considers the thesis put forward by Paul Kennedy in his book *The Rise and Fall of the Great Powers: Economic Change and Military Conflict from 1500–2000*, which, unusually for a serious history book, became a runaway bestseller in the United States on its publication in 1988.

For students who wish to go back and revise particular topics, this book will endeavour to provide a guide to where, in earlier books of the course, particular issues are discussed. But the course as a whole consists of far more than just the five books (including this one) of structured teaching material. There are video-cassettes, audio-cassettes, a Course Reader, an *Offprints Booklet* (or, for general readers, references to periodicals), a *Maps Booklet*, two volumes of documents, and a set textbook by J. M. Roberts. Students of history need to demonstrate skills of presenting balanced and well-supported arguments: such arguments should draw upon all the resources available, and Book V seeks to exemplify how this should be done.

To some extent, though by no means entirely, the authorship of the different topics within the three units has been organized so that the writer of the topic is not the same person that wrote the relevant material in the earlier parts of the course. Bringing a fresh approach to bear, as I've already said, can be very fruitful in helping to fix ideas and evidence in the mind. There *are* differences of approach and, far from trying to conceal this, the course has openly recognized such differences. The authors of this final book are not going to tell you that what a colleague wrote was 'wrong': what judgements you finally come to are up to you. But if you are stimulated to *think* more deeply, that is all to the good. 'Unfair', some students cry. 'How can we decide what to believe if even members of the same course team sometimes disagree? How can different perspectives possibly help us when what we want are certainties with which to approach the exam?' Three answers:

1   Though there may be differences of interpretation or approach, there are no differences about the need to argue *rigorously*, and to base arguments on evidence. It is vital that at this stage you should be completely clear about the basic principles of historical study.

2   In fact, a great deal of historical knowledge on twentieth-century Europe is secure and not subject to serious debate. At this stage, it is very important to be sure what *can* be taken as soundly established information and interpretation.

3   Above all, the ideal state to have reached towards the end of a history course is that of thinking like a historian: to be positive where it is proper to be positive, to be aware of differences of interpretation where such differences are soundly based, to be cautious without forever sitting on the fence, to be sceptical, but not cynical.

The basic activity of practically all academic endeavour is the solving of problems. In essence, an exam invites you to join in that activity. If there are different views worthy of being cited (this very much depends on the nature of the question), by all means cite them: but do arrive at a conclusion of your own. If you argue well, and produce such evidence as has been made available to you, then it will matter not a bit that the examiner would, personally, have arrived at a different conclusion.

At this point, students of the course should refer to Book I, Unit 1. Read again the opening section, 'The course title explained', and note the six aims of the course set out on page 10. If the course has been successful, you should now feel that you can meet the course's aims. Book V sets out to provide detailed help and reinforcement for particular topics encompassed within the six aims. It would be a good idea now to turn to the end of Unit 1, 'Conclusion: three themes'. Re-reading this should help to alert you to the kinds of problems and interrelationships you should be thinking about by this stage of the course.

As a final word in introducing this book, I should like to suggest that it forms the summing up of the entire *spirit* in which A318 has been offered. There has been no attempt to insist that war is the most significant agent of change in the twentieth century, or even to insist that war is an important agent of change. The reasons for focusing on war are: (a) that without doubt the two total wars are unavoidable factual phenomena in twentieth-century European history which, whatever their long-term significance, have touched off much argument and debate among historians; and (b) to force you to think about historical explanation, about processes of change and how they are caused. If you believe that structural and ideological factors are far more important than wars, or that it is the decisions of politicians and political parties which really count, then that is fine by us. The important point is that you should arrive at some thoughts on these matters fundamental to the study of history, rather than just seeing history as a vast array of miscellaneous information. If, in some of the individual sections that follow, it is suggested that other factors are in fact much more important than war, do not despair: this course has not so much been about war, as about the *arguments* (pro and con) over the effects of war, set against the many other possible sources of change.

UNIT 28 THE NATURE AND CAUSES OF WAR

(Sections 1 and 2 are written by Bernard Waites; sections 3 and 4 by Clive Emsley)

Open University students of this unit will need to refer to:

Course Reader: *War, Peace and Social Change in Twentieth-Century Europe*, eds Clive Emsley, Arthur Marwick and Wendy Simpson, Open University Press, 1990

1 THE NATURE OF TOTAL WAR

Aggression may well be innate in human nature, but there is nothing 'natural' about war, let alone total war. Here, 'nature' is simply a term for the essential characteristics of the intensified, societal forms of warfare which have occurred in Europe and Asia in the twentieth century. Ian Beckett argues in an article in the Course Reader (War, Peace and Social Change in Twentieth-Century Europe, edited by Clive Emsley, Arthur Marwick and Wendy Simpson) that the wars which are the focus of this course differed in degree rather than in kind from conflicts in earlier periods; and certainly we will find the 'nation in arms', ideological warfare, horrendous battle casualties, and the extermination of civilian populations, as well as other characteristics of 'total war', in wars before 1900. It would seem axiomatic that no political regime can survive defeat in 'total war', and because the existence of the state is in jeopardy, belligerents are compelled to employ the *total* resources at their command in the fight for survival. By these criteria, the American Civil War was a 'total war', at least for the Confederacy. There is, however, a profound and inescapable reason for regarding World War I as a great watershed in history: it was the first general war in which combatant states could command advanced industrial economies and deploy the tremendous potential for destruction that modern technology, mass production and science-based industry gave them.

This section of Unit 28 will analyse industrialized total war firstly by examining what has been called the 'technological' battlefield, secondly by considering the subjective responses of men to the new conditions of warfare they had to endure (responses which became sedimented in culture), and thirdly by dissecting the multi-dimensional process of escalation which led, in both 1914–18 and 1939–45, to the totalization of warfare.

1.1 The technological battlefield

In August 1914, artillery firepower was the chief embodiment of industrialism's potential for destruction. This firepower accounted for the great majority of battle casualties during the war, and its capabilities *and limitations* largely determined the deadlock on the western front between October 1914 and March 1918, when no attack or series of attacks was able to move the line as much as ten miles in either direction (Fuller, The Conduct of War 1789–1961, 1981, p.160). A generation of technical development had greatly increased the weight, accuracy and rapidity of fire by field guns and heavy artillery. (Very roughly, the former were lighter pieces with low trajectory designed to command an 'open' battlefield; the latter were heavier ordnance with a high trajectory used to reduce fortifications and earthworks.) The epitome of field-gun development was reckoned to be the French 75mm Puteaux which, at a maximum rate of twenty-five rounds per minute, could throw a 12lb high-explosive shell or a 16lb shrapnel shell to a distance of 7,500 yards. The best heavy gun was thought to be the German 150mm howitzer. Before the war, the French General Staff had adopted – even been obsessed by – the doctrine of offensive 'open' warfare, to which the lighter, more manoeuvrable field gun was better adapted. The doctrine had led to the French army being seriously under-equipped, both in numbers and quality, with heavy guns.

Exercise   In what way had a generation of technical development *not* improved artillery? ■

Specimen answer   It had not improved its *mobility*. Once armies had left their rail-heads artillery pieces were horse-drawn and manoeuvred by muscle. □

Exercise   I now want you to attempt an exercise which should bring home to you the lethal character of artillery firepower and dispel a widespread misconception about the trench warfare for which World War I is notorious. From the statistics of war-related deaths reproduced below, I want you to say what was the most lethal *period* of the war, and how the statistics help dispel popular misconceptions about trench warfare. ■

Table 28.1   French war-related deaths among men aged 16–60

1914	1915	1916	1917	1918	Total
306,585	334,836	217,502	121,545	225,733	1,206,203

Table 28.2   German war-related deaths among men aged 15–59

1914	1915	1916	1917	1918	Total
240,805	424,123	332,774	310,876	445,776	1,754,354

(Source: Winter and Wall, eds, *The Upheaval of War*, 1988, Tables 1.3 and 1.12)

Specimen answer and discussion   The statistics demonstrate that the period of open warfare *at the beginning of the war* was, proportionately, the most lethal of the whole war. Twenty-five per cent of all war-related deaths among Frenchmen occurred in those five months when France lost far more men than throughout the whole of 1916 – the year of Verdun. The opening months were not quite so lethal for the German forces, for 14 per cent of all their losses took place in 1914; but had their rate of loss during these five months prevailed over a whole year it would have resulted in 580,000 deaths. These casualty rates were testimony to the lethal character of modern firepower in 'open' warfare. The statistics actually mask just how horrendous the initial battles were, for the French casualties were heavily concentrated in August and September. The statistics should dispel once and for all the misconception that casualty rates were highest during the 'classic' confrontations at Verdun, on the Somme and at Passchendaele.

It is worth pointing out, too, that the motorized, mobile warfare of World War II was often less economic in life: in the six months of *Blitzkrieg* on Russia in June to December 1941, the German army alone sustained more casualties than the French and German armies combined during the ten months' battle of Verdun (Terraine, *White Heat*, 1982, p.209).

Armies entrenched to save lives and to exploit the superiority of the defensive – a superiority much enhanced by the use of barbed wire and the deployment of machine guns in ever greater numbers. It was, however, the discrepancy between the weight of firepower and its relative immobility which proved to be the over-riding factor determining the nature of warfare during 1914–18. By early 1915, all the combatants had exhausted their existing shell stocks, but by instituting greater state control of their industrial economies they were able to augment munitions production to meet their artillery requirements. A key part of offensive strategy became the concentration of huge quantities of shell fire on chosen sectors of the enemy front in order to destroy barbed-wire obstacles and machine-gun posts, silence opposing batteries and break the morale of defenders in preparation for infantry assaults. Twenty-three million shells were fired off by the opposing sides at Verdun between February and July 1916 (Cruttwell, *A History of the Great War*, 1934, p.252). The physical devastation of firepower actually hindered its intended objective – the breakthrough beyond the enemy's lines – for it destroyed roads and churned ground into a morass of shell-holes, and made the movement forward of artillery in close support of advancing infantry extraordinarily difficult. Even the brilliant Brusilov offensive against the Austrians on the more 'open' eastern front, in June to September 1916, ground to a halt because the advancing infantry outstripped its supporting guns (Stone, *The Eastern Front*, 1975).

The generals making war in 1914 confronted a new type of battlefield with a 'mental set' more suited to an earlier style of warfare. The military profession had long required technical competence (particularly in branches such as artillery) and administrative efficiency, but in the 'mental set' of the professional officer these were normally subordinate to the traditional martial virtues of heroism and *élan*. French expectations in August 1914 were that victory would be achieved by the superiority of their troops' offensive spirit; though the price of courage might be high, the battle in which it was paid would be swift and decisive. British professional soldiers had similar misconceptions as to the nature of modern warfare, and similarly emphasized moral qualities of discipline and team-spirit over technical competence. Social Darwinian nostrums and fear of 'national degeneration' had led them to a preoccupation with moral fibre to the neglect of the problems of co-ordinating different arms and exploiting the potential of relatively novel weapons, such as machine guns, or the new technology of wireless communication which allowed for decentralized command in battle. One historian has analysed what he describes as:

> . . . the attempt of senior [British] officers to come to mental grips with a war that had escaped its pre-ordained boundaries and structures. It was a war that had 'got away', so to speak, and the groping towards enlightenment of the 1914–18 period was a continuous attempt to overcome prewar conceptions of a simple and understood form of war, and to find new theories or structures to encompass the new technical warfare. (Travers, *The Killing Ground*, 1987, p.224)

If anything, French military conceptions were even more rooted in the past than were those of the British: they fought on 'the sacred soil' of France and believed that the best form of defence was not to yield a foot of ground. In fact, bitter experience was to show that the elastic defence-in-depth, which allowed the enemy to sweep over a thinly held forward zone, and then subject him to counter-attack from a second or third line of defence, was far more effective. The German army began the war with a similar set of misconceptions (when the stalemate set in late in 1914 the Supreme Command ordered densely packed and rigid defences and the re-taking of every foot of lost ground) but it adapted more rapidly to the technological battlefield. Ludendorff's appointment in August 1916 (see below, p.21) led to new regulations setting out the principles of elastic defence in depth which no longer required ground to be held at all costs, and in February–March 1917 he conceived a superbly executed strategic retirement to the 'Hindenburg' defensive line. It ruined the Allies' strategic planning and 'exchanged a bad, haphazard, bulging line for another well-sited, bristling with every device of the most up-to-date defensive art, and much shorter. It was calculated that thirteen fewer divisions were required as trench garrison' (Cruttwell, 1934, p.401).

Why was the German army more innovative and adaptive? Part of the answer is, no doubt, to be found in what has been called its 'institutionalized military excellence', with its high quality staff work and a much greater ratio of well-trained junior and non-commissioned officers than prevailed in the French and British armies. But deeper, societal reasons have been stressed by historians such as Michael Geyer and Norman Stone. They have argued that Germany was compelled towards tactical and strategic innovation because disparity in man-power and resources forced it to follow a policy of 'scarcity', whereas the Allies – with their combined superiority of resources – followed a policy of 'abundance'. Furthermore, Geyer has argued, there was a fundamental change in the war in 1916 with the arrival at the Supreme Command of military technocrats, wedded to a 'machine culture', who espoused the maximum use of arms and the escalation of violence. These men brought a concept of military efficiency which had a certain family resemblance to the concept of industrial efficiency being advocated in America in the early twentieth century. Industrial technocrats preached the optimal use of machines, the functional organization of work, and the adaptation of human labour to the machine. Military technocrats preached the optimal use of weapons, the functional organization of violence, and the adaptation of the soldier to weaponry. Just as industrial technocrats had their ideology of maximizing productivity, so the military technocrats had an ideology of 'total war' (Ludendorff coined the phrase) around which they mobilized the 'inner' home front. The ideology of 'total war' legitimized the resumption of unrestricted submarine warfare (discussed below) as well as far-reaching measures of industrial mobilization. According to Ludendorff, war, 'far from being the concern of the military forces alone, directly touches the life and soul of every member of the belligerent nations. Total war is thus directed not only against the fighting forces, but indirectly against the nations themselves' (quoted in Falls, *The Nature of Modern Warfare*, 1941, p.8. My discussion is also indebted to Travers, 1987, Epilogue).

The generals were not alone in having to shift from one 'mental set' to another as they strove to master the technological battlefield. The men in the trenches had to adjust their attitudes and values, even their sense of self-identity, to their experiences. This adjustment is, I think, registered in a passage by C. R. M. F. Cruttwell, who was both a combatant in and a fine historian of the war. Here he discusses the furious reaction of Allied soldiers in the first German gas attacks and argues that the reaction did not stem from the effects of gas:

> The real explanation of the fury felt by the soldiers, which invested the war with a more savage character, is to be sought elsewhere. In the face of gas, without protection, individuality was annihilated; the soldier in the trench became a mere passive recipient of torture and death. A final stage seemed to be reached in the whole tendency of modern scientific warfare to depress and make of no effect individual bravery, enterprise, and skill. (Cruttwell, 1934, p.154)

More recent scholars have gone further in exploring this shift from a heroic conception of warfare, and the notion of the battlefield as the site of individual courage, to the modern perception of war as nihilistic farce, with the common soldier as one of its victims. Men went to war, it has been argued, expecting a liberation from the stifling routines of industrial society; in 1914 they had 'a traditional, non-economic and romantic vision of what war was and what it would mean' (Leed, *No Man's Land*, 1979, pp.6–7). But the reality of the technological battlefield was a nightmare intensification of industrialism. Many of the articulate in August 1914 envisaged the war as a test of their authentic selves; what they experienced was a form of warfare which concentrated all the 'alienation' felt by men in an industrial culture. Furthermore, the war involved for many not just the annihilation of individuality, but the shattering of self-identity: exposure to bombardment, long periods of sleeplessness, continuous stress – all combined to produce hundreds of thousands of psychological casualties in the combatant armies. Symptoms of 'shell shock', or what we now call post-traumatic stress, included amnesia, hysterical mutism and the hysterical paralysis of limbs. These novel and alienating experiences of warfare later resonated through its representation in literature, art and film, and permanently affected our repertoire of cultural responses to war. In Britain, it has been argued, these responses are shaped by an ironic sensibility formed and conventionalized during the Great War (Fussell, *The Great War and Modern Memory*, 1975).

1.2 The escalating process of total war, 1914–18

Once industrialized states engaged in general war, the reciprocal exchange between the practice of warfare and the evolution of its technique accelerated at an unprecedented pace. The technique of pre-industrial warfare had changed so slowly that the weaponry and tactics used by Marlborough's troops in the early eighteenth century did not differ greatly from those of Wellington's army a hundred years later.

Consider, by contrast, the extraordinarily rapid development of air power in World War I. Real flight, as opposed to mere levitation by balloon, dates from 1900 with the first Zeppelin voyage. In 1914 the 'dirigibles' rather than the aeroplane (first flown in 1903) appeared to represent the future of powered flight: they could travel further distances, lift incomparably greater weights, and could climb higher and more swiftly than any aeroplane, which was scarcely out of its technological infancy when war broke out (Terraine, 1982, p.27). The success of the Zeppelins led to some (such as H. G. Wells in his book *The War in the Air*, 1908) to prophesy the bombing of cities by air fleets, but military professionals had given very little thought to the tactical and strategic potential of air power before the war. Among European armies, the French showed the greatest enthusiasm for aviation and had used spotter planes and dirigibles for reconnaissance and artillery observation in pre-war manoeuvres, but it had only 136 planes fit for use in August 1914 (Terraine, 1982, p.30). Britain had formed a Royal Flying Corps in 1912, and two years later its naval wing was transformed into the Royal Naval Air Service, but the air services were disadvantaged by the absence of an aero-engine industry, and when war broke out had only about fifty militarily useful aircraft between them. The Western Allies were opposed by a German army air service of about 180 planes. In the East, Tsarist Russia had evolved some of the most technically advanced planes of the day, but was unable to match design competence with an efficient supply of spares. It is safe to say that all the General Staffs had the most modest expectations of this new arm of warfare available to them.

The military utility of aircraft was almost immediately underlined when a pilot detected the 'wheeling' movement of von Kluck's army prior to the battle of the Marne. As the war entered its long entrenched phase, aeroplanes quickly established their virtual indispensability as 'artillery scouts'. Initially, the vast cubic space of the air made it seem that planes could perform their function irrespective of enemy aircraft, but the development of fighter planes made the winning of air superiority a crucial task of modern warfare. To achieve this task, the French air service and the Royal Flying Corps (RFC) entered a constant technological race with Germany. When *The Times*'s war correspondent visited the RFC's headquarters in April 1917, he found Major-General Trenchard, its chief in France, to be 'one of the few indispensable men in the Army'. His Corps now had 2,000 pilots and was confronted by a German air service that deployed two single-seater fighter planes to every artillery scout (Repington, *The First World War 1914–1918*, 1920, vol.1, pp.536–7).

Between this point in the war and the armistice, British air power increased tenfold. By November 1918, what was now the Royal Air Force (and the world's largest air force) comprised 200 squadrons and disposed of more than 22,000 aircraft. A separate (but never self-sufficient) medium of war had come into being, and all the tactical and strategic uses of air power had been put into effect, if only experimentally (Smith, 'The tactical and strategic application of air power on the western front', 1985, pp.53–67). Photographic aerial reconnaissance was now an indispensable part of the meticulous preparations for the Allied advances: before the attack at Amiens in August 1918, 38,000 air photographs were issued to the troops to supplement their large-scale maps (Cruttwell, 1934, p.549). Fighter aeroplanes were used in co-ordination with infantry units to harass enemy trenches and bombers were now being deployed as 'aerial artillery'. An even more momentous decision had been taken which helps to expose the 'nature' of total war: the British Air Board had devised a strategy for bombing German industrial towns, not just (or even primarily) to strike at the productive resources of Germany's war economy, but to undermine the morale of its industrial workers and so help bring pressure on its government to end the war. Its plans for a strategic bombing force of 2,000 bombers, each carrying 1,000 lb and with a range that would take them to Berlin and back, were being put into effect when the armistice was signed.

These plans were scarcely 'realistic' – as subsequent history was to demonstrate – but they had arisen as a seemingly more rational solution to the weaponry-based deadlock on the ground than the strategy of remorseless infantry attacks which Haig had pursued so disastrously at Passchendaele. The British government had some evidence to suggest the scheme might work: the raids by German Gotha planes on London and other south-eastern towns in 1917 had produced a panic quite disproportionate to the casualties inflicted, caused widespread absenteeism among munitions workers, and led to a virtually irresistible demand for reprisals. Very few Gothas were shot down, despite the diversion of considerable numbers of British planes to counter them and the setting up of a network of anti-aircraft defences, so it appeared to be an economic means of waging war. Finally, it is worth noting that the adoption of strategic bombing plans was an outcome of the continuing friction between politicians and generals over the higher direction of the war. Setting up an Air Ministry, and creating an air force with an independent strategic role, was a kind of vote of no confidence by the politicians in the military leadership of Haig and Sir William Robertson (Smith, 1985, pp.64–6).

This multi-dimensional process of escalation – involving rapid technological development, the adaptation 'under fire' of tactical and strategic doctrine, and the erosion of conventional moral and political restraints on warfare – is, I think, inherent in the nature of total war between industrialized societies. How and why does this escalation come about? Is it inevitable? Those contemplating the total destructive resources now commanded by the great (and even lesser) powers pray that it can be avoided, devise strategies for 'limited' thermonuclear war, and even analyse past escalations to help the military professionals prepare for the future. (Thus F. M. Sallagar's book, *The Road to Total War*, 1969 – an analysis of the strategic bombing offensive against Germany – was originally prepared as a Rand Corporation Report for the United States Air Force.)

Exercise What other examples of the process of escalation occurring during World War I can you think of? How and why did they come about? ■

Specimen answer and discussion Two spring to my mind: the use of poison gas as a weapon of mass destruction is a prime example of the way science and technology brought an incremental change in the technique of war. However, still more significant in determining the course of the war was Germany's decision to resume unrestricted submarine warfare in February 1917. These are very different examples of escalation because the causal factors behind the first were primarily technical and behind the second political. These examples are worth considering in some detail because they bring us closer to the nature of total war by showing how science and technology interacted with tactics and strategy, and strategy related to politics and economics. □

The German army's first and ineffective use of gas cylinders (in this case chlorine), which depended on the wind to blow the poison on to the enemy, was on the eastern front in January 1915. In April, at the start of the second battle of Ypres, the Germans deployed cloud gas much more effectively, to the immense indignation of Allied public opinion which believed (wrongly) that poison gas was forbidden by the Hague Convention on warfare of 1899. (In fact, the Convention only forbad gas *shells*.) The Germans' resort to gas is easily explained as one apparent way out of the tactical and strategic impasse of trench warfare and an attempt to avoid the horrendous casualty rates which all armies had already experienced. They achieved a considerable tactical success by causing mass panic among French troops – quite unprepared for the new weapon – whose rout left a four-and-a-half mile gap between the French and British forces. Their own success probably took the Germans by surprise, and they have been accused of throwing away an unrivalled opportunity of victory through the premature and local use of the new weapon. But this ignores the technical limitations of gas warfare *at that time*; cloud gas depended on favourable winds and the irregularity of the front line meant that it could only be used locally (a favourable wind in one sector was an ill wind in another). Gas shells, which could be lofted into enemy trenches by mortar fire, were much less dependent on the wind, but were not developed until a later stage of the war. By then, opposing forces had devised counter-measures and engaged in a technological competition to perfect the new means of warfare. The Allies quickly overcame their scruples about a weapon they had condemned as 'frightful': Haig refused to undertake an offensive in September 1915 unless it was preceded by a gas attack. In early 1916, the Germans began to use gas shells in large quantities to deliver the more deadly phosgene and mustard gases. The Allied armies did not yet have gas shells, but after the French had experienced the formidable and lasting effect of 'yperite' shells during the Battle of Verdun, Foch and Pétain pressed for an enormous order of poison gas and smoke shells (Lloyd George, *War Memoirs*, 1938, p.1264).

Gas is an obvious example of the close dependence of 'total' warfare on science-based industry. One might cite several others from 1914–18, perhaps the most important being the development of a new process for synthesizing acetone by Chaim Weizmann, then a chemist at Manchester University. Acetone is required for cordite explosive and before 1914 was normally produced from wood pulp. Britain was heavily dependent on North America for supplies and in 1915 found itself competing with other purchasers for American output. This was a severe drain on dollar reserves; even worse, a survey of supply sources showed that Britain's military requirements for 1916 could not be met. Lloyd George, then Minister of Munitions, was put in touch with Weizmann, who found a solution to the problem by transforming a laboratory method for producing acetone from fermented maize into a manufacturing process. The political pay-off for these scientific services (which saved huge sums) was momentous. Lloyd George wanted Weizmann to be recommended for an honour, but Weizmann was a leading figure in the Zionist movement and asked for nothing for himself but the British government's commitment to the setting up of a national home in Palestine. At this point in the war – the winter of 1916–17 – Britain was anxious to secure Jewish support in neutral countries, especially the USA. For this, and other reasons, Britain supported the Zionist cause, and in November publicly endorsed the idea of a Jewish state in the Balfour Declaration.

Unrestricted submarine warfare was a potential war-winner; paradoxically, its resumption lost the war for the central powers by irrevocably tipping the balance of industrial resources, on which military might depended, against them. The submarine's viability as a military weapon was first generally recognized by naval staffs during the 1890s when the French developed a 'long-range' prototype. The British Admiralty ordered five submarines in 1900. Initially, German naval doctrine had no place for the new weapon which was thought to have solely defensive capabilities, and Germany did not acquire a U-boat until 1906. Despite (or maybe because of) a late start, the submarines they were producing by 1914 outclassed Britain's in range, speed and striking power: they could travel 5,000 miles and were armed with gyroscopically controlled torpedoes. None the less, Germany had merely twenty-eight of this 'overseas' class which would only 'come into their own' during a long war for survival, when the pressures of war drove the powers to step beyond the hitherto accepted limits of war.

The speed of modern warships meant that they could evade submarines, the likely targets of which were merchant vessels protected, in theory, by the international law of naval warfare. This had evolved mainly out of a need for a *modus vivendi* between a combatant's right to blockade the enemy and the neutral's right to trade. Blockading ships who stopped a merchant vessel with contraband goods were expected to place a prize crew aboard and sail it to harbour. The law recognized that the commerce raiders would sink merchant-men, but only after they had been warned and the crew had taken to lifeboats. At the beginning of the war, neutral powers – pre-eminently the USA – wanted the list of contraband goods defined as narrowly as possible, and insisted on their right to trade with states, such as Holland, which were sending goods on to Germany. It was extraordinarily difficult for Britain to blockade effectively and observe the laws of blockade; in fact it violated all of them, but by small steps which kept American antagonism within bounds. The submarine gave Germany the capability of becoming a blockading power, but only by ignoring the international conventions which robbed the weapon of its chief assets. To deploy it effectively meant taking a large step towards extending the war and intensifying its barbarity. As the British Admiral Fisher wrote in a memorandum on submarine warfare in 1913: '. . . it is freely acknowledged to be an altogether barbarous method of warfare . . .', but he added 'the essence of war is violence, and moderation in war is imbecility' (quoted in Terraine, 1982, p.35).

Germany's first submarine campaign started in February 1915 with the intention of bringing pressure on Britain to withdraw from the war by striking at its vulnerability as a state which imported most of its food. The USA reacted sternly to the German declaration that enemy merchant vessels in a 'war zone' around the British Isles would be sunk without warning; in a note of 13 February President Wilson warned that the German government would be held to strict accountability for losses of American life and property. When 128 American citizens drowned with the sinking of the *Lusitania* in May, the American response was so threatening that Bethmann Hollweg and Falkenhayn (then Chief of the General Staff) were able to persuade the navy to limit its campaign. Unrestricted submarine warfare was resumed in 1917 for two basic reasons: first, Germany's leaders correctly identified Britain as the industrial and financial lynch-pin of the alliance, and regarded its continued participation in the war as the principal obstacle to a negotiated peace favourable to Germany. Britain's military strength was growing and, with the sapping of French power, it was clear that Britain would soon assume the main military burden on the western front. Secondly, the appointment of Hindenburg as Chief of the General Staff in August 1916, with Ludendorff as his adjutant, brought to power a duumvirate determined to wage 'total war' and wrest its political direction from the civilian politicians. Bethmann Hollweg's authority was soon eroded, and his ability to resist the resumption of the submarine campaign gravely weakened by a *Reichstag* resolution that in this matter he should be guided by the Supreme Command. At a meeting called by the military leadership on 8 January, Bethmann was presented with a virtual diktat. Unless submarines were unleashed by 1 February, the Supreme Command would no longer assume responsibility for the future course of operations.

The military leadership took a delicately calculated gamble on time and quantities: Britain had to be forced to negotiate before the next harvest and before the USA became an effective combatant. Naval statisticians calculated that less than half British cargo space was available to meet civilian needs and that only 2 million tons of neutral shipping were available to it. By sinking 600,000 tons a month – a conservative estimate – Britain would lose 39 per cent of its available cargo space in five months. The German Admiralty was confident that by August 1917 Britain would recognize its position as hopeless and would be incapable of waging war. But the gamble took insufficient account of Britain's ability to match the escalation of war at sea with effective counter-measures, and the capacity of its shipyards to replace lost tonnage. It took no great prescience to recognize – as Bethmann Hollweg's secretary did in his diary – that the resumption of the U-boat campaign was a 'fatal mistake' (quoted in Craig, *Germany 1866–1945*, 1981, p.381). The German ambassador in Washington had consistently warned that the USA would declare war and that its resources were inexhaustible. We now know, too, that the decision rescued the British government from a desperate financial situation. By January 1917 its lines of credit on Wall Street were exhausted; there would be no further loans to purchase the American munitions on which the Allies were heavily reliant and Britain had already liquidated all the dollar assets of its own citizens. Furthermore, once the USA was a combatant it discarded all its erstwhile scruples about neutrals' rights and helped enforce a ruthless, world-wide embargo on trade with the central powers.

1.3   The escalating process of total war, 1939–45

If we were to ask what aspect of World War II in Europe most expressed its 'total' character, many would point to the virtual destruction of European Jewry as the quintessence of violence unlimited by moral or political restraint. Others might reply that the culmination of 'total war' between true belligerents was the barbarization of warfare on the eastern front, where Hitler ordered the execution of all political commissars and death in captivity was the fate of millions of prisoners of war (both Soviet and German). The fact that my discussion in this section focuses on the Allied strategic bombing campaign against Germany does not reflect any disagreement with either of these replies. I do, nevertheless, regard the strategic bombing offensive as one aspect of the 'totalization' of war, a process by which weaponry came to be exploited without moral or political restraint: British bombers began the war with the harmless, though untidy, pastime of littering German streets with incitements to revolt. They ended it with the indiscriminate killing of hundreds of thousands of civilians and the destruction of cities of negligible military significance. They created a crucial precedent for the fire-bombing of Tokyo and other Japanese cities, and then for the atomic bombing of Hiroshima and Nagasaki. The bombing of densely populated areas finally eroded the imaginary line between the combatant and the civilian which had once figured on the mental map with which Europeans went to war. It 'brought the realities of war home to more civilians than any other conflict for several centuries' (Bond, *War and Society in Europe, 1870–1970*, 1983, p.191). Since we have already analysed the origins of the concept of strategic bombing, it seems apposite to trace the steps by which it became a reality.

As we have seen, the idea of the independent, strategic use of air power grew out of the weaponry-based deadlock of World War I. In a memorandum of 1928 to his fellow service chiefs, Trenchard (now Chief of the Air Staff) advocated the use of air power to attack the enemy's *sources* of power, instead of being frittered away in an effort to defeat hostile armies and navies.

> It is not . . . necessary [he argued] for an air force, in order to defeat the enemy nation, to defeat its armed forces first. Air power can dispense with that intermediate step, can pass over the enemy navies and armies, and penetrate the air defences and attack directly the centres of production, transportation and communication from which the enemy war effort is maintained. (Quoted in Sallagar, 1969, p.10)

Air power, he claimed, could have the dual effect of undermining the enemy's *ability* and his *will* to resist by striking at industrial targets in populous areas. Trenchard accepted that indiscriminate bombing of a city for the sole purpose of terrorizing the civilian population was illegitimate, but justified terrorizing men and women munition workers into absenting themselves from work. He saw the demoralizing effect created by bombing in such circumstances as the inevitable result of a lawful operation of war – the bombing of a military objective. Trenchard's views were opposed both on grounds of inhumanity and illegality, but perhaps more importantly with the arguments that geography made Britain a more exposed target in unrestricted air warfare than its potential enemies, and that its initiation would encourage unrestricted submarine warfare. Trenchard brushed both moral and strategic arguments aside:

> If restriction were feasible, I should be the last to quarrel with it; but it is not feasible. In a vital struggle all available weapons have been used and always will be used. All sides made a beginning in the last war . . . there is not the slightest doubt that in the next war both sides will send their aircraft out without scruple to bomb those objectives they consider the most suitable . . . we [must] accept this fact and face it. (pp. 12–13)

These assumptions became widely accepted during the 1930s. The Air Staff were expecting 165,000 civilian casualties from bombing in the first twenty-four hours of war and 35,000 daily for several weeks thereafter, and there were predictions that 3 to 4 million people would be driven out of London into the surrounding open country. Initially it was thought that the only strategy to meet the threat was one of deterrence, but in the two years preceding the outbreak of war there was a greater appreciation that the bomber would *not* always get through, and a much higher priority was given to the development of Fighter Command.

Fewer periods of warfare can have been more 'limited' than that in the West in 1939; Britain did not suffer a military fatality until 9 December. There was restraint on both sides in the air as well as on the ground. The opposition of France, who had more to fear from reprisal air attacks, ruled an Allied strategic bombing campaign out of the question in 1939 and Hitler, who had no concrete plans or preparations for a major war with France and Britain, ordered his forces in the West to go on the defensive. He had given little thought to the strategic bombing of the West (for which the *Luftwaffe* was not equipped) and prohibited air attacks on civilians without express permission. Even in Poland the *Luftwaffe* was instructed to confine air attacks to legitimate tactical targets, partly in response to the appeal by President Roosevelt to refrain from bombing civilians. The actual bombing of Warsaw seemed to be a flagrant rejection of the American appeal (and in terms of courting international opinion it was a grave error to celebrate the action in the propaganda film *Baptism of Fire*), but Warsaw was a defended city and aerial bombardment was used in support of ground forces. The evidence is that the Germans *did* restrain the *Luftwaffe* in Poland. Nevertheless, alleged brutalities had a lasting effect on the British, who considered themselves freed from the restraint to which they and the French had agreed in response to Roosevelt's appeal. However, throughout the winter of 1939–40, Bomber Command contented itself with the futile leaflet campaign which appears to have convinced German public opinion that the British and French were not serious antagonists. There was, too, limited war with the West at sea, for at this time Germany observed the international conventions prohibiting the sinking of enemy merchant vessels without warning.

A highly significant step in the escalation of the air war was the German bombing of Rotterdam on 14 May during the assault on the Low Countries and France in 1940. The first reports of 30,000 deaths greatly exaggerated the true number (980), and few were to know that the bombing was originally intended as a tactical operation in support of ground troops. The effects on a congested city of tactical bombing were indistinguishable from the effects of bombing intended simply to terrorize. The exaggerated reports and the misinterpretation of German intentions led the new British Coalition Cabinet to take the far-reaching decision to approve an air strike on targets in the Ruhr. These first night raids were dismal failures: the bombers were 'light', wholly inadequate machines, not yet equipped with electronic aids for night navigation, and they rarely came within five miles of their targets. None the less there was a feeling that 'the gloves were off'. A technological race began to develop radio location systems and 'pathfinding' techniques, but for most of the war moonlight was essential if the bomber crews were to find their targets, which had to be conspicuous enough to be found at night and large enough so as not to require a high degree of bombing accuracy. The logic of these operational limitations meant that 'area' targets (that is, densely populated towns and cities) were selected, although in the first instance the Air Staff maintained the fiction that the bombers were attacking 'military objectives' (such as marshalling yards, power stations and factories) in towns and cities. The inevitable civilian casualties were merely a by-product of the pursuit of military objectives.

Exercise   The moral objection to area targeting was by no means the only one raised. What other objections can you think of? ■

Specimen answer   The strategy was, and continues to be, criticized in terms of its *cost-effectiveness*. A new departure in the conduct of war occurred with the attempt to calculate the effectiveness of military operations using scientific methodology. The armed services created Operations Research teams, whose statisticians analysed the probable consequences of various courses of action. As a result of one such exercise, it was reckoned that bombing capability would be more economically deployed protecting merchant shipping from submarines – in which role aircraft losses were few and the returns on their use high. Now that we appreciate the British army's chronic inferiority in armour, we might also argue that some of the industrial capacity that went into making heavy bombers would have been better employed turning out tanks. In the event, the scientific arguments against area bombing were over-ruled by the political arguments in its favour. □

The political arguments varied, of course, according to the stage of the war and Britain's overall strategic position. In the autumn of 1940 powerful domestic pressure to take the war to German cities arose from the blitz on London and Coventry. The attacks on London were probably triggered accidentally by German bomber crews unloading their bombs after failing to reach their intended target – airfields – during the Battle of Britain. Whatever the case, Churchill authorized an attack on Berlin on 25 August, to which the Germans responded by opening the blitz. One of Hitler's motives may have been to distract attention from his failure to launch an invasion of Britain. Mass daylight assaults on the capital were launched on 7 and 15 September, and were followed by regular heavy night bombing throughout the autumn and early winter. Casualties in London were considerable: in 1940, 13,596 were killed, and 18,378 hospitalized with severe injuries. Though these were far lighter than had been expected before the war, or than German cities were to suffer, they were unprecedented and aroused a huge clamour for reprisal raids.

In addition to responding to this domestic pressure, the government had to make certain delicate calculations about American opinion. By the end of May 1940, American participation in the war was Britain's sole hope for the future, but this participation appeared to Britain to depend a great deal on the re-election of Roosevelt who had not yet decided to run for a third term of office. Had Britain sued for peace with the fall of France, it is unlikely that Roosevelt would have sought re-election. As long as Britain held out, and as long as there remained a chance that German victory might be prevented, Roosevelt would stay in the electoral race. Bombing was the only means Britain had of demonstrating its resolve to engage militarily with Germany. Moreover, in the autumn of 1940 the American administration moved towards a war footing (it introduced selective military service in October) and did as much as it could to assist Britain while maintaining formal neutrality. Many Americans were violently hostile to the Axis powers but deeply suspicious that Britain would use American blood and money to pull the chestnuts of its empire out of the fire. In other words, to be certain of American participation, Britain could not afford to appear supine in the war with Germany.

A final set of political calculations concerned German morale and the German economy: British strategists believed that the Nazi regime enjoyed little popular loyalty and reasoned that morale would break more easily in a totalitarian state. From erroneous intelligence, they argued that Germany's economy was much more overstrained than was in fact the case. These assumptions were eventually embodied in a strategy (advanced by Lord Cherwell, Churchill's chief scientific adviser, in March 1942) of 'de-housing' a substantial proportion of Germany's urban population by aerial bombardment with the aim of 'breaking the spirit of the people'. Whatever else we think of this strategy, it is testimony to the way total war brutalizes all combatant states.

The chain of events by which Britain arrived at this strategy was complicated. Throughout 1941, the bombing of Germany may have appeased domestic opinion and helped convince the Americans that Britain was serious, but it did precious little else. Bomber Command operated under a directive of October 1940 which struck an uneasy compromise between two conflicting aims: it was to carry out the precision bombing of oil installations (identified as a key weakness of the German economy) *and* undertake area bombing in order to break civilian morale. It was equipped for neither: precision bombing required navigational aids and techniques which did not yet exist, while to be in any way effective area bombing demanded great concentrations of planes in time and space which Bomber Command could not yet muster. Fire and other emergency services could deal with the effects of bombing dispersed over time and space, but saturation bombing started self-sustaining fires, disrupted water supplies, and made roads impassable. Only when this concatenation of blows fell on a city's infrastructure did area bombing achieve its intended material effect, and even then it did not achieve its intended effect on morale. Throughout 1941, evidence accumulated from photographic reconnaissance of Bomber Command's chronic failure to hit precision targets. This was very disillusioning, and prompted calls to abandon the offensive altogether. In the event, it led to the single-minded pursuit of the second aim – the destruction of civilian morale. A memorandum from the Chiefs of Staff of July 1941, which discussed the conditions in which Britain could contemplate a resumption of the land war against Germany, had stated that before an invasion:

> We must first destroy the foundations upon which the [German] war
> machine rests – the economy which feeds it, the morale which sustains it,
> the supplies which nourish it and the hopes of victory which inspire it.
> Then only shall we be able to return to the continent and occupy and
> control portions of his territory and impose our will upon the enemy . . . It
> is in bombing, on a scale undreamt of in the last war, that we find the new
> weapons on which we must principally depend for the destruction of
> German economic life and morale.

The memorandum went on to give bombers first priority in production. Not until
the early months of 1942 were the debates over the higher direction of the war
finally resolved into a decision to put the memorandum's strategy into effect. A
new political consideration was the desire to put heart in the Russians. Furthermore, Bomber Command wanted to take maximum advantage of a radio navigation device (GEE) within the six months Germany would require to learn to jam it.
Finally, the appointment of Sir Arthur Harris as Chief of Bomber Command
brought a commander dedicated to the area bombing strategy and willing to
exercise considerable initiative in executing it. It was *not* Harris's personal
strategy. The Air Staff's directive of February 1942 – under which Bomber
Command operated for most of the rest of war – stated: 'The primary object of
your operations should now be focussed on the morale of the enemy civil
population and, in particular, of industrial workers.' As we have already noted
(p.25), this strategy became linked with Cherwell's argument that, given sufficient bombers, the RAF could 'de-house' a third of Germany's urban population.

The raids launched under Harris's command soon showed what could be done
by concentrations of force: in March almost half of Lubeck was destroyed; in April
Rostock was extensively damaged in raids which had the valuable by-product of
destroying the city's Heinkel factory; in May more than 1,000 bombers were
assembled for an attack which reduced Cologne to a blazing ruin, wrecked its
railway marshalling yards and rendered 45,000 people homeless. The raids were
achieving – or appeared to be – the general disruption of industrial activity (by
striking at a city's infrastructure and creating mass absenteeism among its
workforce) which Harris regarded as the primary objective of area bombing. They
had their greatest effect where prolonged hot weather and a considerable volume
of inflammable material created fire-storm conditions after incendiary bombing.
In July and August 1943, these conditions were met at Hamburg, where the
fire-storm killed two-thirds as many people as did all the German raids on Britain
throughout the entire war, and a million residents were driven to seek refuge
outside the urban area (Wright, *The Ordeal of Total War*, 1968, p.179). Albert Speer,
who had been appointed Minister of Armament Production in early 1942, was
later to testify that had destruction on this scale been repeated in four or five other
cities the war would have come to a rapid end.

Speer's claim is often cited by those defending the rationale of area bombing,
but we must treat it with some reserve. Speer also testified that the American
daylight raids on specific industrial targets 'were by far the most dangerous. It
was in fact these attacks which caused the breakdown of the German armaments
industry' (quoted in Wright, 1968, p.182). It has been calculated that, in 1943,
bombing reduced Germany's total production by only about 9 per cent, and in
1944 by 17 per cent; and less than half of this reduction was in armaments (ibid).
Bombing's most signal contribution to victory was the destruction of Germany's

oil installations in September 1944 – which grounded the *Luftwaffe* and caused havoc with transport – but this was a triumph for precision targeting and only came about after the Allies had established day and night command of the air.

Furthermore, we must bear in mind that there was a fortuitous element to fire-storm conditions which were only to be repeated in Europe when successive night and day raids incinerated Dresden. The city was swollen with refugees fleeing from the east, so civilian deaths were appallingly high, although the destruction was so terrible that they could not be reliably estimated. Rightly, photographs of Dresden have become thickly textured with meaning – for we see not just ruins, but gratuitous destruction and the degradation of the Allied cause – and have entered that repertoire of cultural images which represents for us the 'totality' of twentieth century war. It was not, alas, the end of the bombing offensive: in March 1945 German targets received a weight of bombs almost equal to that dropped by Bomber Command during the entire year of 1943.

We noted earlier how the experience of trench warfare interlaced with its representation in literature and other cultural forms to produce a particular way of remembering World War I. Strategic bombing has made a similar – though perhaps slightly less significant – contribution to modernist sensibility towards war. Almost as soon as hostilities were over in Europe, powerful voices were declaring that the RAF's offensive was an enormous waste of Britain's stretched resources which, with its costly expenditure of machines and highly trained air crews, had inflicted as much harm on Britain as on Germany. This judgement came on top of an official shunning of Bomber Command and its leader; the former was denied the campaign medal which its courage and losses certainly merited, the latter the public honours given to lesser commanders. The controversy has seeped into philosophical discussion of the morality of war; in a notable study, Michael Walzer argued that while the refusal to honour Harris and his men was itself morally ambiguous, it 'at least went some distance towards re-establishing the rules of war and the rights they protect' (Walzer, *Just and Unjust Wars*, 1980, p.325). One of the indirect consequences of the moral revulsion against strategic bombing was to give a fillip to the campaign for nuclear disarmament in the 1950s and 1960s – for experience seemed to show that once aerial warfare began the process of its escalation was irresistible; even the best-intentioned powers would slaughter civilians without compunction. Better, therefore, to disarm now. Finally, it is worth noting how aerial bombing has contributed to particularly powerful fictional images of war. If – as seems plausible to many – bombing civilians was morally dubious, more harmful to the assailant than the defender, and took a terrible toll on air crews, then the whole enterprise was a black farce. It is the image of war in Joseph Heller's *Catch 22* or Kurt Vonnegut's *Slaughterhouse 5*.

2 THE CAUSES OF WAR

In this series of books you have studied the origins of two wars, and it is quite likely that Open University students will be asked in the exam to compare and analyse their causes. This section will, I hope, help them to do so. At the same time, it will review some of the methodological issues which have formed a sub-theme of the course.

Exercise   What preliminary distinctions should we make when comparing the causes of different wars? ∎

Specimen answer   It is important to distinguish between *immediate* causes, which occasioned the outbreak of a particular war, and longer-term causes. Furthermore, many have argued that there were general causes of war which made international conflict a recurrent feature of the European state system between the late fifteenth century (when the system originated) and 1945, and we shall consider some of these arguments shortly. □

Exercise   What were the immediate causes of war in August 1914 and September 1939? What was common to the expectations of the men responsible for the outbreak of war on each occasion? ∎

Specimen answer and discussion   Identifying immediate causes is not necessarily a simple matter: was the assassination of Archduke Ferdinand on 28 June 1914 the immediate cause of the outbreak of a general European war? Or was this simply seized on by Austria-Hungary as a pretext for dealing 'once-and-for-all' with Serbia, and should we locate the immediate cause in the Austrian ultimatum to Belgrade issued (after Berlin had given its 'blank cheque') on 23 July? Most would argue the latter, but would not consider Austria to have been the prime mover during the July crisis. The documentation assembled by Immanuel Geiss shows conclusively that the German government bore responsibility for escalating the crisis and deliberately risking general war (Geiss, *July 1914*, 1972). Shortly after the outbreak of war, when Austria-Hungary required German military assistance against the superior Russian armies, the Hungarian prime minister advised the Austro-Hungarian foreign secretary to tell Berlin that 'we took our decision to go to war on the strength of the express statements both of the German Emperor and the German Imperial Chancellor that they regarded the moment as suitable and would be glad if we showed ourselves earnest' (Fischer, *Germany's Aims in the First World War*, 1967, p.88).

The immediate cause of war in 1939 does not appear to present the same problems: the German attack on Poland (August 31) was for Britain and France, both guarantors of Polish independence, the *casus belli*. It is worth emphasizing, however, that it was they who took the decision to turn a limited war into a *general* war by issuing ultimata to Germany. In explaining the outbreak of World War II we have, therefore, to accord as much attention to the calculations of the British and French governments as we do to Hitler's miscalculations.

The actual war that ensued in both 1914 and 1939 was quite different from the war expected by the men responsible for its outbreak. In August 1914 nearly everyone thought the war would be over within six months, if not by Christmas, and the delusion must be considered part of the atmosphere that caused the war. The men of 1914 were not exceptional in deluding themselves, for similar misjudgements had been made before the start of many previous wars (Blainey, *The Causes of War*, 1973, p.40). In late August, early September 1939, Hitler thought the conflict with Poland could be isolated while Britain and France thought Nazi Germany could be defeated by blockade and economic warfare. On both occasions, false expectations contributed to the outbreak of conflict. □

The longer-term and general causes of war are much more difficult to establish than the immediate. My intention is to help you analyse them by reconsidering the course material in the light of some theoretical analysis of international conflict. Now theoretical analysis is abstract thought in which we scrutinize concepts and hypotheses, and you may well ask 'What good is abstract thought to me as a student of the two world wars? These were unique events brought about by flesh and blood individuals. The way a historian understands them is by using the available evidence to construct a narrative which displays the unfolding of those events in time. The ideal account is that where the fullest documentation makes for a seamless sequence of events. We know why World War I broke out when we know how things followed from one another.'

Exercise   Whose views on the origins of World War I do these sentiments echo? ■

Specimen answer   A. J. P. Taylor's. If you were unsure re-read the extract from *War by Timetable* in
and discussion   Book I, Unit 6, pp.217–8. □

These views are quite widely shared among historians, particularly those identified with the so-called revival of narrative history, but I do not find them persuasive. We should note first that if the two world wars were literally unique events, then there would be no point in trying to compare their causes because 'unique events' are by definition incomparable. Comparison is equally futile if the historian's ideal account is the seamless narrative, for in this narrative World War I is part of the sequence that led to World War II. To attempt to compare the causes of the two would be like performing *Hamlet* in two halves and then comparing the dramatic unity of each half. Real comparisons – our narrative historian will tell us – can only be made of coexistent independent entities, and the two world wars certainly don't fulfil these conditions.

But, of course, these wars were not unique events in the full sense of the word: they fall into a class or category of historical phenomena. As the philosopher Patrick Gardiner remarked: 'The attribution of the term "unique" to any event or thing logically presupposes prior classification' (Gardiner, *The Nature of Historical Explanation*, 1952, p.43). We describe this category with a finely shaded vocabulary: limited war, general war, total war, lightning war, undeclared war, defensive war, a just war, unprovoked aggression – these are some of the concepts we use to discriminate between events classed as 'war'. These discriminations are indispensable for interpreting the evidence available to historians which is always evidence *for* something and never a historical fact in itself. Furthermore, these discriminations are intrinsically comparative – the concept of limited war implies a state of limitless war which we can conceive even if it has never actually occurred – and we could not make these discriminations without at least implicit historical comparisons. (Thus, when the term 'limited' is applied to eighteenth-century European warfare it is usually by contrast with the seventeenth-century Thirty Years' War and the French Revolutionary and Napoleonic Wars.)

Moreover, though narrative is the device a historian chooses to give an intelligible account of the past, we must not be fooled into thinking the device is inherent in the events so described. Narratives (more especially seamless narratives!) are literary and rhetorical artefacts, the effects of which depend upon the selection and 'pointing up' of events. In constructing his or her narrative, the historian similarly has to 'point up' events and attach to certain actions a significance (for the future) of which the actors themselves could not have been wholly aware. Alternatively, the historian may have to deny significance to certain events if they disrupt the overall shape of his or her narrative.

My point is not to deride narrative – for nearly all history seeks to establish sequentiality, whether it be of long-persistent structures or declarations of war – but to emphasize that establishing what followed from what is an achievement of the historian, not a *datum* in the documents.

Exercise This may seem a bit remote from the causes of the world wars, but think back to the historiographical controversy surrounding each, and ask whether you have encountered certain events or evidence being 'pointed up' or 'played down' in the interest of the narrative coherence of an historian's account of war origins. ■

Specimen answer I can think of two: Fritz Fischer placed a particular significance on the 'War Council' of 8 December 1912 in reconstructing the sequence of events which led to the outbreak of general war in August 1914 (something discussed in Book I, Unit 6 and the article by Mommsen in the *Offprints Booklet*). By contrast, A. J. P. Taylor chose to minimize the significance of the Hossbach Memorandum in his account of the origins of World War II because (as Norman Rich rightly says in an article in the Course Reader) this evidence did not fit Taylor's *theories* of the war's origins. (If you are unclear about the controversy surrounding Taylor's handling of the Hossbach Memorandum, you should re-read Book III, Unit 20, pp.251–2.) □

The concepts historians use are not, unlike the mathematician's, purely theoretical constructs. They refer to real events, and they are modified and adapted to the stream of human experience. The notion of 'a just war' is an ancient one, but the doctrine can be, and has been, defended and modified in terms of recent history. 'Genocide', by contrast, was a term coined in 1944, but we now use it to refer to instances of racial extermination which long pre-dated Hitler's 'Final Solution'. Historians' concepts are bounded on one side by their internal, logical coherence and on the other by their empirical validity. A concept which has no valid correspondence with human experience is of no use to historians, although – as the history of racial exterminations indicates – our conceptual vocabulary will often lag behind the experiences it defines. The abstract tasks of refining that vocabulary, considering the logical relations between its terms, and framing hypotheses, are not ends in themselves, but means of critically evaluating evidence and fashioning that evaluation into an explanation of the past.

2.1 Historical causality

Before we go on, it is worth asking what historians do when they specify the cause or causes of any event in history. There is no single answer to that question but we can discern in philosophical debates about historians' methods two broad schools of thought. (Arthur Marwick has at several points referred to these debates.) One stresses that the subject matter of history (and other humanistic disciplines) differs from that of the physical and natural sciences because it is concerned with meaningful action. According to this school, historical events are the 'external' expression of the intentions, wishes, desires, and so on, of social actors, and the historian has specified the cause of an event when he or she has managed to reconstruct or 'relive' those intentions. In a technical sense this is an 'idealist' theory of historical explanation; its best-known exponent is R. G. Collingwood, who provides the following example:

When a historian asks, 'why did Brutus stab Caesar?' he means 'what did Brutus think, which made him decide to stab Caesar'. The cause of the event for him means the thought in the mind of the person by whose agency the event came about: and this is not something other than the event, it is the inside of the event itself. (Collingwood, 'Human nature and human history', 1936)

Exercise   This is a much trickier exercise than it looks. Imagine you have been asked to explain the outbreak of general war on 3 September 1939, and you have come across the following passage from Hitler's speech to his Commanders-in-Chief on 22 August 1939 when he justified the forthcoming attack on Poland. I want you to say why it should lead you to raise important objections to Collingwood's theory.

Now it [the planned attack on Poland] is also a great risk. Iron nerves, iron resolution.

The following special reasons strengthen my idea. England and France are obligated [i.e. by their guarantees to Poland], neither is in a position for it. There is no actual rearmament in England, just propaganda . . . The English speak of a war of nerves. It is one element of this war of nerves to present an increase in armament. But how is British rearmament in actual fact? The construction programme of the Navy for 1938 has not yet been filled. Only mobilization of the reserve fleet. Purchase of fishing steamers. Considerable strengthening of the Navy, not before 1941 or 1942.

Little has been done on land. England will be able to send a maximum of 3 divisions to the continent. A little has been done for the air force, but it is only a beginning . . .

England does not want the conflict to break out for two or three years . . . England's position in the world is very precarious. She will not accept any risks.

France lacks men (decline of the birth rate). Little has been done for rearmament. The artillery is antiquated. France does not want to enter this adventure . . .

The enemy had another hope, that Russia would become our enemy after the conquest of Poland. The enemy did not count on my great power of resolution. Our enemies are little worms. I saw them at Munich. (Reproduced in Overy, *The Origins of the Second World War*, 1987) ∎

Specimen answer and discussion   At first blush, this document might appear to be precisely the type that vindicates Collingwood's theory of historical explanation, but in my view it serves to expose its fundamental flaw. You have been asked to explain the outbreak of general war, and I think you would agree that the document is good evidence for the theory that a general war resulting from the German attack on Poland was something Hitler *did not expect and did not intend*. Like his contemporaries, Chamberlain and Bonnet, he acted in the light of imperfect knowledge and of expectations we now know to have been mistaken. On the basis of evidence such as this, we can argue that the outbreak of general war on 3 September was an *unintended consequence* of false expectations. This is a type of historical event which historians routinely attempt to explain and by definition they cannot do it simply by reference to 'the thought in the mind of the person by whose agency the event came about', for the event is not an 'external' expression of the agent's wishes, desires, and so on. □

Now although an event may be unintended, there is no such thing as an *undetermined* historical event in the sense of not having causal antecedents, just as (outside sub-atomic physics) there is no such thing as an undetermined natural event. Because determinism is an apparently universal feature of the world we know, many philosophers of history (and the social sciences) have argued that when we specify the cause of an historical event we should follow the method so triumphantly successful in the natural sciences. They constitute our second broad school of philosophers, and they are usually termed 'positivist' – a label derived from Auguste Comte who proposed, as a central tenet of his 'positivist' philosophy, the methodological unity of the natural and social sciences. According to the positivists, the central characteristic of scientific method is that the causes of particular events are deduced as uniform with general, covering laws. Thus, if we wanted to explain why a hot air balloon is able to defy the force of gravity we would offer a general physical law that hot air rises relative to the cooler air surrounding it, and that given certain conditions (a canopy of such and such a size, a sufficient source of heat, a basket and crew of a maximum weight . . .) a balloon will ascend. To explain certain other events – let us say mechanical flight – we might need to refer to a number of covering laws which are all subsumed under the general theory of physical dynamics. This model of explanation is called nomological-deductive and it can be written in technical notation thus:

Given C_i, . . . C_{ii}, . . . C_{iii} etc
and assuming L_i, . . . L_{ii}, . . . L_{iii} etc
then E follows

where the Cs are the certain conditions, the Ls the covering laws, and the E the event we want to explain.

It should be added that this model is not proposed as an actual picture of how scientists formulate their explanatory accounts, but rather as an explication or rational reconstruction of a mode of explanation. Can historians' accounts be rationally reconstructed in the same way? There cannot be much dispute that historical accounts of, say, price inflation or unemployment rest upon general laws of economics, although these laws may often be implied rather than explicitly stated by economic historians. Do historians' accounts of wars, revolutions, and so on, rest upon analogous general laws of political behaviour? Neo-positivist philosophers, such as C. G. Hempel, say they do, although they admit that the explanatory content of an historian's account will often be very sketchy, both because the causes of political behaviour are so manifold that their totality cannot be determined precisely, and because the general laws explaining them are so obvious they are not worth stating explicitly.

Hempel argues that even 'rationalist' accounts of historical events couched in terms of a particular actor's reasons or intentions of doing something can be constructed as explanations which state that: given a situation of a certain type, and the disposition or intention to act in a particular way, then any person of that disposition finding himself in that situation would have acted in that way (Hempel, 'Explanation in science and in history', 1962).

Exercise   You might well ask: what possible advantages can there be in reconstructing 'rationalist' accounts in such a way? Is it not so much simpler to use the actor's reasons to explain events? ∎

Specimen answer   Simpler, maybe, but also simplistic. A positivist would, I think, respond like this: people's actions are dictated not just by rational calculations but also by inner drives and impulses which their 'reasons' do not disclose. Developments in the behavioural sciences (psychology, ethology) have led to theories – or covering laws – which explain how these drives govern our dispositions and actions. There are no grounds for believing that our psychic structures and the causes of human behaviour were fundamentally different in the past, and historians' accounts will be all the richer if they are sustained by the laws of the behavioural sciences. But, perhaps more importantly (and here I paraphrase Hempel), the fact that 'rational-ist' explanations can be construed as nomological-deductive suggests 'that the nature of understanding, in the sense in which explanation is meant to give us an understanding of empirical phenomena, is basically the same in *all areas of scientific inquiry* . . . [It is] one important aspect of the methodological unity of all empirical science'. (I have emphasized the phrase because I think historians ought to welcome the designation of their studies as an area of scientific inquiry.) □

Exercise   The philosophical debate I have outlined is often presented as a dichotomy between the *interpretation* of meaning and the *explanation* of phenomena (or, to use the German terms, *verstehen* and *erklaren*). In recent decades many have argued that the dichotomy is needless and sterile. I cannot go into all the arguments here, but I can ask you to attempt an exercise which should bring home to you, as students of the causes of war, why *both* interpretation and explanation on nomological lines should figure in your methods. Here is a passage from Quincy Wright's book *A Study of War* (1942), and it is followed by an extract from the report of Hitler's conference with the heads of the armed forces on 23 May 1939. I want you to read them and say: (1) what general theory of the causes of war is proposed; and (2) why the document makes clear that this general theory itself demands the interpretation of meaning from the historian.

> Among the hypotheses suggested to explain the recurrence of war is the difficulty of maintaining a stable equilibrium among the uncertain and fluctuating political and military forces within the system of states. The phrase 'the balance of power' has sometimes designated the achievement and sometimes the effort to achieve the difficult task. The concept of the balance of power provides the most general explanation for the oscillations of peace and war in Europe since the Thirty Years' War. (Wright, 1942, p.756)

> [Hitler was recorded as saying] Our situation *vis-à-vis* the surrounding world has remained the same. Germany was outside the circle of the Great Powers. A balance of power has been established without Germany's participation.
>   This balance being disturbed by Germany claiming her vital rights and her reappearance in the circle of the Great Powers. All claims are regarded as 'breaking in' . . .
>   Living space proportionate to the greatness of the State is fundamental to every Power. (Given in Overy, 1987, p.103) ■

Specimen answer   1   The general theory is that, in the system of sovereign states – more particularly in the relations between the great powers who have dominated the system – peace depends on the maintenance of an equilibrium between states. (We will return to the explanatory value of this theory later.)

2   The document makes clear that, as well as being an explanatory hypothesis,

the 'balance of power' was an idea in the heads of historical actors whose meaning for those actors the historian needs to interpret. It was also an idea expressed in diplomatic and strategic practices and we can say that interpretations of the balance of power (by Louis XIV in the seventeenth century, Lord Palmerston in the nineteenth, Hitler in the twentieth) actually helped constitute both the concept and its referent. This example does seem to expose an irreducible methodological difference between the humanistic and natural sciences: whatever scientists theorize about nature and the physical universe is quite meaningless to these entities. But historians' explanatory concepts are distilled from the idiom of the historical and social world and cannot be wholly purged of the interpretations which constituted them in 'everyday' language and practices. □

2.2   Political science and the study of war

For a variety of reasons, the positivist approach to the study of political behaviour has been most influential in America where it produced the single most exhaustive study of war, Quincy Wright's 1,600 page volume, quoted above. This synthesized Wright's own prodigious labours and the work of more than sixty scholars engaged, since 1926, on the University of Chicago's Causes of War project. Wright assembled a mass of information on the frequency, intensity and duration of war, its changing techniques, its political and social functions, its relations to nationalism and other forms of social integration, the attempts to codify war through international law, and so on.

Wright recognized that there is no single cause of war and that peace is an equilibrium between many forces. However, he argued that in international relations there had been a general tendency for change 'in procedures of political and legal adjustment to lag behind economic and cultural changes arising from contacts [between states]' and he regarded this 'political lag' as 'an outstanding cause of war in contemporary civilization'. In his view, the geographical expansion of the sovereign state had seen no concomitant growth in world government to adjust relations between states. Although economic growth, the spread of commerce, and the evolution of technology had profoundly affected relations between states at the level of material co-operation and interdependency, these had not produced – at least among the major powers – a corresponding political interdependency. All the major powers clung to their untrammelled sovereignty. (Minor powers were often economically and politically dependent on a major power and had their sovereignty severely curtailed; Egypt, occupied by Britain in 1882, and Morocco by France in 1912, are cases in point.)

Wright went on to argue that there was an inverse correlation between the efficiency of government within the state and the efficiency with which international relations were regulated. Sovereignty eliminated tensions within the state, but this augmented external tensions. 'International relations become a "state of nature". War . . . among states claiming sovereignty tends to be primarily related to the balance of power among them' (p.1286).

Wright's argument seems to me to be true, but not to take us very far. If the principal cause of war lay in the absence of international government and the absolute sovereignty of the major states, why was there a long period of peace in Europe between 1871 and 1914 (when sovereignty claims were at their apogee) and between 1945 and the present? One answer might be because decisive victory leads to long periods of peace since it demonstrates unambiguously the military superiority of the victor over the vanquished: France's defeat in 1871 was conclusive, Germany's in 1945 still more so. The outcome of World War I rather confirms this line of reasoning: although Germany was defeated in the West in 1918, in the East it was victorious. Its post-war statesmen, such as Rathenau and Stresemann, never accepted the 'Eastern' settlement imposed on Germany because it did not correspond to the military realities of 1918.

We can draw on Wright's study to advance a further reason for the two exceptionally long periods of peace among the European powers. He argued that 'War tends to increase in severity and decrease in frequency as the area of political and legal adjustment (the state) expands geographically . . .' Each period (1871–1914, and 1945 to the present) began with the effective expansion of a major state – Germany in 1871 and the Soviet Union in 1945. To establish the German Empire Bismarck deemed it necessary to fight three limited wars (against Denmark, Austria and France). But in the 1880s it was aptly said of him 'Bismarck – c'est la paix', for his life's work was now the preservation of the peaceful status quo, and in pursuit of this he made Berlin the centre of a network of defensive alliances. The post-1945 situation of the Soviet Union was scarcely an exact parallel (did anyone say 'Stalin – c'est la paix'?) but there were certain similarities. The Soviet Union made all its significant territorial and strategic gains in the closing months of World War II, and from that point was (like Bismarck's Germany) a satiated power with a pronounced lack of concern in matters lying outside its own 'sphere of influence'. Soviet power had grown at the expense of the sovereign state power of the countries in this sphere – as Hungary in 1956 and Czechoslovakia in 1968 were to learn. Though this had tragic consequences for the internal politics of Eastern bloc countries, Europe and indeed the world as a whole benefited from the existence of a cautious super power principally concerned to maintain the status quo. (For evidence of this caution we might point out that neither in the Korean nor the Vietnam War did the Soviet Union commit its forces to its allies; unlike the United States which was militarily engaged on both occasions.)

2.3 The three 'images' of the causes of war

1 Innate aggression

We will revert to some of Wright's ideas, but at this point I want to draw upon a more manageable work of American political science to help us categorize theories of international conflict. In his book *Man, the State and War*, Kenneth Walz examined a heterogeneous body of writing on war and asked of it '*Where* are the major causes of war to be found?' The question enabled him to group accounts of war around three 'images' of bellicosity, each defined by where writers have located the nexus of important causes. In the first image, human nature appeared as the primary cause of war. The second image focused on the internal structure of individual states, with writers identified with this image arguing that certain types of state were more prone to aggression than others. The third image shifted to the system – or more accurately lack of system – in which states competed with each other, and attributed the primary cause of war to this international 'anarchy'.

You might reasonably be tempted to argue that these images are not mutually exclusive and that causes of all three types have been implicated in the outbreak of many wars. But the debate is about how we rank causes in order of importance, and in, say, analysing the outbreak of war in 1914, we cannot attribute *most* importance to those clustered under *both* the second and third images.

Our first image encompasses the long-standing belief that wars result from humankind's innate aggression, or from the pathological psychology of individuals or collectivities. For example, the seventeenth-century philosopher Spinoza explained violence by reference to human imperfections: passion displaces reason, and consequently men, who out of self-interest ought to co-operate with one another in perfect harmony, engage endlessly in quarrels and physical violence. Modern versions of this thesis tend to explain warfare by drawing analogies from ethological studies of animal, especially primate, behaviour. During World War I the philosopher Bertrand Russell – who in early August 1914 had discovered to his amazement that average men and women were delighted at the prospect of war – analysed the causes of war in a lecture series. He was not, of course, privy to the secret diplomacy which had preceded it, but it is to be doubted whether confidential knowledge would have altered his view of the war's basic causes:

> . . . war, like all other natural activities, is not so much prompted by the end which it has in view as by an impulse to the activity itself. Very often men desire an end, not of its own account, but because their nature demands the actions which will lead to the end. And so it is in this case: the ends to be achieved by war appear in prospect far more important than they will appear when they are realised, because war itself is a fulfilment of one side of our nature. If men's actions sprang from desires for what would in fact bring happiness, the purely rational arguments against war would have long ago put an end to it. What makes war difficult to suppress is that it springs from an impulse, rather than from a calculation of the advantages to be derived from war. (Russell, *The Principles of Social Reconstruction*, 1916, p.55)

Exercise   I want you to consider these extracts from the *Berlin Diary* of the American journalist William Shirer, and say what arguments they would lead you to pose against Russell's views.

> *Berlin, September 27 (1938)*
> A motorised division rolled through the city's streets just at dusk this evening in the direction of the Czech frontier. I went out to the corner of the Linden where the column was turning down the Wilhelmstrasse, expecting to see a tremendous demonstration. I pictured the scenes I had read of in 1914 when the cheering throngs on this same street tossed flowers at the marching soldiers, and the girls ran up and kissed them. The hour was undoubtedly chosen to-day to catch the hundreds of thousands of Berliners pouring out of their offices at the end of the day's work. But they ducked into the subways, refused to look on, and the handful that did stood at the curb in utter silence unable to find a word of cheer for the flower of their youth going away to the glorious war. It has been the most striking demonstration against war I have ever seen . . . What I've seen to-night almost rekindles a little faith in the German people. They are dead set against war.

> *Berlin, August 31 (1939)*
> Everybody [here] against the war. People talking openly. How can a country go into any major war with a population so dead against it?

Berlin, September 3
I was standing in the Wilhelmplatz about noon when the loud-speakers suddenly announced that England had declared herself at war on Germany. Some 250 people were standing there in the sun. They listened attentively to the announcement. When it was finished, there was not a murmur. They just stood there as they were before. Stunned. (Shirer, *Berlin Diary*, 1941, pp.119, 154, 159) ∎

Specimen answer and discussion

Russell erred in concluding from his experience of August 1914 that 'war fever' arose from innate, timeless human impulses rather than – as I would argue – the particular historical conditions of the epoch, with their culture of imperialism and Social Darwinism. Shirer's testimony (and that of many others) shows conclusively that there was no popular impulse towards war in Germany in the late 1930s, despite the Nazis' glorification of struggle. It is not hard to suggest why: most adult Germans in the late 1930s would have had memories of suffering and bereavement during World War I. Indeed, in all the former combatant states the horrors of the Great War appear to have immunized – at least temporarily – people from 'war fever'. Once you have rejected the argument for innate impulses, the evidence might have led you further to say that popular mentalities were largely irrelevant to the causes of both wars: in 1914, the statesmen's decision for war fortuitously coincided with a popular bellicosity that arose from ignorance of what industrialized war would really entail. In 1939, statesmen decided on war despite people's well-founded fears that it would be long, brutal and devastating. □

The assumption that the fundamental causes of war lie in a fixed human nature seems to me refuted by the events of our own 'century of total war'. Aggression may indeed be 'natural' in the sense of having an innate component, and understanding its innate dimension may give us insights into combat motivation and the perpetuation of hostilities through time. But humans live, not in nature, but in societies, and I think it more rewarding to look for the causes of twentieth-century wars in the organization and tensions of societies. This leads us to our second image.

2   International conflict and the internal structure of states

The image that locates the causes of war in the instability within states is as old as the modern state itself. We find it in the writings of Macchiavelli, who regarded all dynamic 'healthy' polities as conflict-ridden, and for whom foreign war (and the organization of the state for war) was a necessary source of unity and authority within the state. Nineteenth- and early twentieth-century liberals abhorred such political 'realism' but can be identified with the image, for it was a common liberal belief that wars frequently served as diversions from domestic ills and were provoked for that purpose. In the liberal view, war and foreign conquests did not pay; peace and free trade were objectively in the interests of all states. Just as harmony would arise in a society where individuals pursued their rational self-interests, so international society would be harmonized by states pursuing their rational self-interests. The best-known statement of this thesis was in Norman Angell's book *The Great Illusion* (1910), written during the Anglo-German naval race in order to show that the attribution of economic well-being to military power was 'a gross and desperately dangerous misconception' (p.25).

In the liberal analysis, militarism, imperialism and war arose in authoritarian, anti-democratic states whose rulers were not responsible to public opinion. Many liberal historians would still argue that the decisive cause of the failure to preserve peace in July 1914 was the subordination of Germany's political establishment to its military leadership. For liberal economists (such as Joseph Schumpeter) who believed that capitalism was essentially irenic, the militaristic aspects of Imperial Germany – Europe's most successful capitalist society – were to be explained by 'atavisms' in its social structure and the persistence of a quasi-feudal ruling élite. In 1917–18 the liberal prescription for peace followed closely from its analysis of the causes of war. As Woodrow Wilson told Congress: 'A steadfast concert for peace can never be maintained except by a partnership of democratic nations. No autocratic government could be trusted to keep faith within it or observe its covenants . . . Only free peoples can hold their purpose and their honor steady and prefer the interests of mankind to any narrow interest of their own' (quoted in Walz, 1954, p.118; see also 'Wilson and self-determination', Book III, Unit 20, p.235).

Exercise   Certain themes of this liberal analysis should be familiar to you from your course reading. To whose views am I referring? How would you summarize them? ∎

Specimen answer   I am referring to the views of Arno J. Mayer, expressed in *The Persistence of the Old*
and discussion   *Regime*. (You may have noted that at several points Mayer acknowledges his indebtedess to Schumpeter.) Mayer's thesis is that the 'old order' of Europe was, in 1914, 'thoroughly pre-industrial and pre-bourgeois'. Except in Britain, agriculture remained the largest economic sector and the most important source of livelihood. He argues that the dominant political élites in all European societies were drawn from a traditional agrarian ruling class whose values and outlook suffused the rest of society. With the exception of republican France, the nobility and the church were the vital constituents and pillars of monarchical states in which the crown continued to be a crucial source of power and political integration. The industrial and financial bourgeoisie was, in Mayer's view, a distinctly subaltern class: the modest growth of the capital-goods industries and finance capitalism meant that its economic base was narrow, and the bourgeoisie had failed to develop its own distinctive social and political ideals which would, in Marx's terms, have made it a class 'for itself'. Instead, it had succumbed to a social and cultural 'feudalization' by imitating the manners and style of the life of the nobility, and adopting its political ideas. The predominant culture of old-regime Europe remained, in Mayer's view, classicist and anti-modern. It is a central postulate of his study that 'The Great War was an expression of the decline and fall of the old order fighting to prolong its life rather than of the explosive rise of industrial capitalism bent on imposing its primacy.' (Much of Mayer's argument strikes me as highly questionable but I have reserved my criticisms for section 3 in Unit 29.) ☐

Although Mayer claims that his book is 'a Marxist history from the top down, not the bottom up', his views are completely at variance with the traditional Marxist analyses of imperialism and the causes of World War I, which date back to the works of Rosa Luxemburg, Rudolf Hilferding and Lenin's wartime pamphlet *Imperialism, the Highest Stage of Capitalism* (1916). The crux of the Marxist theory was that the 'new imperialism' had economic roots in a specific new phase of capitalism which led to the territorial division of the world among the great capitalist powers, and intensified competition for markets and the raw resources of the Second Industrial Revolution (rubber, oil, tin and other, tropical, products). When Lenin first analysed the war's causes in the autumn of 1914 he acknowledged that 'the dynastic interests of the more backward Eastern European monarchies' had been among them. But the 1920 re-issue of *Imperialism* purported to have 'proved that the war of 1914–18 was imperialist (that is, an annexationist, predatory war of plunder) on the part of both sides; it was a war for the division of the world, for the partition and repartition of colonies and spheres of influence of finance capital, etc' (quoted in Lichtheim, *Imperialism*, 1974, p.106).

Exercise What, then, do Mayer's views have in common with the Leninist position? ■

Specimen answer They can both be assimilated to our second image which relates the causes of war to the internal structure of states, but in Mayer's view war sprang from the traditional, backward-looking forces within the European powers, while in Lenin's view competition between the most modern elements of their capitalist economies was the dynamic behind international conflict. □

Discussion Marxism is now a very variegated tradition and few Marxists still treat Lenin's dicta as eternal verities. It is important to note, however, that much of the documentation on German war aims published by Fischer and others gives some substance to Lenin's analysis. In particular, the now notorious Memorandum of 9 September 1914, in which the German Chancellor set down notes on peace terms, called for the cession of the French iron-ore field of Briey, 'which is necessary for the supply of ore for our industry', a commercial treaty which would make France economically dependent on Germany and secure French markets for German exports, the reduction of Belgium to a vassal state that would make it economically a German province, and the creation of a Central European economic association which would be 'in practice under German leadership and must stabilise Germany's economic dominance over Mitteleuropa'. The memorandum also referred to the creation of 'a continuous African colonial empire' (Fischer, 1967, pp.103–5). Although the emphasis was on using war to secure economic domination in Europe rather than in the undeveloped world, the connection between politico-military force and economic expansion was plain. The document does not, of course, prove that Germany went to war to realize these aims (which may represent opportunist capitalization on apparently imminent victory) but there is evidence that specific demands – such as the Briey ore fields – had been named as potential war aims by spokesmen of German heavy industry as early as 1913 (Fischer, *World Power or Decline*, 1975, p.37).

In German historiography there has long been something of a middle position between Mayer's and the Leninist interpretation, first delineated by Eckart Kehr (whose influence is discussed in the Mommsen article in the *Offprints Booklet*). Kehr argued that the ruling interests of Imperial Germany were determined by a conservative alliance of reactionary Prussian landowners and leading industrialists, an alliance first cemented in the mid-1870s and periodically reinforced by policies of protective tariffs, anti-socialist measures, social welfare legislation, imperialist expansion, 'world policy' and the naval arms race. According to the 'Kehrites', these policies constituted a defensive strategy on the part of the ruling élites attempting to curb and restrain the dynamics of the industrial world, in particular the political claims of the increasingly organized working class. (Claims which, in Prussia, were blocked by the class suffrage of the *Landtag*.) This interpretation of the imperial power structure does not neglect its reactionary, quasi-feudal component but regards that structure as a condominium of aristo-crats and bourgeois. Although there are different nuances among historians adopting Kehr's position, generally they agree that German war aims, and Germany's foreign policy before 1914 and during the July crisis, were critically influenced by a determination to defend the traditional social structure.

Exercise   So far I have not discussed the causes of World War II in terms of our second image, partly because when I worked through the course material I found interpretations which I could assimilate to the image that so conflicted with each other as to give me a depressing sense of the futility of the exercise. Still, there is a value in trying to distinguish between causal explanations of the outbreak of war in 1939 which give priority to 'internal' factors, and those emphasizing 'inter-national' relations. I want you now to try to list all those you would categorize under the former. I will postpone purely 'international' explanations until the next section, but if you can recall any arguments for the breaking down of the internal/international distinction, please put them forward. ∎

Specimen answer   Let me begin with the final point:
and discussion
1   There is a persuasive argument put forward by MacGregor Knox (in the Course Reader) that in Hitler's ideological vision (as in Mussolini's) the conquest of domestic and foreign enemies was inextricably entwined. Hitler's political categories of race and racial struggle superseded the ideas of the nation-state and the international balance. The dictator was determined to re-shape by force German society and Europe, even the world, to fit his ideological vision, and his domestic and foreign conquests were part of the same process.

2   There is a very different position which tends to discount Hitler's ideology and 'uniqueness' by arguing that there was a fundamental continuity in German history between 1871 and 1945 determined by the primacy of *Innenpolitik* (inner or domestic policy). Thus, some scholars have argued that the pursuit of aggressive, expansionist policies abroad as part of the conservative élites' defensive strategy against the working class (a strategy summarily defined as 'social imperialism') characterized both the Wilhelmine and Nazi Reichs. The parallels between the rampant annexationism espoused by many Germans in World War I and Nazi annexations are often adduced in this context.

3   A not dissimilar, but much more specific, argument focusing on the outbreak of war in 1939 claims that both Hitler's decision to attack Poland and risk general war, and the type of war the Nazis fought, were greatly influenced by domestic crisis and the fear of domestic crisis. According to this line of argument, as a result of breakneck rearmament the regime was confronted by interlocking problems of labour shortages, material bottlenecks, inflation and widespread working-class truculence. It was also haunted by memories of late 1918 when the civilian burdens of total war had brought the nation to revolution and near anarchy. A 'lightning war' of plunder, which would pay for rearmament and yet spare German consumers the terrible austerity of 1916–18, was – accordingly – the regime's solution to its domestic crisis.

4   This specific argument can be complemented by 'functionalist' interpretations of the Nazi state, which emphasize the internecine competition between its governing and party agencies, the absence of clear chains of command, the

'weakness' of its dictator, and its perilous reliance on charismatic authority to provide the sole integrating principle of government. These – it is claimed – were the causes of a cumulative and destructive radicalization in both domestic and foreign policies.

5   It must not be supposed that 'intentionalist' historians, who trace the causes of war to a fairly consistent political 'programme', necessarily disavow our second image. Hitler's ideology and the fact that he could impose it on his movement and the state were, after all, phenomena of German domestic politics. □

Exercise   The categorization of such mutually inconsistent positions under our second image indicates its limited utility, but it has a certain usefulness in drawing together explanations of the outbreak of war which have something fundamental in common. What is it? ■

Specimen answer   They are all 'German-centred', and can all be distinguished from explanations which locate the nexus of important causes in the international system. This brings us to our third image. □

3   International conflict and international anarchy

For about 500 years those states which have considered themselves 'sovereign' have recognized no supranational authority and regarded war as the final arbiter of disputes between themselves. As Tony Lentin argues (Unit 20, pp.262–3), international law is entirely consensual, and attempts to regulate relations between states, or indeed enforce 'collective security', are conditional on those states' compliance. Our third image derives from these realities and is loosely 'Darwinian', for it locates the causes of war in an environment of dearth and constant struggle: states, in this image, are competitive species whose lineaments are determined by geography, demography and material resources, and for whom ideology is mere camouflage for 'reasons of state'. There is much to be said for this argument: Protestant England fought mercantilist wars against the Protestant Netherlands; Republican and Napoleonic France pursued strategic objectives not dissimilar to Louis XIV's; the Soviet Union resorted to the foreign policy aims of the Tsarist Empire and more or less succeeded in restoring its boundaries. Moreover, our image helps us see why a state like Poland, occupying a strategically exposed position between more powerful polities to the east and west, has had such a precarious existence.

Given an environment of constant struggle the periods of peace between great powers stand just as much in need of explanation as do the wars, and (as we have already noted) it is the concept of a balance of power which provides the most widely advanced explanation for both. The Darwinian analogy can again be drawn on to expound the concept: in certain environmental circumstances the competition between species achieves a natural equilibrium. Jackals coexist with the lion. Disturbances in the environment – such as climatic change or the introduction of new diseases – destroy this equilibrium, and raise competition to an intense pitch of struggle which does not subside until a new equilibrium is established.

The analogy – which is *only* an analogy – does not dispose of all the ambiguities in the balance of power concept, but let us say that an international equilibrium of force, derived from a rough parity of territory, population, productive resources and weaponry (such as maintains between the USA and the USSR), is favourable to peaceful coexistence, and a disequilibrium makes war more likely.

Exercise

What arguments can you advance in support of the view that the two world wars had common cause in imbalances (both actual and potential) within the great power system? ■

Specimen answer and discussion

One might preface an answer by saying that the multipolar world of 1914 and 1939 was inherently more unstable than the bipolar world created by World War II and the nuclear stalemate. On the eve of World War I, eight powers (France, Britain, Germany, Austria-Hungary, Russia, Italy, United States and Japan) had the capacity to sustain industrialized warfare against each other. Although they were highly unequal in their resources, the disparity between them was not such as to create a super-power hegemony and each was free to pursue aggressive adventures abroad. (Japan attacked China and Russia, Italy fought Turkey over Libya, and the United States went to war with Spain.)

Having said that, a more threatening source of international instability lay in an historically novel type of imbalance that had arisen between the established imperial and continental powers, and the insurgent power of Germany. Britain and France were global states by virtue of their Asian and African empires; for both, pacifying and conserving imperial possessions was a major aim of national policy which (despite the 1898 war scare known as the Fashoda crisis – see Roberts, p.126) they were able to pursue without mutual antagonism or disturbing the international balance. The United States and Russia were steadily expanding into their vast land masses and – whatever their military and political weaknesses – their status as great powers was assured by their territorial, demographic and material resources. Germany's political class felt that their country's position within the great power system was anomalous: it was indubitably Europe's leading industrial and military state, but (it was thought) it did not exercise a global power commensurate with its economic strength, demographic vitality and military traditions. Whether these perceptions were 'objectively' valid is beside the point, for from 1897 they led Germany to embark upon a conscious and determined quest for 'world power' status, and to challenge British naval supremacy by laying down the High Seas Fleet. Germany's opinion-formers justified this threat to British naval hegemony by conjuring up fears of 'encirclement', but the naval arms race actually turned the fears it was meant to dispel into reality. Britain formed an entente with France: in January 1906 there began secret conversations between their General Staffs, and in 1912 Britain undertook naval commitments to France so binding that it is highly likely it would have been drawn into a Franco-German war even if Germany had not violated Belgian neutrality.

Restoration of the equilibrium which had been disturbed by Germany's 'world power' policy was, for Britain, the motive for the entente with France and Russia. Many would argue, too, that the British decision for war in August 1914 was principally determined by the conviction that a German victory would destroy the existing balance and create a new one totally inimical to British interests. The balance of power concept does, therefore, help us understand both the realignment of international forces in the early twentieth century and Britain's participation in the war (which was contrary to Germany's calculations – do not forget my point about the cardinal significance of false expectations). But (and here the

Darwinian analogy breaks down) we cannot invoke the balance of power concept as if it was some kind of natural law. My exposition has referred to the *perceptions* of Germany's political class, the *motives* behind British foreign policy, and – by implication – how opinion-formers in both states *interpreted* the concept of the balance of power. The balance of power concept is simultaneously a highly generalized explanation for the outbreak of conflict and an idea in the heads of individual historical actors in specific situations – such as Sir Edward Grey, the British foreign secretary, and Prince von Bulow, the pre-war German imperial chancellor. It was, moreover, a controversial idea, contested by contemporaries such as Norman Angell, Karl Kautsky – the German social democratic theorist – and Lenin, who all had different visions of international politics.

Now let's consider the new perspectives our third image affords us on the causes of World War II. Basically it establishes a framework of explanation that is no longer 'German centred', and focuses on the relations between states rather than the socio-political relations within one of them. It brings the calculations of Britain, France and the Soviet Union into the picture, and helps us to see that whatever Hitler's unique moral responsibility for the outbreak of war (which is not our concern *qua* historians), political responsibility must be shared by Chamberlain, Bonnet and Stalin.

For a long time 'Hitler' was sufficient answer to those enquiring as to the causes of World War II, and A. J. P. Taylor's famous study must be credited for having disabused many of such misleading simplicity. In his own words, Taylor's book 'has little to do with Hitler. The vital question . . . concerns Great Britain and France. They had the decision in their hands. It was perfectly obvious that Germany would seek to become a Great Power again; obvious after 1933 that her domination would be of a peculiarly barbaric sort. Why did the victors not resist her?' (Taylor, *The Origins of the Second World War*, 1964, p.9). □

Exercise   How would you answer that vital question? ■

Specimen answer   France, though it remained Europe's foremost military power until the later
and discussion   1930s, was gravely weakened by a chronically low birthrate and the huge losses of young men during World War I. Its pre-eminent foreign policy concern was for security against Germany, a state whose industrial and demographic resources were clearly superior to France's own, and whose relative strength in Central-East Europe had actually increased with the collapse of Russia and the 'Balkanization' of that region. France regarded strict adherence to the Versailles Treaty as essential to its security, but the failure of the Ruhr occupation undermined its will to enforce the treaty single-handedly, caused it to look still more to Britain to guarantee its frontiers, and drew it into a defensive strategic mentality. By stages, France conceded the initiative in the Western powers' dealings with Germany to Britain. The Locarno Pact, though it guaranteed its frontiers and re-affirmed the de-militarization of the Rhineland, was a French diplomatic defeat because it left Germany's eastern frontiers open to revision, and so threatened the integrity of Poland, France's ally. While the 'Locarno spirit' lasted, many French people could convince themselves that war in Western Europe was a thing of the past; Aristide Briand, foreign minister at this time, is remembered as an apostle of European political unity and '*le pèlerin de la paix*' – the pilgrim of peace.

The rise of Nazi Germany was immediately recognized as a threat to France by its political leaders because no one had demanded the revision of Versailles more vehemently than Hitler. But France's ability to respond to this threat was much weakened by the Great Depression, which hit it later than it did other economies but from which it recovered more slowly, and by its chronic political instability, manifested most acutely in savage riots in February 1934, which threatened the integrity of the state. A small minority of French fascists or neo-fascists welcomed the Nazi regime as a bulwark against Bolshevism; a larger one considered Léon Blum, the French socialist leader of Jewish origin, no less an enemy of the 'real' Catholic, conservative France than Hitler. Despite these weaknesses and divisions, in 1935 France attempted to secure itself against Nazi aggression by allying with the only continental power capable of defeating a rearmed Germany, the Soviet Union. But for reasons not entirely within French control, the alliance was not followed up by a military convention, or even serious military conversations. The pact gave Hitler a pretext for repudiating Locarno and re-militarizing the Rhineland; although French leaders fully appreciated the strategic significance of Hitler's move, they were hampered in their response to it by a governmental crisis, fear of financial instability, military unpreparedness and, above all, their dependence on the British. In 1936, France 'in effect surrendered its foreign policy to Britain' (Book III, Unit 20, p.261).

Since 1919, many in Britain had considered the Versailles Settlement morally invalid and politically and economically inept, and their opinions had a corrosive effect on Britain's will to enforce the treaty. It was invalid in denying to people identifying themselves as German the national self-determination which was supposed to be the treaty's legitimating principle. Since many believed that chief responsibility for the war (into which 'we had all stumbled') lay in the old diplomatic system of secret diplomacy, the settlement was unjust in pinning sole guilt for the war on Germany. It was politically inept to imagine that such a potentially strong state as Germany would long tolerate the limitations on its forces or the de-militarization of part of its territory, or to think that in an age of nationalism it would not advance claims on regions where, if given the choice, the majority would elect to be German citizens. It was economically inept to impose a reparations burden on one of the world's leading economies if this hindered the revival of international trade and the liquidation of war indebtitude. Such was the case for 'appeasing' Germany.

All Germany's significant claims before and after 1933 were confined to Continental Europe, and British political leaders could regard them with a greater degree of detachment than could the French. Britain was not a continental power, had traditionally avoided continental diplomatic entanglements, and quickly abandoned the conscript army which was required to play a military role in Europe. What military strength Britain had was further dissipated by the fact that its primary foreign interests were imperial. The peace settlement gave the illusion of being the zenith of Britain's empire, for it acquired former German colonies and became the mandate authority in Palestine. But Britain lacked the military and financial strength needed to meet its imperial commitments, which for long led it to regard states other than Germany as greater potential enemies. Fascist Italy threatened the British presence in the Middle East, and its enmity was assured after Britain concerted the unsuccessful international opposition to the invasion of Abyssinia. The expansion of Japan threatened Britain's position in the Far East.

British leaders, like the French, were answerable to a public opinion in which the memory of one abhorrent war was fresh, anxiety about future warfare acute, and 'campaigning' for peace (by the Peace Pledge Union and other groups) was effective. They had good evidence that rearmament was electorally unpopular, and their Treasury officials were convinced it was unaffordable. Very few in Britain actively opposed the appeasement of Germany; most supported it as apparently the only way to preserve international peace; some welcomed a strong Germany as a bulwark against Bolshevism. British Conservative leaders had a strong distaste for co-operation with the Soviet Union, and even when war was imminent were extraordinarily dilatory in pursuing a Soviet alliance.

Without a Soviet alliance, the military-strategic obstacles to direct, effective resistance to Nazi expansionism were insurmountable. Except for the re-militarization of the Rhineland, all Hitler's moves were made in Central and Eastern Europe. For France and Britain to have opposed them effectively would have meant a swift invasion of Germany for which they were not equipped and had not planned. Their strategic thinking was geared to a long war of blockade during which they hoped their superior economic resources would slowly wear Germany down (or encourage the emergence of a more tractable regime). Since such a strategy could do nothing in the short term for the victims of Nazi aggression, the British and French were loath to adopt it on the victims' behalf. □

Exercise Why, then, did they eventually oppose Hitler? ∎

Specimen answer and discussion Not because they regarded Poland as more deserving of their support than Czechoslovakia, but because they saw it as in their interests to do so. An unopposed attack on Poland would have left Britain and France passive spectators to Germany's total domination of Central-East Europe. After the diplomatic coup of the German–Soviet pact, Hitler was assured of an ally in the east which loyally fulfilled its obligations to supply Nazi Germany with war *matériel*. At some point in the future Hitler would have been able to turn on France with overwhelming force and without fear of a war on two fronts. To oppose him in September 1939 – rather than face his attack at some future date – made sense to the Western powers because they had been rapidly rearming and believed that the balance of force was more favourable to them now than it would be later. Their intelligence services led them to believe that the German economy was weaker than was really the case, and that Hitler's dictatorship was less secure than it turned out to be. Their own economies were dangerously overstretched by rearmament. As democratic states with independent labour movements, they could not (unlike Nazi Germany) contemplate all the measures needed to sustain a 'war economy' without actually being at war. Moreover, in March 1939 a great revulsion of public opinion had followed the German occupation of the vestigial Czech state. Nearly all felt that Hitler 'had to be stopped' and the declaration of war in September was supported by a wide consensus in both Britain and France. Altogether, the Polish crisis appeared to be an unrepeatable opportunity to challenge Germany's expansion. ⊔

2.4 The Thirty Years' War thesis: for

I began with the intention of helping you to analyse and compare the causes of the two world wars, and I hope we have gone some way to fulfilling that aim. In conclusion I want to consider an argument which – if sound – would vitiate comparative analysis. This is the thesis that the two wars were really a single conflict and, therefore, did not have distinctive causes which we can usefully compare. It is certainly a familiar argument: Churchill prefaced his history of World War II with the claim that it formed a continuation of the story of World War I which he had set out in *The World Crisis*: 'Together, they cover an account of another Thirty Years' War' (Churchill, 1948). In more recent historiography the thesis takes the form that the wars constituted the prolonged disintegration of Europe's old order – though its proponents seem unsure whether the wars were cause or effect of disintegration, and cheerfully settle for both. But, flippancy aside, there are several good reasons for seeing the wars as two acts of the same drama, with the inter-war years as a mere interlude.

Exercise   Can you suggest some reasons? ■

Specimen answer and discussion

1   The simplest reason of all arises from the circumstances that in November 1918 Germany's armies stood on foreign fields, and were all basically intact and capable of prolonged resistance. Germany's frontiers were inviolate and its military and political leaders did not, as in 1945, surrender unconditionally but requested an armistice. These circumstances lent colour to the legend that Germany had not suffered military defeat but had been forced by the cracking of the 'Inner Front' to accept a truce, and of course they encouraged nationalists to lay the blame for the humiliation of a dictated peace on the Weimar regime. A cold-blooded realist might argue that until Germany experienced final military defeat, the aberrant nationalism in its political life would not be expunged and the major cause of international conflict in Europe removed.

2   Even if we believe Germany was defeated militarily in 1918 – and I do – we might still argue that both wars arose from 'the German problem', that the solution attempted in 1919 failed and that resolution awaited the total defeat, occupation and division of Germany in 1945.

3   From the near identity of the opposing coalitions in the latter phase of each war (at least in Europe – Japan had joined the Allied powers in World War I) one could argue that the wars were fought for the same geopolitical and strategic objectives. To substantiate this thesis one could, for example, point to the fact that the proposals for the German economic domination of Western Europe put forward in the September 1914 'programme' were realized in 1940, after the defeat of France.

4   Then there is the argument that World War I disrupted (and in places destroyed) the political, economic and social systems of Europe, and the peace 'settlement' failed to establish a new order in their place, leaving chronic frictions which eventually flared up into renewed war. This argument for the fundamental defectiveness of Versailles has international and socio-political dimensions. To touch on the former: the peacemakers of 1919 looked to the last great European peace settlement of 1815 for guidance, but their own efforts produced nothing equivalent to the early nineteenth-century Congress System and the Concert of Europe. True, there were circumstances, such as the failure of the USA to ratify the treaty and its withdrawal from European affairs, which were beyond their control, but critics of the international settlement might argue that it should have allowed either for the speedy return of Germany to great power status (such as France was permitted after 1815) or it should have been dismembered. It was sufficiently harsh to foment nationalist grievance, but too lenient to destroy Germany's capacity to rectify that grievance. Moreover, with the collapse of the Austro-Hungarian and Tsarist Empires, the peacemakers were confronted with

an anarchic international situation in Eastern Europe for which there was no precedent to guide them. Before 1914, Austria-Hungary had been a major source of stability in the ethnic patchwork of Central-East Europe and Russia the counterweight ally of France in the European balance. The successor states, with their welter of claims on each other, constituted a region of chronic instability, and none was able to play the counterweight role of pre-war Russia (though the French had placed some hopes on the military prowess of a 'strong' Poland).

To touch on the socio-political defects of the settlement: it left an estimated 19 million people as national minorities in nine major states, out of a total population of about 98 million. About one-fifth of Poland's citizens were not ethnic Poles and one-third of Czechoslovakia's neither Czechs nor Slovaks (Bell, *The Origins of the Second World War in Europe*, 1986, pp.24–5; see also Book III, Unit 8, section 1.2 on the Versailles Settlement). These minorities provided recruits for political terrorism and could be used by enemy powers to undermine a state from within (as with Henlein's Sudeten German Nazis in Czechoslovakia). Nor should we neglect the economic defects of Versailles, the reparations clauses of which appeared to place an impossible strain on the German economy, and involve it in permanent balance of payment difficulties, because it would be furnishing exports for which it was not paid, or earning foreign exchange which was not for its own use but for the purposes of making reparations payments (Bell, 1986, p.20, following the argument of Keynes). Attempting to enforce reparations exacerbated German inflation, and thus accelerated one of the most socially disruptive processes in twentieth-century advanced societies.

In sum, these arguments would lead us to believe that World War II followed inexorably from the causes and defective settlement of World War I. □

2.5   The Thirty Years' War thesis: against

The first point to be made against this thesis is a philosophical one: inexorability has no place in the explanation of such complex events in human society as general wars separated by two decades. Intermeshing political, economic and international systems are 'open-ended' in the sense that they always allow for various possible outcomes. We can envisage many plausible 'might have beens' – or counter-factual situations, to use the jargon – which would have diminished the threat of a second general European war, if not removed it entirely. Such speculation is far from pointless if it helps us see (as it sometimes does) the specific operative causes behind particular events.

The second point is a historical one. Reasons (2) and (3) above seriously distort both the origins and character of World War II by promoting the facile idea that it was merely a replay of the first. Even if we exclude from consideration the war with Japan, there are obvious and significant differences, such as the fact that a major area of British military commitment was the North African–Mediterranean war against Italy. A far more important difference is revealed, however, if we consider when and how the main military adversaries became engaged in war. From July–August 1914, the coalitions which bore the brunt of the fighting were at war (France, Russia and Britain versus Germany and Austria-Hungary). Though the entry of Turkey into the war in November and Italy in May 1915 brought important extensions of the conflict, it did not shift the battle-front where the outcome of the war would be decided: France and Flanders. Nor did the USA's entry in March 1917. By contrast, the main military adversaries in World War II (Germany and the Soviet Union) were at peace until June 1941, and it was not until then that the war's decisive battle-fronts in Europe were opened. (Three-quarters of Germany's military casualties occurred on the Russian front.) An explanation of the causes of World War I which terminates in August 1914 is true to the 'core' realities of the war that followed. An explanation of World War II which stops short at September 1939 greatly distorts its 'core' realities.

Furthermore, the similarity of German geopolitical and strategic objectives in the two world wars should not blind us to the striking differences in the aims and policies pursued by Germany after 1939, which point us to different causes behind World War II. The military defeat of Poland enabled the Nazis to put into effect policies of subjugation and extermination inspired by their racist ideology which were actually dysfunctional in terms of strategic objectives. Poles in the new Government-General were to be 'natives' in the most pejorative, racist sense – unable to own property, form associations, receive education beyond the primary level, or be employed in any managerial capacity. They were to have only Germans as their masters; there was to be no mixture of blood between Germans and Poles, and Polish leaders and intellectuals were to be executed. Nazi rule over Poland was such as to deprive it of economic usefulness to the Germans; a territory which might have been a valuable source of agrarian produce and raw materials became a giant Golgotha (Bell, 1986, pp.271–2). The contrast between the actions of the central powers in Poland in 1914–15, when the Polish legions had subordinated themselves to Austria-Hungary and Varsovians had collaborated with advancing German armies, and of Nazi Germany in 1939, is tragic evidence that this was much more than a 'replay'.

Of course, it is indisputable that, because of its place in the ideology of *Lebensraum*, an attack on Russia had long been Hitler's central military objective. Serious planning for it began in August 1940 and Hitler signed the top-secret directive 'to crush Soviet Russia in a rapid campaign' on 18 December. But these facts do not mean that the twenty-two months between the invasion of Poland and the launching of Barbarossa were simply a lengthy pause while destiny waited in the wings of the future.

For a start, specific frictions arose in these months from German eastward expansion and Soviet westward expansion, which themselves contributed to Hitler's decision to attack Russia: Germany encroached on Finland, Romania and Bulgaria, states which the Soviet Union considered in its sphere of influence. But additionally we must bear in mind that not all plans are realized, and Hitler had always matched ideological fixity of purpose with strategic and tactical flexibility. There were good reasons why he might have postponed the attack on Russia or even pursued other grandiose goals. While invasion plans were being drawn up in November 1940, he made some efforts to involve the Soviet Union in a grand coalition with Germany, Italy and Japan to break up the British Empire, and instructed Ribbentrop to present Molotov with a draft agreement for dividing the world into spheres of interest. As long as Britain was undefeated, and many of the world's markets closed to Germany, the alliance with the Soviet Union was very advantageous to Hitler. A commercial agreement of February 1940 stipulated that the Soviet Union should provide Germany during the next year with considerable quantities of cereals, oil, cotton and metal ores, and make purchases in third countries of other goods (such as rubber) on Germany's behalf. The Soviet Union fully discharged its obligations and, in return, received industrial and military technology. The agreement was renewed in 1941 and a further agreement signed in April 1941. Economic co-operation was matched by close collaboration between the Gestapo and NKVD: German communists were handed over from Russia in exchange for Russian *emigrés* and Ukrainians from Germany.

One needs to add, too, that although Stalin's resort to the Nazi–Soviet pact is sometimes justified as buying time to prepare against later Nazi aggression, German invasion plans were something in which he refused to believe and which the Soviet staff did little to counter. The first intelligence of Barbarossa reached him (via the USA) in January 1941, and further information flowed in during the next six months. He consistently discounted it as an imperialist plot to involve the Soviet Union in a war with Germany. After the conquest of Yugoslavia (April 1941), Stalin acted as if he believed that a policy of total appeasement would ward off a German attack. We can speculate that the course of events would have been different had the Soviet posture towards Germany been different; if British and French negligence was a contributory cause of the 1939 war, so too was Soviet negligence of the 1941 war.

Exercise Such brief consideration of events between September 1939 and June 1941 will have indicated that there were certain immediate, local causes of the 'core' conflict in World War II to which the Thirty Years' War thesis blinds us. But there are weightier reasons for scepticism. Can you suggest some? ■

Specimen answer and discussion 1 In the mid- and later-1920s, Stresemann displayed great skill in mitigating the terms of the dictated peace by diplomacy and 'finesse'. Germany entered the League, reparations were scaled down, it became a favoured field of foreign investment. Co-operation with the Western powers might have continued had it not been for

2 the shattering effect on German domestic politics and international relations of the Great Depression – a major source of discontinuity in world history. All national economies tried to protect themselves by autarky which accelerated the collapse of world trade – the total value of Europe's trade in 1935 was only two-fifths of what it had been in 1925 – and extreme nationalism was a common political response to the crisis throughout Central-Eastern Europe.

3 In Germany, it brought to power a movement whose leader was motivated by a racist vision of the world, and whose pre-eminent goals were eastward expansion and the destruction of the Jews. He and his movement exulted in the barbarization of political life and of warfare. Hitler's 'world view' represented a qualitative leap from German annexationism in World War I.

4 Similarly, though in many respects Hitler continued the revisionist policies of his predecessors, he did so with radically different methods, which represented a qualitative leap from the foreign policy of Weimar Germany.

5 Hitler committed Germany to rearmament on a scale which caused considerable economic strain and at a pace which could only be continued by wars of plunder. □

There were, of course, many continuities linking the total wars of twentieth-century Europe, but each sprang from a causal matrix sufficiently different to make our comparative analysis valid and instructive.

3 *GERMAN GUILT?*

Of all the combatants of the two world wars Germany has most commonly been singled out as bearing the lion's share of the 'guilt' for causing the wars. The charge was levelled at the peace conference at Versailles, where Germany was compelled to agree to the notorious Article 231 by which it accepted the responsibility 'for causing all the loss and damage to which the Allied and Associated Governments [had] been subjected as a consequence of the war imposed upon them by the aggression of Germany and her allies'. This clause subsequently caused embarrassment among some of those who had been at Versailles, and arguably it contributed to the policy of appeasement pursued during the 1930s. It also contributed to Hitler's success in winning electoral support during the 1920s and early 1930s; his subsequent actions overturning the Versailles Settlement are generally regarded as helping to maintain the continuing support which the Nazi regime enjoyed.

> We had all – teachers as well as pupils – been caught up long since in the giddy whirl of the new regime's great successes. The growth of Germany's power impressed us.
>
> The mood in March 1938 was particularly thrilling. I stood in front of the display copy of the local newspaper and read and re-read the news: 'The Greater German Reich has been formed. Austria, the Eastern March, is part of Germany once more!' A gentleman standing by said to me: 'Yes, my boy, you can be proud – we are living in great times!' And I felt this too. We were living in great times, and their creator and guarantor was Hitler. Adolf Hitler, for us, was the impressive Führer figure. We took the picture we were given for the man. This did not prevent us from mimicking the stereotyped openings of his speeches, as a joke. But we awaited each speech with the tingling expectation that he was about to announce a new German success. We were seldom disappointed. (Hans Gunter Zmarlik, 'Einer vom Jahrgang 1922', quoted in Detlev J. K. Peukert, *Inside Nazi Germany*, 1989, p.149)

The question of 'guilt' for World War II was levelled at Hitler and the Nazi Party by the victorious Allies, and in 1945 they embarked on policies of denazification. In the Russian sector this involved eradicating the 'classes' which had supported Hitler and in the Western sectors it meant seeking out former members of the Nazi Party and punishing or re-educating them. Perhaps it is understandable that the victors will lay the blame on the vanquished, but Hitler and the Nazi Party were a singularly evil bunch of villains and there has rarely been any serious attempt to suggest, as has often been the case with World War I, that all of the major combatants should share the blame for the outbreak of World War II. As far as the German people were concerned, the evidence suggests that their response to the outbreak of war in 1939 was as muted as it was elsewhere in Europe; similarly there was no popular enthusiasm for Operation Barbarossa in June 1941. However, it has been suggested that there was a degree of continuity in German policy contributing to the outbreak of both world wars.

In 1951, in a new edition of *The Course of German History* (first published in 1945), A. J. P. Taylor posed the question:

The German problem has two sides. How can the peoples of Europe be secured against repeated bouts of German aggression? And how can the Germans discover a settled, peaceful form of political existence? The first problem is capable of solution. Germany is in the centre of Europe and had scored repeated successes by playing off her neighbours to east and west. If these neighbours are united, or even reasonably friendly, then the Germans will not harm us nor even themselves. Nowadays the problem is put in a different form: how can we build up Germany as a Great Power and use her as an ally against the Soviet Union without risk of turning against us? The answer to this is also simple: it is not possible, and those who attempt the impossible will sooner or later pay the penalty. It may be that agreement with the Soviet Union is also impossible. The experiment was abandoned after a few months of sceptical effort; the experiment of living with Germany as a Great Power has been tried, with harsh results, for the last half-century. (A. J. P. Taylor, *The Course of German History*, 1951, p.9)

Ten years later Taylor published *The Origins of the Second World War* which argued forcefully that there was continuity in German foreign policy linking the two wars. The same year saw the publication of Fritz Fischer's *Griff nach der Weltmacht*, which caused a furore in Germany by suggesting not only that the Kaiser's government was quite prepared to risk war in pursuit of their general aims in 1914 but, more seriously, that as soon as the war began they were developing plans, already discussed, for large scale annexations of territory and the creation of a German-dominated new order in Europe. The point was not lost on Taylor.

In 1961 a German professor reported the result of his investigations into German war aims. These were indeed 'a blueprint for aggression' or, as the professor called them, 'a grasp at world power': Belgium under German control; the French iron-fields annexed to Germany; the Ukraine to become German; and, what is more, Poland and the Ukraine to be cleared of their inhabitants and to be resettled with Germans. These plans were not merely the work of the German general staff. They were endorsed by the German foreign office and by 'the good German', Bethmann Hollweg. Hitler, far from transcending his respectable predecessors, was actually being more moderate than they when he sought only *Lebensraum* in the east and repudiated, in *Mein Kampf*, gains in the west. Hitler merely repeated the ordinary chatter of rightwing circles. Like all demagogues, Hitler appealed to the masses. Unlike other demagogues, who sought power to carry out Left policies, Hitler dominated the masses by leftwing methods in order to deliver them to the Right. This is why the Right let him in. (A. J. P. Taylor, 1964, p.23)

Of course, this kind of argument for the continuity of an aggressive German foreign policy linking the Second and Third Reichs has not gone unchallenged.

Exercise Read the essay by Norman Rich, 'Hitler's Foreign Policy', in the Course Reader and answer the following questions:

1   On what grounds does Rich challenge Taylor's assertion that, with reference to foreign policy, there was little difference between Hitler and 'virtually all Germans'?

2   What difference does Rich pinpoint contrasting Hitler's treatment of the Slavs with that of his predecessors? And why does Rich consider this a point worth considering?

3   To what extent does Rich criticize the conclusions of Eberhard Jäckel? Why does he do so? ■

Specimen answers   1   Rich warns that 'more careful scholars' might be less willing to assume a knowledge of what the Germans did or did not want (something which you should, of course, bear in mind when writing your own essays or examination answers). It is probably true to say that the Versailles Settlement provoked resentment in Germany, but it would be difficult to substantiate the argument that virtually all Germans shared Hitler's expansionist aims, or even that previous German diplomats and foreign ministers had shared them; and, as you should have noticed, Rich himself notes inconsistencies in Taylor's comments in this respect.

2   Rich makes the point that while Hitler set out to exterminate the Slavs, his predecessors (and there is only the example of the Prussian rule of Poland which can be deployed as a comparison) sought to Germanize them. The reason for making this comparison is simply to call in question the simplistic assumption that if Germany had won World War I, then the Kaiser's troops and officials would have received similar orders, and behaved in a similar way, to Hitler's. I will return to the question of the extermination of Jews and Slavs later.

3   Generally speaking Rich agrees with Jäckel's conclusions, but he parts company with him when Jäckel suggests that there was a long-standing tendency in the history of Germany for imperialistic territorial conquest. Rich believes that this kind of 'fundamental forces' argument is profoundly unhistorical because it leads to a concentration only on those events which foreshadowed the Third Reich, thus ignoring or underestimating other important aspects of the nation's past which, conceivably, may have been even more significant. Furthermore, this argument suggests that whatever individuals or nations do, there is nothing that will enable them to escape a pre-ordained fate. □

Discussion   I think that there is a problem of two issues converging in this debate which should be thought about separately:

1   responsibility for the outbreak of war in 1914 and in 1939–41;

2   whether the nature of German expansionist plans in 1914–18 and 1939–45 were at all similar.

It is much easier to argue a similarity case for (1) than for (2). All that (1) requires is to show that German policies were designed to alter the status quo, that German decision-makers consciously embarked on a path to achieve their ends which included a readiness to fight wars, and that when their policies got them into a situation in which they actually had to fight a war, then they went ahead. What the precise territorial objectives might have been, and what kind of political order was envisaged after a successful war, are rather different things. Furthermore, perhaps it needs to be stressed that while Fischer's arguments were about the guilt of the decision-makers, he did not raise the question of the German people. Again this distinction needs to be borne in mind when looking at 1939 and 1941, where it becomes contentious because of the more deliberate divorce that historians (and others) have made between the Nazis and the German people compared with that between the Wilhelmine government and the German people.

Taylor's book deals with the outbreak of war in 1939, and there is some justification for arguing that the war did not become a 'world' war until 1941, with the beginning of Germany's war with Russia and the broadening of the conflict in the Far East. As far as Europe is concerned there can be no doubt that the truly titanic struggle was fought on the eastern front between Germany and the USSR. This was the real war as far as many Germans were (and are) concerned. Professor Andreas Hillgruber argued forcefully that the tragedy of World War II was the destruction of Central Europe and the advance of Soviet power. For Hillgruber, one of the principal dynamic forces in modern history was national consolidation. However, Germany's attempts to achieve such consolidation had a serious effect on the international system because the numbers of ethnic Germans, the position of the territories which they inhabited, and the economic richness of those territories, meant that Germany could not be brought together without dominating the international system in Europe. The potential of this domination, in turn, produced massive coalitions to prevent it. In *Zweierlei Untergang: die Zerschlagung des Deutschen Reiches und das Ende des Europäischen Judentums* (literally, *Two kinds of ruin: the breaking of the German Reich and the end of European Jewry*), published in 1986, Hillgruber argued that atrocities committed by the Red Army, and the fear of such, justified the ferocious resistance of the German army and also solved the moral dilemma of their fighting to preserve Hitler's Germany. He urged readers to emphasize and identify with the German soldiers struggling to protect their people and their country against the Red hordes intent on rape and plunder, who were enabling the escape of many thousands of the inhabitants of the Reich's eastern provinces.

But most of the death camps were in the east, and the longer the German army held up the Soviet advance the longer these camps could function. And this leads us on to the other issue of German 'guilt', which has also been taken up in Germany both by historians and others – politicians, journalists, and so on – anxious to come to terms with their country's recent history, and particularly with the question of whether or not Hitler and the Nazis were an aberration or something peculiarly and specifically German.

One of the most controversial books on the question of Nazism is Ernst Nolte's *Der Faschismus in Seiner Epoche: Die action française, Der Italienische Faschismus, Der Nationalsozialismus* (1963, published in English in 1965 as *Three Faces of Fascism*). Nolte argues that Fascism was a European phenomenon of which Hitler and the Nazis were only one variant. 'Fascism', for Nolte,

> . . . is anti-Marxism which seeks to destroy the enemy by the involvement of a radically opposed and yet related ideology and by the use of almost identical and yet typically modified methods, always, however, within the unyielding framework of national self-assertion and autonomy. (Ernst Nolte, *Three Faces of Fascism*, 1965, pp.20–1)

Nolte also suggests that the Holocaust was part and parcel of this development in as much as it was the mirror image of the class murder committed by the Bolsheviks: the European bourgeois (a term used by Nolte) terrified of, and threatened by, the Bolsheviks, turned on a part of itself – namely the Jews. The book was controversial when it was first published, but the whole issue blew up again following an article written by Nolte in the *Frankfurter Allgemeine Zeitung* in June 1986.

The *Historikerstreit* (historians' controversy), which Nolte's newspaper article sparked, raises several philosophical problems, but essentially it focuses on two historical questions:

1   Was the Nazis' mass murder of Jews, as well as of other minorities and 'deviants', something unique, or can it be compared with other historical examples of mass murder and genocide?

2   Was there a causal connection between mass murder by the Nazis (and the acceptance and involvement of ordinary Germans in the Holocaust) and the actions of the Bolsheviks which predated it?

Exercise   Turning back to Rich's essay, how does he describe Jäckel's analysis of the Holocaust? ■

Specimen answer   Jäckel does not attempt to exonerate the German people from their support for Hitler and the voluntary obedience of men to his criminal orders. However, he does stress the lack of information available to most Germans in the Nazi period, and he argues that, although Hitler's programme was outlined in *Mein Kampf*, there is no evidence that he was given power simply to implement this programme. □

Discussion   Jäckel, like most of his contemporaries, participated in the journalistic conflict of the *Historikerstreit*. In particular, he was one of those who pointed out that Nolte's suggestion of a causal relation between mass murder by the Bolsheviks and mass murder by the Nazis was based on the flimsiest of evidence. Jäckel stressed that a considerable amount is now known about the elements that contributed to the way in which Hitler viewed the world and the process of history, and Russian atrocities scarcely figured in this.

The principal problems for individual Germans who were fully aware of the violence and the atrocities of the regime were what they could do about it, and at what point they should have protested. The Holocaust was a very gradual development in Nazi policy. Generally there seems to have been widespread support for a tough 'law and order' policy in Germany during the 1930s. The assault on the Left which followed the Nazi take-over received widespread support, and the first of the concentration camps, at Dachau near Munich, which was established in March 1933, was regarded by many non-Nazis as an acceptable way of dealing with 'troublemakers' and 'revolutionaries'. The extermination of Rohm and the SA in 1934 appears to have been accepted on the grounds that Rohm and many of his lieutenants were homosexuals and the SA were thugs; Hitler, many could believe, wanted decency in everyday life and this was one way of establishing it. As Detlev Peukert notes:

> Many older people today looking back on the Third Reich still see it as having had two strong points in its favour that made up for a lot: people could leave their bicycles unlocked outside their front doors; and long-haired layabouts were hauled off into Labour Camps. Even if such attitudes fell short of a demand for the death penalty or the gas chamber (though these demands were common enough), they testify to the existence of popular consent to a specific form of terror, namely dealing with non-standard behaviour, or non-standard categories of person, by

bundling the individuals concerned into camps and subjecting them to drill even if not to annihilation. It should not be forgotten that a complementary part of the stock folk memory about unlocked bicycles that were safe against theft was the knowledge that gypsies were being arrested as 'theft suspects' and imprisoned in concentration camps. (Peukert, 1989, pp.xx)

The *Kristallnacht* pogrom of November 1938, in contrast, appears to have provoked obloquy for the regime among the population and to have ensured that when the Final Solution began to be implemented in 1941, information about it was circulated by the authorities with considerable circumspection and caution. Protest at this point may have been met with disbelief; it may also have been branded as unpatriotic since the Final Solution began only after the struggle on the eastern front had also begun.

4 THE RISE AND FALL OF GREAT POWERS

Exercise   Thinking back over the course note down:

1   Which great powers dominated Europe in 1914?

2   Which great powers dominated Europe in 1945? ■

Specimen answer   1   In 1914 there was something of a balance between a cluster of 'great powers' in Europe: there were the two great multinational empires of Austria-Hungary and Russia to the east, and the two great imperial powers of Britain and France to the west; in the centre was the newly formed (1871) German Empire; to the south was the newly created Italian state, probably the weakest of the cluster, but with aspirations for an overseas empire like Germany.

2   In 1945 there were two great powers dominant in Europe and the world: the USA and the USSR. □

Discussion   Great powers are generally defined by their economic and military dominance and I don't think that there can be much dispute about the answers given above. Italy scarcely made great-power status even in 1914, and it was badly mauled in the two wars. Austria-Hungary was destroyed as a result of World War I; and Germany was destroyed as a united nation state in the aftermath of the Nazi defeat in 1945. Tangentially, it is interesting to note here the emphasis which some German historians have recently put on Germany's geographical position as a determinant of its status and its relations with other powers. In the discussion of German 'guilt' in section 3, Andreas Hillgruber's analysis of the problems inherent in German national consolidation was mentioned. Hillgruber's work has been taken a stage further in a series of essays and books by Michael Sturmer, who stresses the problems emanating from the *Mittellage* (middle position) of Germany in Europe; this position has proved both a temptation and a curse in Sturmer's estimation. His views have been heavily criticized, however, on the grounds that they appear ultimately to reduce international politics and war solely to matters dependant on geography. Britain and France clung both to empire and to great-power status in 1945, but they can only be construed as middle-ranking powers beside the two super powers of the USA and the USSR. Of course, rather more complex questions follow the pattern of great-power development outlined in the answers to the exercise above and this discussion: what caused this emergence of a bipolar world? was it simply the two world wars?

During the time that this course was being planned and written Paul Kennedy published *The Rise and Fall of the Great Powers: Economic Change and Military Conflict from 1500–2000* (1988). The central chapters of the book deal with the emergence of the bipolar world. Kennedy insists that it is essential, when assessing the strengths and weaknesses of great powers, to do so relatively and in the light of the broader economic and technical changes affecting the world as a whole. Keeping these issues in mind he argues that the origins of the bipolar world were discernible at the close of the nineteenth century. *Fin de siècle* France, for example, was wealthy and industrially advanced, but when comparative economic data are deployed it becomes clear that France was way behind Britain, the United States, Russia and, most significantly, its neighbour and major rival, Germany. Britain was also having to cope with a relative decline in its economic powers, while its new rivals were presenting a potential military threat which was making the difficulties and the costs of protecting sea lanes and empire enormous. The economic and military potential of both the United States and Russia was apparent by the turn of the century, but was held in check in the former by American isolationism, and in the latter by administrative chaos and relatively limited industrial development. Germany, with enormous muscle, was a possible challenger to these emerging giants. The efficiency of German industry and its national organization gave it a tremendous advantage over its Eastern neighbour during World War I. Moreover, the war revealed that the entente powers were incapable of beating Germany and its allies on their own; it was aid from the USA which tipped the balance.

Exercise   If Kennedy is right about the bipolar world being on the cards by the end of the nineteenth and beginning of the twentieth century, why do you suppose – thinking back over the material you have studied in the course – did it not come about as a result of World War I? ■

Specimen answer   In the aftermath of World War I both the USA and the USSR largely disappeared from the international scene: the United States retreated once again into self-imposed isolationism; the USSR became isolated for different reasons – revolution and civil war. □

Discussion   To quote at length from Kennedy:

> The swift post-1919 American withdrawal from foreign engagements, and the parallel Russian isolationism under the Bolshevik regime, left an international system which was more out of joint with the fundamental economic realities than perhaps at any time in the five centuries covered in this book. Britain and France, although weakened, were still at the centre of the diplomatic stage, but by the 1930s their position was being challenged by the militarized, revisionist states of Italy, Japan and Germany – the last intent upon a much more deliberate bid for European hegemony than even in 1914. In the background, however, the United States remained by far the mightiest manufacturing nation in the world, and Stalin's Russia was quickly transforming itself into an industrial superpower. Consequently, the dilemma for the *revisionist* 'middle' powers

was that they had to expand soon if they were not to be overshadowed by the two continental giants. The dilemma for the status quo middle powers was that in fighting off the German and Japanese challenges, they would most likely weaken themselves as well. The Second World War, for all its ups and downs, essentially confirmed those apprehensions of decline. Despite spectacular early victories, the Axis nations could not in the end succeed against an imbalance of productive resources which was far greater than that of the 1914–18 war. What they did achieve was the eclipse of France and the irretrievable weakening of Britain – before they themselves were overwhelmed by superior force. By 1943, the bipolar world forecast decades earlier had finally arrived, and the military balance had once again caught up with the global distribution of economic resources. (Kennedy, 1988, p.xxi)

You might quibble, of course, that this paragraph is redolent with hindsight. To what extent were the politicians and diplomats of the inter-war years thinking in terms of the interrelationship between middle powers and giants? It is doubtful whether Hitler and Mussolini or Chamberlain and Churchill thought in such terms. Furthermore, the paragraph might be charged with a kind of economic determinism. But these are traps which Kennedy is much too good a historian to fall into. In answer to the first charge it is only fair to tell you that the quotation is taken from the wide-ranging introduction which encapsulates the general argument of the book. In answer to the second charge it must be stressed that throughout the book Kennedy explains how economic superiority can be checked, albeit often only temporarily, by other factors. Thus, he suggests, at the end of 1944 – even though it was still occupying vast territories outside the boundaries of the pre-war Reich, and facing Anglo-American forces with a superiority of 20 to 1 in tanks and 25 to 1 in aircraft, not to mention the massive Russian onslaught from the east – the German military held out because of the generally superior calibre and training of its staff officers and NCOs, and the effectiveness of its flexible, decentralized decision-making process on the battlefield.

By the same token the decisions and actions of individuals might accelerate decline, and there are other ways of assessing the decline of individual great powers. It was noted earlier how some German historians have stressed Germany's geographical position as a key determinant in its rise to great-power status and its ultimate destruction as a single nation state. In *The Audit of War*, Correlli Barnett, analysing the decline of Britain since 1945, starts by posing the question: why, given that it was a victor in World War II, did Britain's position deteriorate in such an astonishing way over the next forty years to:

> . . . fourteenth place in the non-communist world in terms of Gross National Product per head, with a balance of payments deficit in goods other than North Sea oil of over £11 billion and a deficit in manufactured goods of £3.6 billion; with little more than a third of West Germany's manufacturing output per head and half that of the United States; with mass unemployment standing at over 13 per cent of the insured population, and a rate one-third worse than in West Germany . . . and with the wasting short-term asset of North Sea oil alone standing between her and economic catastrophe [?] (Correlli Barnett, *The Audit of War*, 1986, pp.7–8)

Barnett concludes that Britain's impressive wartime production had been possible only because of lend-lease and sterling-area credit, and that these masked an out-of-date industrial system. Moreover, he insists that British decline in the aftermath of World War II was overwhelmingly the result of conscious (and wrong) decisions made by the country's ruling élite. During and after the war, he argues, the élite, schooled in Edwardian notions of Britain as a great power both economically and militarily, failed to appreciate the changing nature of industry elsewhere in the developed world. They concentrated on social reform and the construction of a New Jerusalem; they ignored the trend towards large-scale enterprise and sophisticated technology, often government sponsored but always requiring a technologically literate workforce which could only be created through a thorough-going reform of the educational system. The failure to recognize the changes in the world and to implement the necessary reforms left British industry with archaic plant, an archaic institutional framework in which to work, and a workforce incapable of meeting the demands of modern industry. Barnett's case is forcefully argued, though it might be countered that where he employs comparison to highlight a British failure, he scarcely analyses the historical context of the successful rival to demonstrate the particular circumstances which contributed to success. Whether his implied alternatives for Britain were viable in the circumstances of World War II and its aftermath remains a moot point.

References

Angell, N. (1910) *The Great Illusion*, Heinemann.

Barnett, C. (1986) *The Audit of War: The Illusion and Reality of Britain as a Great Nation*, Macmillan.

Bell, P. M. H. (1986) *The Origins of the Second World War in Europe*, Longman.

Blainey, G. (1973) *The Causes of War*, Macmillan.

Bond, B. (1983) *War and Society in Europe, 1870–1970*, Fontana.

Collingwood, R. (1936) 'Human nature and human history', reproduced in R. H. Nash (ed.) (1969).

Craig, G. (1981) *Germany 1866–1945*, Oxford University Press.

Cruttwell, C. R. M. F. (1934) *A History of the Great War*, Oxford University Press.

Falls, C. (1941) *The Nature of Modern Warfare*, Methuen.

Fischer, F. (1967) *Germany's Aims in the First World War*, Chatto and Windus.

Fischer, F. (1975) *World Power or Decline*, Weidenfeld.

Fuller, J. F. C. (1981) *The Conduct of War 1789–1961*, Greenwood.

Fussell, P. (1975) *The Great War and Modern Memory*, Oxford University Press.

Gardiner, P. (1952) *The Nature of Historical Explanation*, Clarendon Press.

Geiss, I. (1972) (ed.) *July 1914 – the Outbreak of the First World War: Selected Documents*, Norton.

Hempel, C. G. (1962) 'Explanation in science and in history', reproduced in R. H. Nash (ed.) (1969).

Howard, M. (1983) *The Causes of War*, Harvard University Press.

Kennedy, P. (1988) *The Rise and Fall of the Great Powers: Economic Change and Military Conflict from 1500–2000*, Unwin and Hyman.

Leed, E. (1979) *No Man's Land: Combat and Identity in World War I*, Cambridge University Press.

Lichtheim, G. (1974) *Imperialism*, Penguin.

Lloyd George, D. (1938) *War Memoirs*, Odhams.

Nash, R. H. (ed.) (1969) *Ideas of History*, Dutton.

Nolte, E. (1965) *Three Faces of Fascism: Action Française, Italian Fascism, National Socialism*, Weidenfeld and Nicolson.

Overy, R. J. (1987) *The Origins of the Second World War*, Longman.

Peukert, D. J. K. (1989) *Inside Nazi Germany: Conformity, Opposition and Racism in Everyday Life*, Penguin.

Repington, C. C. (1920) *The First World War 1914–1918*, Constable.

Russell, B. (1916) *The Principles of Social Reconstruction*, Unwin.

Sallagar, F. M. (1969) *The Road to Total War*, Van Nostrand Reinhold.

Shirer, W. (1941) *Berlin Diary*, Hamish Hamilton.

Smith, M. (1985) 'The tactical and strategic application of air power on the western front' in P. H. Liddle (ed.) (1985) *Home Fires and Foreign Fields*, Brasseys.

Stone N. (1975) *The Eastern Front*, Hodder and Stoughton.

Taylor, A. J. P. (1951) *The Course of German History*, Hamish Hamilton.

Taylor, A. J. P. (1964) *The Origins of the Second World War*, Penguin.

Terraine, J. (1982) *White Heat: The New Warfare, 1914–18*, Sidgwick and Jackson.

Travers, T. (1987) *The Killing Ground: The British Army, the Western Front and the Emergence of Modern Warfare, 1914–1918*, Allen and Unwin.

Walz, K. (1954) *Man, the State and War*, Columbia University Press.

Walzer, M. (1980) *Just and Unjust Wars*, Penguin.

Winter, J. and Wall, R. (eds) (1988) *The Upheaval of War: Family, Work and Welfare in Europe, 1914–1918*, Cambridge University Press.

Wright, G. (1968) *The Ordeal of Total War*, Harper.

Wright, Q. (1942) *A Study of War*, second edition 1965, University of Chicago Press.

UNIT 29 THE PROCESSES OF CHANGE

(Section 1 is written by Arthur Marwick; section 2 by John Golby; section 3 by Bernard Waites)

1 *ASSUMPTIONS AND THEORIES*

Let me share a little secret. The part of the course that most worried my course team colleagues was the section of Book I, Unit 1, where I introduced the distinction between nomothetic and idiographic approaches; fortunately my revised attempt is easier to understand than the original. (Bernard Waites, in Unit 28, presented the distinction in slightly different terms, 'positivist' and 'humanist'.) It would be true to say that conventionally history courses do not bother to go into matters of this sort, and that academics in general prefer their basic assumptions and theories to emerge obliquely from their writings, rather than to state them explicitly at the outset. I hope that this course has demonstrated the value of, as it was put in the Introduction to the Course Reader, 'knowing your historian'. But I would go even further than that and say that it should be fundamental to the make-up of all educated people that they scrutinize all assumptions, particularly their own, with great care. A very large element in arguments and debates over major contemporary issues (and history students, above all, should be qualified to participate in such debates) centres not on facts, but on assumptions. Does one automatically assume a primacy to the 'laws of the market', 'sound finance', 'good housekeeping', the inherent inability of different ethnic or racial communities to live together peacefully, the inevitability of males endeavouring to continue to asset a traditional 'superiority' over females? Does one automatically assume that high public spending is a good thing, that there is something 'right' about victory for the Left, and 'wrong' about victory for the Right, that racial disharmony and the brutality of men towards women are both caused by capitalism? It's about fifteen years since my book *Women at War 1914– 1918* was published, but I still clearly remember one short review, written by a woman, which began along the lines of, 'Why has this book about women been written by a man?', and went on to denounce me for not recognizing that World War I was 'an imperialist war'. That particular label for World War I, as will be clear to all students of this course, begs far too many questions: it derives from a theory of history which, in this case, is utterly incompatible with any sensible, serious study of World War I. The other assumption – that a man cannot write on aspects of history relating to women – is, to say the least, highly debatable.

How does all this relate to the point you, as Open University students, have now reached in your studies? Well, your answers to examination questions will be better to the extent that they will not be based on unstated assumptions: by all means adopt a Marxist approach towards class, or deploy the concepts of élites, or of corporatism, or of modernization, but make it clear what you are doing and, still more importantly, make it clear that *you* are clear about what you are doing. There is a great temptation in academic work to play around with fancy technical terms. Some forms of argument absolutely depend upon such terms, but you are likely to trip up if you use such terms without fully understanding the theory upon which they depend. It is very hard to write history without at some stage using words such as 'ideology' and 'hegemony': if you use such words, be sure that you do know the sense in which you are using them (if in any doubt here, go back and re-read pages 30–40 of Unit 1).

That advice concerns *how* to write exam answers; the following discussion relates to *what* to write in exam answers – or at least *some* exam answers, for it very much depends on the question asked. There are very many possible topics relating to what happened in Europe in the aftermath of World War I which it would be difficult to discuss without referring to the ideas of Charles Maier. In turn, these ideas are difficult to discuss without referring to the basic theories or assumptions which lie behind them. Maier, standing firmly in the tradition of Max Weber, holds a 'class-conflict model' of society, and hence feels it necessary to explain how and why 'stabilization' was attained. It would be a good idea to re-read the extracts from Maier in the Course Reader now, together with the comments in the Introduction and, most importantly, the discussion of Maier in Book III, Units 14 and 15.

If you want an up-to-date account of British society in the twentieth century you could not do better than refer to Harold Perkin's *The Rise of Professional Society: England since 1880* (1989), where the discussion of the effects of the two world wars is very judicious (see chapter 6, and section 1 of chapter 9). However, in considering Perkin's insistence that there was a 'crisis of class society' between 1910 and 1926 (this is rather similar to Maier), and his central thesis that 'professional society' has now taken over from 'class society', it is vital to be aware that Perkin is a Weberian with a 'class-conflict model' of society. His statement that: 'Every society contains the seeds of its own decay' (p.436) is, in the grand manner of the nineteenth century, redolent of that 'idealism' with which Schuker reproached Maier (Unit 27), and might be thought out of place in a historian writing at the end of the 1980s.

But what such a statement also shows is that Perkin has a clear conception of how social change comes about. And this, above all, is what you must be *thinking* about as you reach the end of this course. You will be getting further guidance on this in the remainder of this unit, and also in sections 2 and 4 of Unit 30. Meanwhile, it would be a good idea to go back and re-read Unit 5, where I set out some general ideas on how to discuss the ways in which social change takes place.

Some of you, I know, will have a strong interest in feminist approaches to historical study. In Units 8–10, section 2.8, I suggested some of the reasons for the general resistance of feminist historians to the view that wars had any positive effects on the position of women. Feminism may imply no more than a particular interest in subjects relating to women, or it may mean a whole set of assumptions, often closely related to the cultural theory and post-structuralism referred to in Unit 1. We noted in Unit 27 that, although Simone de Beauvoir did recognize a connection between the experiences of World War I and women in Britain gaining the vote, she was a strong progenitor of the increasingly influential notion that women are shaped by society. As I noted in that unit, whether one regards all phenomena relating to human beings in society as being *determined* by society, or simply as *influenced* by society, is really central to the way in which one approaches many historical issues. Were there, for example, genuine feelings of national unit in 1914, genuine attachments to royalty, or were these sentiments simply 'socially constructed' in the interests of the ruling classes? These really are fundamental issues for you to think about.

If you do feel attracted to Marxist analysis then two points should be noted here: first, you do have to show that you have grasped the more idiographic (or empirical) approaches presented in most of our units; second, it is unwise to talk airily about Marxism unless you really have a good grasp of what Marx actually said.

One assumption we all share is that fundamental to all historical study is the critical analysis of primary sources. As you know, you will be asked in Part I of the exam to write commentaries on two extracts from the sources contained in your two documents' volumes. The first point is to be absolutely sure you are clear what you are being asked to do: the question asks you to say what the document is, to set it in its historical context, to comment on points in the text, and to sum up its significance for the study of war, peace and social change. Be very sure that that is exactly what you do. Don't, for instance, write a general essay vaguely related to the subject matter of the extract. Some of you may remember the unseen documents exercises I set in the *Introduction to History* in the Arts Foundation Course: there the exercise was almost exclusively in technique and did not call for detailed historical knowledge. In this course, in addition to adopting the correct technique (that is to say, doing exactly what you are asked to do), you need to have a considerable amount of historical knowledge in order to give the historical context, and in order to be able to sum up the significance of the extract. The exercise is designed to bring you as close as possible to the actual practices of a working historian though, of course, there is inevitably something artificial about it. Historians work from whole documents, and indeed from whole bundles of documents, not from single extracts. We have preselected documents for you, with a clear idea in our own minds of their historical significance. Working historians would seldom be likely to accept the testimony of one single document without checking it against many others. You have to take it on trust if we tell you that a particular document is in fact representative of a number of similar documents. The best way of ensuring that you have got the right technique for writing commentaries on documents is (a) to look back to the first document-TMA that you did and to the comments your tutor made on it; and (b) to look back to those places in the course where you were given a very full example of how to do this kind of exercise (Unit 1, pp.27–30; Unit 5, pp.202–3; Units 22–25, pp.131–3). In a moment, I will talk you through just one more example.

What other advice can I give you about preparing to cope with this aspect of the exam? In the exam you have a choice of two extracts out of six. This suggests that it would be wise to prepare yourself thoroughly on at least half the total number of documents. If you have been working systematically through the course, following our directions, you will already have encountered almost all of the documents; some you may have made use of in your TMAs. The documents are an astonishingly rich and varied collection, which can be read for enlightenment and pleasure. I recommend that you look through both volumes trying to see if, at least in a general way, you know why we have chosen each particular document – that is to say, what its significance is. The documents to revise most thoroughly are the ones that fall within subject areas that particularly interest you. It is important that you are familiar with the entire content of these documents: in the exam, you just get a short extract, but in order to be able to comment effectively on it you have to know what is in the rest of the document. (Don't misunderstand me here: in commenting on the extract you refer to the extract in front of you, but, nevertheless, to do this effectively you will nearly always have to make some reference to what else is in the whole document, or about where in the document the extract you are commenting on comes from.) In the *Introduction to History* in the Arts Foundation Course, I spell out all the individual critical questions a historian asks of a document: we now take it for granted that you know to look out for questions of dating, of how biased, or how representative, the author of a particular document is, and so on.

The following extract is similar to one you might encounter in Part I of the exam:

> During the many years of peaceable neighbourly existence, the two countries have become united by many ties, and a social upheaval in the one is bound to affect the other. That these troubles will be of a social, and not a political, nature cannot be doubted, and this will hold true, not only as regards Russia, but for Germany as well. An especially favourable soil for social upheavals is found in Russia, where the masses undoubtedly profess, unconsciously, the principles of Socialism. In spite of the spirit of antagonism to the Government in Russian society, as unconscious as the Socialism of the broad masses of the people, a political revolution is not possible in Russia, and any revolutionary movement inevitably must degenerate into a Socialist movement. The opponents of the government have no popular support. The people see no difference between a government official and an intellectual. The Russian masses, whether workmen or peasants, are not looking for political rights, which they neither want nor comprehend. (P. N. Durnovo, memorandum to the Tsar, February 1914)

Now, what I suggest you do (something you couldn't do in the exam, of course!) is turn to the entire document in *Documents 1* (extract I.28). (In fact, this is not the entire document, but extracts the course team has chosen.) You will see there that we give you some important information about Durnovo (we generally only do this where such information is not readily available to you in the course units or in Roberts). I suggest that you now read carefully everything that we have printed about Durnovo's memorandum.

As you will have readily noted, this is an immensely rich document, covering both foreign and domestic issues. Thus, while the general significance of whatever extract you are given to comment on might be roughly the same, its particular significance will depend upon the particular extract in front of you. But you will see also how the extract I have selected takes on much more meaning once you are aware of how it fits in to the memorandum as a whole. Thus, ideally, you should bring with you into the exam room, locked away in your mind (with respect, that is, to dealing with this particular extract), a broad knowledge of all of the selections from the memorandum that we have printed for you, the knowledge provided about Durnovo, relevant information about previous developments in Russia from Units 2–5, about the origins of the war from Unit 6, and about subsequent developments in Russia from Units 11–13. You should be able to make use of that knowledge in at least one essay question.

Let us look at the individual questions you have to answer.

What is the document?

To repeat that it is a 'memorandum' doesn't take us much further, but it is still worth stating clearly what the document is. You could then say that it is a piece of private advice being offered to the Tsar by an elder statesman, someone who is (and this is important) representative of the extreme reactionary elements in Russia, who were, of course, both numerous and influential among the upper classes.

What is the document's historical context?

Here the date is clearly of crucial importance. This is seven months before the outbreak of World War I, six months before the fateful assassination of Archduke Franz Ferdinand. The context is one of an international alliance system which has been lining up the powers in two armed camps, and of a series of international crises which, to a right-wing politician like Durnovo, suggested that general war was imminent. He would, of course, be particularly sensitive to the implications of the Balkan Wars. The precise element which has provoked Durnovo's memorandum is the way in which Russia has become embroiled (as he sees it) in an alliance with Britain and France, which puts it in the opposite camp from Germany and means that, if war breaks out (which he believes to be very likely) Russia will be forced to fight against Germany. The purpose of the memorandum is to persuade the Tsar to reverse this policy before it is too late. Essentially the document as a whole consists of a range of arguments in support of this plea. Durnovo's fundamental conviction is that, because of their economic rivalry, war between Germany and Britain is inevitable (interesting how this extreme reactionary presents arguments which are also vintage Marxism!), and that many other powers will then automatically be drawn in to an immensely destructive war. His basic point is that, as the two great conservative powers, Russia and Germany are natural allies. (These two sentences are good examples of contextual points which are derived from knowledge of the entire document.)

What are the specific points in the text?

The first phrases which call for discussion are 'peaceable neighbourly existence' and 'united by many ties'. Again we find explanations earlier in the document: there is the point about Russia and Germany being the two leading conservative, autocratic and imperial powers, but more important with regard to the second phrase is the question of heavy German investment in Russian industry. From more general historical knowledge, one might comment that the phrase 'peaceable neighbourly existence' is not entirely accurate: under Bismarck it had been a principle of German policy never to come into conflict with Russia, but 'Germany's drive to the east', as seen, for example, in its investment in Turkey, was a potential cause of friction with Russia, and, still more, its support for Austria meant an embroilment in a sharp conflict of interests in the Balkans. The whole sentence forms an important link in Durnovo's argument against Russia becoming involved in a general European war. He argues in the previous paragraph that defeat in such a war would entail social revolution, and he then reasons that because of the close links between the two countries, social upheaval in the one would inevitably lead to social upheaval in the other – thus even if victory might be envisaged, it still would not be worth becoming embroiled in a war.

The distinction Durnovo makes between 'social' and 'political' is interesting and revealing: what he means only becomes clear once one has read the whole paragraph. It becomes clear that by 'political revolution' he simply means a change in the ruling group; what he means by 'social revolution' becomes fully clear from the beginning of the paragraph that immediately follows our extract (yet another example of the advantages of knowing the document as a whole); social revolution means the peasants gaining land, the workers taking over the capitalist profits of the bosses. The tenor of Durnovo's argument, then, is that the result of war will be much worse than mere political change; it will be complete social upheaval. The soil, he goes on to say, is especially favourable in Russia. There were, of course, developed socialist parties in Russia at this time, particularly the Bolsheviks led by Lenin; but this 'unconscious' socialism that he speaks of seems to be akin to what is often spoken of as the 'land hunger' of the peasants. Undoubtedly that existed.

Durnovo goes on to show his contempt for the political opposition in Russia (presumably he is thinking of the Kadets) who have failed to make the spirit of antagonism to the government conscious. Even more interesting in this sentence is the apparent contrast between Russian society, which he seems to be limiting to those who have some feelings about the nature of government, and the broad masses of the people. This is very characteristic of the arrogance and contempt for the Russian people shown by many in Durnovo's class. Because of a lack of political consciousness, the argument goes, any revolution will be a socialist one. Once again he stresses the horrific consequences of war. Again he points to the distinction between the political classes and the popular class, where the former have no real support. On the whole this is in itself a shrewd judgement and the Bolsheviks, indeed, were very aware that they would have to provide the revolutionary leadership.

The final two sentences are again very contemptuous of the Russian people. The jibe about intellectuals (that is those of liberal sentiments) appearing to the people as indistinguishable from government officials is very typical of the kind of reactionary stance Durnovo represents. There is, of course, much truth in what he says: Russia *was* a backward country and, what is almost worse, a leading member of the upper class expresses a kind of scoffing acceptance of this. But the last sentence may represent something of the kind of fatal miscalculation people like Durnovo were liable to make: not *all* workmen and peasants were so ignorant; some, particularly among the workers, were already showing political aspirations.

What is the document's significance in the study of war, peace and social change?

Even within this extract you can see that Durnovo is, in February 1914, envisaging war as a very real probability. With regard, then, to the question of the origins of World War I, this document is significant in showing that a senior politician fully expected war, which, in turn, serves to support the thesis that the question is not why war broke out in August 1914, but rather why it did not break out earlier. Within the extract, we can see that Durnovo is arguing that Russia should withdraw from an alliance which will involve it in war with Germany. So we can see that some conservatives in Russia, just as much as liberals in Britain, thought that an alliance between Britain and Russia was indeed unnatural. However, what the extract is mainly about is the perception that Russian society is so backward, and so divided, that war will inevitably lead to social revolution. The resigned pessimism of political figures like Durnovo was, of course, one of the things that was wrong with Russia, an attitude that made political reform so difficult. But the central significance is that we have here evidence of an experienced politician perceiving, *in advance*, the relationship between war and revolution.

Note that I have not here been providing a 'specimen answer'. Here I have been talking you through the *thought processes* in preparing yourself to write a commentary on an extract from a document.

2 SOCIAL CHANGE 1900–1955

In discussing social changes in Europe in the first half of the twentieth century, I am reminded of the advice given by Josef L. Altholz when writing about religion in Victorian England: 'The most important thing to remember . . . is that there was an awful lot of it' ('The warfare of conscience with theology', 1976). The same can be said for the social changes in the first half of the twentieth century which were so intensive and wide-ranging that the Europe existing in 1955 was a vastly different and largely unrecognizable place from that of Europe before 1914.

The subject of the extent, nature and causes of social change between 1900 and 1955 in Europe is the first of the six stated aims of the course, clearly set out in Book I, Unit 1, page 10. But in a course which is concerned with war, peace and social change, it is impossible to keep this aim separate from the others, particularly aim (4) which concentrates on enabling 'students to argue in an informed way about the causes of twentieth-century social change, and in particular to evaluate the significance of the two total wars with respect to this change relative to "structural" . . . political and ideological forces'. What I intend to do in this short section is to refresh your memory about how we have examined social change over this period, and in doing so I shall discuss three basic and overlapping questions: What is meant by social change? How does social change come about? How do we measure change? Later, in sections 2 and 4 of Unit 30, I shall look briefly at the extent of some of these changes when I discuss the debates over the impact and consequences of the two world wars.

What is meant by social change?

This was the first question you were asked at the start of the course. It is also, with a slight but important variation, the first question posed by the editors in their introduction to the Course Reader, where they shift the direction of their question by asking 'What do *we* mean by social change?' The editors do so because in this course we have tried to explore this question primarily through the examination of ten interrelated areas of social change, which by now must be firmly embedded in your minds. But this is only one particular method (although I hope you have found it a rewarding one) of answering the question of what is meant by social change. Other historians, such as Charles Maier and Arno J. Mayer, would approach the question in much broader terms of class conflicts and changing structures of power. The major difference between our approach and Maier's is that while we place more emphasis on an investigation of the ten areas of social change, Maier attempts to apply theory and to give greater emphasis to long-term structural changes. In the introduction to the Course Reader, and again in Units 1 and 27, Arthur Marwick refers to this distinction by writing of an 'idiographic' and a 'nomothetic' approach. But even here, as Marwick admits, the distinction is blurred because 'The division is not a hard-and-fast one; most historians recognize that their subject does differ significantly from any of the natural sciences, while, at the same time, most of those who avoid general theories do recognize the need for generalization and the exploration of structural interrelationships: many historians, it could be said, incorporate elements from both approaches' (Course Reader, p.3).

Nevertheless, although there may be degrees of difference rather than sharp distinctions, the particular approach of a historian is crucial to his or her interpretation of the next question we are about to examine, that of how change comes about.

How does social change come about?

In section 2.4 of Unit 1, Arthur Marwick, while discussing the place of the two total wars in assessing social change in the twentieth century, states that although there is no attempt in this course to argue that war is the most important cause of major social change, it is necessary 'to evaluate the significance of war as against all other possible factors' (p.21). He elaborates upon these other factors in Unit 5 and describes them as:

1   *Structural*: those factors that 'refer to the broader forces in society which, irrespective of the intentions of individuals or groups of individuals, bring about changes affecting, willy-nilly, large sectors of the population. Industrialization, application of technology, economic growth, population growth, and the emergence of new social classes and groups, involve changes in the very *structure* of society' (p.168).

2   *Ideological*: great movements of ideas such as socialism, democracy and modernism.

3   *Political or guided*: change brought about by the actions of individuals or groups. For example, individual politicians, trade unions or other pressure groups.

Arthur Marwick refers to another factor – contingency – which covers chance events and occurrences which affect social change. In Unit 1, page 17, Arthur Marwick cites the assassination of Archduke Franz Ferdinand as an example of contingency, although he readily admits that there were other longer-term and deep-seated forces which led to this 'chance event'. Perhaps a better example of contingency is the importance of the Colorado beetle epidemic in France in the 1930s, mentioned in Unit 15.

Again, as Arthur Marwick points out, these different headings are not totally distinct from each other. For example, it could be argued that human actions are responsible for the way in which technology is applied, and therefore non-structural elements are present in the 'structural' heading, although Arthur Marwick counters this by arguing that in the last resort the classification must be structural because the effect of the application of technology 'has ramifications for whole societies which go far beyond the conscious decisions of individuals or groups' (Unit 5, p.168).

During the course of your studies this year you have come across the writings of a wide range of historians, all of whom have their own various interpretations and explanations of how change came about in the first half of the twentieth century. In relation to the first aim of the course, it is especially important to appreciate the analysis of the period before World War I made by Arno J. Mayer. In the Preface to his book, *The Persistence of the Old Regime* (1981), Mayer declared he was writing 'a Marxist history from the top down, not the bottom up, with the focus on the upper rather than the lower classes'. One of Mayer's basic arguments was that other historians had underestimated the strength of the *anciens régimes* in pre-1914 Europe.

> For too long historians have focused excessively on the advance of science and technology, of industrial and world capitalism, of the bourgeoisie and professional middle class, of liberal civil society, of democratic political society, and of cultural modernism. They have been far more preoccupied with these forces of innovation and the making of the new society than with the forces of inertia and resistance that slowed the waning of the old order. (p.4)

While Mayer argues for the persistence of the old regime, Charles J. Maier claims that pre-World War I Europe was essentially bourgeois-dominated. His thesis, expounded in *Recasting Bourgeois Europe*, claims that what emerged after World War I in Germany in particular, but also to a lesser extent in Italy and France, was a growth of what he called corporatism. This is discussed in Unit 14 and in the Introduction to your Course Reader, pages 25–7. In Unit 27, Arthur Marwick uses extracts from an article written by Maier in 1981 in which he attempted to extend his thesis to the period following World War II.

Although Mayer and Maier disagree entirely in their interpretation of society before 1914, both their approaches fall into the category that Arthur Marwick terms *nomothetic*. Arthur Marwick and John Roberts, on the other hand, as liberal humanists or pluralists, would regard themselves as having *idiographic* approaches. But adopting these labels would not prevent them from admitting the importance played by structural forces in any analysis of social change in the twentieth century. Of course, Marxist analysts of social change in Europe in this period have continually emphasized the primacy of long-term structural as opposed to non-structural forces. Consequently, in the debates that we have followed in this course on the significance and impact of the two world wars on social change, Marxist historians have usually dismissed 'the effects of wars as being of minor account compared with longer-term structural forces' (Unit 5, p.169). But we must not fall into the trap of believing that one has to be a Marxist historian to take this particular line. As Arthur Marwick states in Unit 1 (p.21), 'Very many historians, both non-Marxist and Marxist, would contend (and it does indeed seem very difficult to disagree) that the great changes of the twentieth century – higher living standards for the mass of the people, expanded welfare provision, greater (if still circumscribed) freedom and new roles for women, a key position in society for the mass media, and so on – are essentially the product of long-term economic, industrial and technological processes.'

The problem, however, as Arthur Marwick has pointed out from time to time throughout the course, is that those historians who continually ascribe change to long-term factors, whether these factors be structural or ideological, are in danger of failing to ask important questions such as why did things happen when they did, and in the way they did. As Arthur Marwick wrote in his introduction to *Total War and Social Change* (1988):

> The ultimate concern of the historian is not with what might have happened, or what would have happened, but with what actually did happen. The purely temporary and short-term must, of course, be winnowed out from the lasting and long-term, and, of course, the latter is

much more worthy of attention than the former. But it is important, too, to remember that historians are concerned with the lives of real human beings. Within the short lifespans allotted to us all, it may matter very much indeed whether child welfare clinics are introduced when we are 22 or 37, or the right to study for the bar when we are leaving school or when we are about to retire, or decent living standards at one point in time or twenty years later. (p.xiii)

Because of their insistence on the primacy of certain long-term factors, some historians have ignored asking specific questions about why certain events occurred at particular times, and instead have resorted to generalizations. For example, in Unit 1, page 22, Arthur Marwick quotes Wolfgang J. Mommsen who, in discussing Germany and World War I, argues that the war only accelerated the 'processes of change in economy and society which had already been under way for a considerable time'. Again, in Units 22–25, page 152, Tony Aldgate quotes from Angus Calder's book, *The People's War*, 1971, in which Calder claims that the effect of World War II on Britain, 'was not to sweep society on to a new course, but to hasten its progress along the old grooves'. Whether or not Calder and Mommsen are right or wrong in their overall analyses of the effects of the wars on Britain and Germany is not really the major point here, but in their anxiety to argue in favour of long-term forces, they are forced into using words such as 'accelerate' and 'hasten', which do not help to answer the questions of why World War I accelerated change in Germany and World War II hastened Britain 'along the old grooves'.

But even if we ask all the questions concerning how and why change comes about, this still does not answer another concern of the course, namely, how we measure these changes.

How do we measure change?

The simple answer to this question is to apply both the qualitative and quantitative approaches mentioned by Arthur Marwick in Unit 1, page 40, to the ten areas of social change with which the course is concerned. However, as you have learned by now, it is of little value attempting to assess the effects of war on social change merely by looking at the state of Europe in 1939 and comparing it with its condition in 1945. Mark Roseman's article, printed in the Course Reader, argues clearly that to answer this sort of question, consideration must be given to the changes carried out by the Nazis in their six years of rule before the outbreak of war. Again, a large section of Unit 5 was devoted to stressing how important it was, in any analysis of the part played by World War I in the major social changes which occurred in the twentieth century, to understand the fundamental features of pre-1914 societies, and what changes were already taking place within these societies before 1914. Incidentally, if you constructed an exercise chart of the changes already taking place in Europe before 1914, as Arthur Marwick suggested in Unit 5, you will have an excellent document with which to start your revision. This, together with Units 26 and 27, will enable you to assess the extent of social change which has taken place in Europe over the period 1900 to 1955.

3 CONTINUITY AND STABILITY IN EUROPE, 1890–1950

Any European born in 1890 and entering old age in 1950 would have sensed that his or her life had been encompassed by an enormous disruption in history caused primarily by war and violence. When G. D. H. Cole (1889–1958), one of the best-informed minds of his day and a person not given to rhetorical excess, concluded *The Intelligent Man's* [sic] *Guide to the Post-war World*, he warned his readers: '. . . the plain truth [is] we are at the crisis of our civilisation . . . hope for the future depends on our success in keeping the knowledge of what is good alive among men, even if, under stress of the times, their collective deeds are terribly evil' (Cole, 1947, p.1083). This sense of crisis induced by massive collective violence – a crisis which had broken traditions of legality and civility – was shared by many contemporary intellectuals. Hannah Arendt (b.1906), who did much to articulate the consciousness of crisis, claimed in 1950 that 'On the level of historical insight and political thought there prevails an ill-defined, general agreement that the essential structure of all civilizations is at the breaking point' (Arendt, *The Origins of Totalitarianism*, 1951, Preface).

It would be perverse to deny the objective realities that prompted this 'general agreement'. For the inhabitants of Central and Eastern Europe, in particular, the upheavals of war, revolution, state coercion and forced migration had cut the present loose from the past. A sixty-year old Pole would have grown to maturity as the subject of an autocratic monarchy, spent his or her thirties and forties as a citizen of an independent East European republic, watched helplessly as Nazi Germany and Soviet Russia partitioned his or her country, endured the barbarities of occupation, and seen a new, socialist Polish state founded, with its centre of gravity shifted considerably to the west, and from which German speakers were ruthlessly expelled. Far more than a change of name distinguished the new Wroclaw from the old Breslau: in the late nineteenth century Baedeker had described the latter for prospective tourists as a thoroughly German town. When its garrison finally succumbed to Soviet and Polish forces in 1945, the town's empty shell was given a Slav name and completely repopulated with Polish refugees from the east. Similar new settlements on old sites were made throughout the so-called Recovered Territories of post-war Poland and in all the former Polish cities incorporated after 1945 into the USSR (Davies, *God's Playground*, 1981, pp.512–14). A complete break is no less evident in the industrial history of Poland: in the generation before 1914, manufacturing industry had 'taken off' in the Tsarist Polish lands as a result of the influx of Western capital and machinery and the protection of the imperial tariff. The industrial sector's performance had peaked in 1913. After World War I, the authorities of the new state had struggled to integrate parts of hitherto different economies. 'Their tentative steps were rudely terminated by the Second World War, whose conclusion, as in most spheres of Polish life, necessitated a completely fresh start' (Davies, 1981, p.164). Even the religious monopoly of Catholicism in post-war Poland – which apparently links the society with the traditions and culture of Western Europe – is the unlooked-for outcome of war and violence: about a third of the citizens of the pre-war Republic were non-Catholics. This minority included 3.3 million Jews who comprised about 10 per cent of the total population and more than a quarter of town dwellers.

Given these circumstances, to focus on 'continuity' and 'stability' in Polish political and social life would be like admiring the marine architecture of the sinking *Titanic*. But Poland is, I think, an extreme case. If we turn our attention to other societies, particularly those of Western Europe, the elements of continuity in their economic, social and demographic history between the late nineteenth and mid-twentieth century appear exceptionally strong. By this I mean that we can trace over this sixty-year period clear trends in economic development, population growth, and social organization and institutions which indicate the persistence of long-term forces for change of a different order to the short-term fluctuations associated with war and violence. Furthermore, if we examine Western societies around 1950 we find that in certain significant ways they had changed remarkably little over fifty years. Britain represents, I think, the extreme case in the steady continuity of its development and the stability of its political and social institutions: its industrial structure in 1950 evinced a joint inheritance of nineteenth-century staples (coal, textiles, heavy engineering, shipbuilding) and newer industries (organic chemicals, electrical engineering, automobiles), the origins of which lay mostly in the period between 1890 and 1914. The impact of war resulted in only marginal perturbations in British demographic history. The stability of Britain's social structure can be demonstrated by the constancy over time of a relatively low rate of social mobility from the manual working class to other social strata (relative, that is, to the rates of social mobility observable *since* 1950).

In the context of the course as a whole, to focus on the extreme case of continuity and stability would be as misleading as focusing on the extreme case of discontinuity. This should not lead us to that favoured stratagem of British dialectics: 'on the one hand . . . and on the other . . .' We can sustain a general argument that, as we move east through Europe, then we observe an intensification of the combined effects of war and political coercion on social development, whereas as we move west we see development arising autonomously from within civil society.

This (very approximate) geographical differentiation is itself a continuation of long-standing differences in the histories of East and West Europe since the post-feudal period: serfdom was imposed later, but lasted much longer in Eastern Europe where the towns did not win (as they did in the West) autonomy and self-government from the feudal nobility. Consequently, the development of civil or bourgeois society was comparatively attenuated. In many parts of Eastern Europe, Jews made up a quite disproportionate number of town dwellers and middle-class entrepreneurs; their civil disabilities and the climate of prejudice made it virtually impossible for them to play a political role comparable to that of the Western bourgeoisie. In Tsarist Russia, the political environment of the patrimonial state, the rulers of which regarded monopoly on productive wealth as a natural complement to autocracy, long exercised a stifling effect on private commerce and industry. Under the 'old regime', which persisted until about 1880, trade and manufacture were centred in the countryside, and urban society was markedly different in character from that in the West, for the commercial and industrial classes did not constitute the bulk of the urban population. Cities had a long history of regimentation by the state, and the forcible movements of populations after 1945 were the revival of a not-so-distant tradition (Pipes, *Russia Under the Old Regime*, 1977, pp.194–203). When the Russian 'old regime' began a rapid process of industrial modernization, the state had to act as a substitute for the autonomous forces of civil society in the West by itself promoting railway construction, encouraging foreign investment, and imposing harsh indirect taxes on basic necessities in order to fund economic growth.

My point is this: while twentieth-century war and political coercion have massively disrupted Eastern Europe, they disrupted it from a path of development which was already different, in important respects, from that of the West. (Czechoslovakia is the critical exception to this sweeping assertion: it had inherited 70 per cent of the industrial capacity of the Austro-Hungarian Empire and was the most economically developed state in Central-East Europe. It was also integrated with the Western economies through international cartels. Zauberman, 'Russia and Eastern Europe, 1920–1970', 1976, pp.595–602.)

As you will know, economic recovery from World War II followed different paths: states within the Soviet sphere of influence were forced to adopt the Stalinist pattern of development and were incorporated within the largest economic unit in the world, Comecon. They attempted to centralize and regulate their economies through national plans; they concentrated investment in the capital goods industries, enforced rigid price control, denied consumers many of the goods which were now being mass produced in the West, and (with the important exception of Poland) collectivized their agriculture. It would be churlish to deny that there were important social benefits to this form of development in the universal provision of health and educational services and unprecedented opportunities for social mobility. Furthermore, the initial phase of planned industrialization was spectacularly successful: Hungarian heavy industrial production increased five-fold between 1949 and 1953; the engineering industry was seven times more productive in 1953 than in 1938. But this growth was grossly distorted: wages and salaries fell far behind prices, the peasantry was demoralized by forced collectivization and the denial of agricultural investment, and the pent-up social resentments flowed into a detestation for the police state which broke out into political rebellion in 1956, not just in Budapest, but in Warsaw and Poznan too (Fejto, A History of the People's Democracies, 1974, pp.362–4).

The pattern of development in the 'mixed economies' of Western Europe during their longest secular boom did, it is true, display certain relatively novel features: the state and para-state agencies had important (but not entirely unprecedented) roles in promoting economic reconstruction and industrial growth in France, Italy and Austria. Generally, the balance of private and public power had shifted towards the latter, and the Keynesian-inspired doctrine that government could and should 'manage' aggregate demand to maintain full employment through manipulation of the fiscal system won considerable intellectual support, although in practice governments were rarely confronted with shortfalls in demand. But these were novel features of a basically familiar economic system. Andrew Shonfield put the point well when he defended the title of his book, *Modern Capitalism* (1969):

> . . . I have decided to stick to the old-fashioned capitalist label . . . because I believe that our societies continue to possess many characteristics which are inextricably connected with their antecedents in the nineteenth and the first half of the twentieth centuries; the word helps to emphasize the continuity. There are, after all, still large areas of economic activity which are open to private venture capital, and in these areas its success or failure is determined by the familiar ingredients: the amount of liquid funds available, the efficiency with which they are manipulated, the personal

initiative of the controllers of this private wealth and the enterprise of competing owners or managers of private capital. Moreover, the prizes for individual success are still large, and they convey on those who win them considerable economic power. (p.3)

Let us identify some of the continuities in capitalism between 1890 and 1950. This economic system has consistently falsified J. S. Mill's prediction that it would reach 'a steady state' and Marx's that it would burst asunder its 'integument' of private property relations. On the contrary, it has shown a more or less constant capacity to increase total output and productivity within a general framework of private ownership. In the 1890s there began, however, a major transformation in that framework (usually referred to as the rise of the corporate economy) which has continued to this day, not – I hasten to add – in a steady progress but in surges which have brought an increasing volume of economic activity within the control of giant firms. In Britain's manufacturing industry, the largest 100 firms accounted for barely 15 per cent of output in 1900; their share rose steadily until about 1919, then at a quicker pace until 1930, by when they accounted for over a quarter of output. During the Depression and World War II their share fell back somewhat, but after the late 1940s it increased constantly until, by the mid-1970s, the 100 dominant firms accounted for nearly half total output. This transformation has resulted from both the internal growth of individual firms and waves of business mergers: the first in 1898–1900; the second in 1918–1920; the third at the end of the 1920s; and the fourth biggest and most prolonged wave from the late 1950s to the late 1960s (Hannah, *The Rise of the Corporate Economy*, 1976).

The concentration of industrial capital has been a general feature of national economies in the twentieth century, notwithstanding very significant differences within and between them. Small firms have held their own in industries where the capital-threshold is relatively low, the product diverse and subject to frequent change, and entrepreneurs have been able to exploit low-paid outwork. Academic publishing would fit this bill, but the clothing and fashion trades are the classic example. Where industrial processes have demanded a high capital threshold in order to exploit the scientific and technological innovations of the late nineteenth century (as in the chemicals, electrical and automobile industries), giant firms have been the order of the day. They have tended to grow 'horizontally', by merging with other manufacturers, and also 'vertically' by integrating the control of raw material resources and the marketing of their final products within professionally managed, multi-unit, hierarchically organized corporations.

Compared with the United States and Germany, the degree of concentration in the British economy before World War I was low. Since America led the world from about 1890 in pioneering organizational changes in capital, and in the industrial labour process, we need to take a glance at its economy. Tendencies to monopoly were evident from the 1870s, and Anti-Trust legislation enacted to control it had the unintended effect of encouraging business take-overs because it outlawed agreements between separate firms to limit competition. The American industrial boom of the later 1890s was accompanied by a great wave of mergers, many of them speculative ventures on the part of financial 'tycoons' which did not last, but others which permanently altered the organization of capital in large sectors of American industry. In particular, those areas of manufacturing which were capital-intensive, relied on continuous or large-batch technology, and were capable of standardized production for mass markets, fell under the domination of large corporations. (Procter and Gamble and Eastman Kodak are examples of large-batch, continuous-process producers; the Singer Sewing Machine Company of a monopoly producer of standardized products for a mass market. All three firms were dominant in their respective markets by the later 1880s.) One very important side effect of the merger boom was the acceleration of the 'managerial revolution', for to profit fully from the economies provided by merger, firms had to integrate vertically (thus gaining control of supplies and distribution) and create a hierarchy of salaried managers to co-ordinate operations and supervise many distinct operating units. These new, managerial hierarchies internalized within the firm functions which had previously been co-ordinated by market and price mechanisms (and in more traditional business sectors remained so) (Chandler, 'The United States', 1980, pp.9–29).

In roughly the same period as the rise of the corporate economy, professional mechanical engineers were effecting sweeping reforms in factory organization by rigorously applying principles of mechanical and economic efficiency to the labour process. 'Scientific management' – as it came to be called – found its leading exponent and publicist in F. W. Taylor, whose best-known innovations are 'time–work study' (in order to determine the most efficient use of labour) and incentive-wage systems to encourage the worker to maximize output. In fact, Taylor's role in the emergence of the modern factory went far deeper than these measures: he pioneered the development of high-speed chromium steel, introduced the sequential ordering of machines in factories so that production would 'flow' as smoothly as possible, and brought an enormous technical creativity to the invention and adaptation of machine tools. He preached a philosophy of centralized management and functional foremanship which was intended to strip the individual craftsman of autonomy and expertise; though far from realized in its entirety, it had a considerable impact on factory labour throughout the industrial world.

If Taylor was the most representative figure of the American 'factory revolution', then the Highland Park factory, built by Henry Ford in 1908–1910 to manufacture the model 'T', was its quintessential material result. Here the assembly-line production of a multicomponent consumer durable was perfected. To achieve continuous production, Ford scrapped his existing machinery and invested massively in specially designed machine tools. Gravity work-slides and rollways were installed to ensure the constant movement of components throughout the factory. As a result of innovations in production methods, assembly times were drastically shortened, output soared and unit costs were lowered. High wages had to be introduced to retain the machine-minders who otherwise left their excruciatingly boring jobs in droves, but Ford knew that a mass consumer market required high wages and that labour costs could be absorbed by a sufficient volume of sales. The original price of the model 'T' was $950; by 1916, Ford was making well over half a million vehicles a year and the price was $360. In 1923, annual production peaked at 2 million vehicles, and in 1924 the price reached a low of $295.

Readers of Aldous Huxley's dystopia *Brave New World* (1932) will recall that the future is dated 'From the Year of Our Ford' – a tiny sacrilege which captures the giant impact of 'Fordism', firstly on Europe's imagination, then later, and more slowly, on its material civilization. The first 'moment' or level of 'Americanization' in Europe began with the diffusion of scientific management in the decade before

World War I when French automobile engineers introduced some of Taylor's technical prescriptions (high-speed steel, sequential machine lay-out, and so on) and experimented with time-work study and incentive wages. After early 1915, the need for huge increases in the output of war *matériel* greatly accelerated the pace with which managerial innovations were effected in France (as elsewhere), although many did not survive the outbreak of peace because war industrialism was a system for meeting 'emergency' needs, and could only operate with a suspension of 'normal' industrial relations. Along with managerial changes came a rapid extension of assembly-line methods for the manufacture of aircraft engines, tanks and lorries by the automobile firms Renault and Berliet. The war's impetus to the technological diffusion of American industrial methods was by no means clear cut, however. Military needs often led to the refinement and diversification of products which militated against mass-production techniques. After 1918, the French motor-car manufacturers (who had from the first been Europe's most dynamic auto engineers) took the lead in adopting the assembly line for peacetime production. Citroën started a line for its first post-war model in 1919, Berliet in 1920, and Renault and Peugeot in the next two or three years. They were somewhat in advance of their German, Italian and Czech rivals and more than a decade ahead of Morris, the leading British manufacturer, who did not install a moving assembly line at Cowley until the factory was rebuilt in 1934 (Fridenson, 'The coming of the assembly line to Europe', 1978, p.162). This vitality of France's auto industry was symptomatic of its overall industrial growth in the 1920s, when it was Europe's most rapidly expanding economy and led the way in the development of the mechanical industries.

Here we can see the material – and as yet modest – impact of American industrialism. The ideological and political impact of 'Americanism' on European élites attempting to re-stabilize their societies after the upheaval of war was far greater. It was felt in the Bolshevik East, as well as the West: in April 1918, Lenin defined the study and application of the Taylor system as one of 'The Immediate Tasks of Soviet Government', and throughout the 1920s and 30s 'Taylorism' was one element in Soviet industrial theory. In the Western bourgeois societies, 'Taylorism' and 'Fordism' appeared to be the keys to a new industrial and social order of boundless productivity in which all classes could prosper (Maier, 'Between Taylorism and technocracy', 1970). Hitherto, capitalist industrialization had had the appearance, at least, of a 'zero-sum game': the economic power of the bourgeois élites had grown at the expense of artisans and industrial workers. Capitalist Europe had bred within it its antithesis – socialism. American industrialism created for its own workers a material abundance to which many European bourgeois could not aspire. Socialism in America had been marginalized; it was the home of 'business unionism' and a new technocracy. Such, in brief, was the ideological cluster attached to 'Americanism' in the 1920s. It was registered at a cultural level by intellectuals such as Luigi Pirandello who, in an interview for an Italian literary magazine in 1929, asserted: 'Americanism is swamping us. I think that a new beacon of civilisation has been lit over there' (quoted in Gramsci, *Selections from the Prison Notebooks*, 1971, p.316).

In fact, the economic and political obstacles to 'Americanization' at this time remained formidable. American mass manufacturing catered for a huge domestic market whose average standard of living had for several generations been far higher than that in Western Europe. A chronic labour shortage during industrialization had meant that manufacturers had long been accustomed to paying higher wages and had systematically sought to substitute machines for labour and eliminate manual skill from production with the use of interchangeable parts. These were the background factors which made the mass production and consumption of the automobile possible by 1914. Two decades later, by contrast, European manufacturers were still making basically a luxury product for a small market. In 1929, the peak inter-war year for global private motor-car production, France – the leading European manufacturer – turned out 248,000 vehicles; America produced 5.358 million. The USA exported more cars (excluding parts exported for assembly abroad) than Europe produced in aggregate. In the late 1930s, a new French car cost twice the average worker's annual wage; as late as 1954, only 11 per cent of French townspeople owned a car, and among non-car owners, the number with sufficient disposable income to afford one was small (Zeldin, *France 1848–1945*, 1980, pp.281, 294).

During the 1930s, the political obstacles to 'Americanization' – as the term was understood at the time – were also formidable, particularly in Germany and Italy. In these dictatorships, the state was highly interventionist, and used its powers to control investment, regulate the labour market, strengthen (in Nazi Germany) the existing producers' cartels, and (in Fascist Italy) impose a corporatist organization of industry. This interventionist political context was quite hostile to 'free market' industrial capitalism. As one percipient mind noted:

> Americanisation requires a particular environment, a particular social structure (or at least a determined attempt to create it) and a certain type of State. This State is the liberal State, not in the sense of free-trade liberalism or of effective political liberty, but in the more fundamental sense of free initiative and of economic individualism which, with its own means, on the level of 'civil society', through historical development, itself arrives at a regime of industrial concentration and monopoly. (Gramsci, 1971, p.293)

These remarks, will, I think, seem particularly prescient when we consider the 'Americanization' of West German industry after 1945, but before turning to that topic it is necessary to revert more closely to our theme of the basic continuity of capitalist development.

The distinctive features of the 'organized capitalism' of late nineteenth and early twentieth-century Germany were the role of joint stock banks in the promotion of industrial growth and the control exerted by industrial cartels over the domestic market. The facility with which German industrialists could draw upon banking capital meant that companies grew much faster than they would have done had they relied on internal funding (as tended to be the case in Britain). German bankers were, it seems, prepared to take 'the long view' and invest heavily in science-based industry. The connection between investment banking and company growth was particularly evident in the electrical industry, where initial capital outlays were very large, and led to the rapid concentration of production in a few firms (the largest being AEG and Siemens). Bankers were also extending current account facilities to firms for their fixed and working capital on a scale much greater than in Britain or France. Bankers are by profession more cautious than industrialists and, in order to protect their investments, the German banks encouraged agreements among producers to maintain prices and limit competition. In this they were aided by a decision of the Imperial Supreme Court making agreements by firms in Germany to restrict competition legally enforce-able. Cartelization was particularly evident in the heavy industries of the Ruhr, and this peculiarly German form of organized capitalism was long associated with schemes for an autarkic, German-dominated, large economic area (*Grosswirtschaft-sraum*). The newer industries of the Second Industrial Revolution were rather more internationalist in outlook, and in them the tendency to industrial concentration was closer to the American pattern of 'trusts'. A mesh of financial trusts began to link the different firms in the organic chemicals industries in 1904, the year in which Hoechst and Casella, and later BSAF and Bayer, formed associations. In chemicals, it was recognized that future production would flow from, and be closely integrated with, increasingly expensive basic scientific research. The time-lag between scientific discovery and the first commercial production was often twenty or more years; among the major synthetic polymers – which are the basis of modern plastics – polystyrene was discovered in 1835 but not commercially produced by IG Farben until 1930, while polyvinyl chloride was discovered in 1871, but not commercially exploited until 1931. The chemicals firms entered agreements to pool profits, pay the same level of dividends and allocate part of the capital to a common holding company in order to cope with the high costs of their research programmes and minimize risks to their investments. Agreements were reached to share patents and licences to manufacture, and extended to market sharing and price fixing (Milward and Saul, *The Development of the Economies of Continental Europe 1850–1914*, 1977, p.52; I have drawn heavily on their discussion of the 'new' German capitalism, pp.46–53). The emergence of giant firms in the German producers' goods industries led (as had happened in America) to new hierarchies of salaried managers – men who were often technically and scientifically qualified, and who brought to business management a different ethos from that associated with the entrepreneurs of an earlier generation. There was not a complete change in attitudes, for the giant firms continued well-established traditions of industrial paternalism, but scientific and technical expertise increasingly substituted for personal and familial authority in the routines of business, and greatly reinforced trends towards professionalism and scientific management in industry (Kocka, 'The rise of the modern industrial enterprise in Germany', 1980, pp.92–7).

This transformation in German capitalism was perfectly evident before 1914. Contemporary Marxists, notably Rudolf Hilferding and Rosa Luxemburg, analysed the phenomenon as a desperate response of the economic system to the problems of the falling rate of profit and the realization of surplus value (if clarification is needed, see the brief discussion of Marx's economics in Book I, the Appendix to Unit 1). Against them, Walther Rathenau, a businessman who typified the 'new capitalist', argued that the economic system was entering a new phase of social responsibility when the growth of production and productivity would benefit mankind as a whole. For our purposes a more pertinent issue is reconciling – if that is possible – the 'new capitalism' with the picture of Imperial Germany as an 'old regime', with which you are familiar from Arno J. Mayer's work.

It is true, of course, that the designation 'old regime' refers principally to the polity, and the reactionary character of the Prusso-German monarchy and *Junker* élite is not in question. However, Mayer's argument does have very important economic dimensions: the size of the agricultural sector, the importance of artisanal and small-scale production, and so on. (See the summary in Unit 28, p.38.) While these are undeniable, the significance Mayer attaches to them is questionable. Not dissimilar features were evident in the American economy:

agriculture was still the largest source of employment in the USA in 1920, one half of the population lived at that date in communities of fewer than 2,500 people, the tertiary service sector (in which businesses were small) was larger than the secondary manufacturing and construction sector (and even in manufacturing, small-scale employment was very common). But to describe the USA as economically an 'old regime' would be only slightly less absurd than calling it a political 'old regime': modern manufacturing had been the dynamo behind the growth of its national product and productivity in the late nineteenth and early twentieth centuries and made it the foremost industrial power in the world.

The dynamic force of German industry in the development of its economy was equally palpable: the output of the industrial sector increased by 3.8 per cent annually over the period 1850–1914, while that of agriculture increased by only 1.6 per cent. Although in 1910–13, agriculture, fisheries and forestry still employed 35.1 per cent of the labour force, this sector accounted for only 23.4 per cent of net domestic product. By contrast, industry, handicraft and mines employed 37.9 per cent and accounted for 44.6 per cent of total product. Germany's industrial growth after 1870 was more constant than Britain's (where the effects of trade depressions were more severe and prolonged), the volume of its domestic investment in the Second Industrial Revolution was far greater; it educated more of its workforce to high levels of technical competence, and its reward was that by 1914 it had firmly established itself as Europe's foremost industrial power. The indices of its economic modernity by 1913 are well known, but will bear repeating: it produced two-thirds of all European steel output, and 20 per cent more electrical energy than Britain, France and Italy combined (Milward and Saul, 1977, pp.19–20).

Germany was by a great margin Europe's second most populous state and in much of its territory the economic and social pattern was (for want of a better word) 'traditional'. As in all national economies, industrial growth was acutely regional and the cause of considerable internal migration. One might argue, therefore, that though the national economy was modernizing, the regions of considerable economic backwardness within Germany lend support to the 'old regime' picture: in 1907, the *Junker*-dominated provinces of East Prussia, West Prussia and Posen had, respectively, 58.2, 54 and 57.9 per cent of the labour force in agriculture. By contrast, Westphalia and Rhine-province had 19.2 and 19 per cent; income per head in these centres of German industry was about 80 per cent higher than in East Elbia. But it is not enough to note these regional disparities; we must grasp, too, the dynamic relationship between them. The higher wages of the industrializing West drew surplus labour away from the impoverished Eastern provinces – away, that is, from the traditional social context dominated by the squire and pastor – and thrust them into the burgeoning towns where the working class had its own politics and culture. About 1.8 million people left the three Eastern Elbian provinces between 1881 and 1910, while by contrast the Rhineland and Westphalia received about 800,000 internal migrants. People moved within provinces, as well as between them, and went above all to industrial towns where the traditional bonds of 'old regime' society were moribund. Between 1880 and World War I, Germany experienced 'the most extensive and rapid process of urbanisation yet seen in Europe, creating large new industrial cities out of mere villages such as Gelsenkirchen and Bochum . . . Only in the most thriving parts of the United States was there anything to compare with this increase in new urban households' (Milward and Saul, 1977, pp.45–6).

Mayer is right to point to 'the forces of perseverance' in European society in 1914, but in my view to emphasize the economic conservatism of Germany leads to a grossly one-sided caricature, and we compound our error if we neglect the social consequences of Germany's rapid modernization. More critically still, an over-emphasis on 'old regime' characteristics blinds us to the sources of Germany's military power: it was its industrial strength which twice gave it the capacity to wage war for the political domination of Europe. Finally – and our most pressing concern here – there was a strong element of continuity between its industrial growth in the imperial period and its post-1945 industrial resurgence. Schonfield put the point with characteristic vividness:

> The defeat, division and chaos which Germany suffered in the 1940s did not wipe out the legacy of the past; it only lifted temporarily the pressure of history. When the Germans began to reconstruct their economy, they built upon the familiar structural foundation and plan, much of it invisible to the naked eye, as if guided by an archaeologist who could pick his way blindfold about some favourite ruin. (Schonfield, 1969, p.240)

One clear indication of this 'legacy' is the survival of the major corporations that I have already mentioned; although the two biggest combines of the Nazi era, IG Farben and Vereinigte Stahlwerke, were compulsorily broken up after 1945, Germany's corporate structure remained otherwise intact. (It is worth noting that the constituent parts of IG and VS were in any case very big by European standards.) Moreover, despite the upheavals of war and denazification, there was a strong degree of continuity in the personnel of Germany's industrial élite; many of the men who had risen to leading positions in the Nazi economy remained in (or had re-entered) the élite echelon in the 1960s. Indeed, despite total defeat and devastation, the social structure in the Western zones proved resilient; there was no upsurge in social mobility, such as occurred in Eastern Europe (Berghahn, *The Americanisation of West German Industry 1945–1973*, 1986, pp.41,111). With the restoration of the economy, the concentration of production proceeded much as it did in Britain: by 1960 the hundred biggest firms were responsible for nearly 40 per cent of total industrial turnover, and they employed one out of every three workers in industry.

Continuity can be an extremely blunt tool of analysis. It is useful if it reminds us of the long-term growth of capitalism and points us to the contrast with the state socialism of Eastern Europe after 1945, but it is downright misleading if it blinds us to the fact that the reconstruction of the German economy was accomplished by the imposition of a form of organized capitalism different from the highly cartelized system of the Wilhelmine and Nazi periods. The United States had made the destruction of the autarkic, cartelized economic 'empires' of Germany and Japan a principal war aim, and its politicians and leading industrialists hoped to create after the war a liberal, competitive multilateral world trading system – a global economic order they would lead, but not dominate. In pursuit of this policy, their occupation officials were instructed to dismantle the German industrial cartels and reintroduce competition into German industry. Despite the fact that the Ruhr's heavy industrial area was occupied by Britain, whose Labour government was nationalizing coal (and threatening steel with the same), the option of taking industry into public ownership was not seriously contemplated. Instead, German industry was broken into competitive units which were nevertheless still viable in the international market. The vertical links between the coal and steel producers were severed, as were the horizontal links between firms which had kept prices up. Initially, too, German banks which had provided the 'middlemen' of the old, uncompetitive organized capitalism were forced to restrict their operations. This policy of introducing oligopolistic competition into the Allied zones was spurred on by the recognition that German economic recovery would be the motive force for the material reconstruction of Europe as a whole, and by the worsening tensions of the Cold War. The United States saw successful private enterprise economies as the most effective response to the threat of communism (Berghahn, 1986, pp.84–110).

Moreover, the 1949 Federal Constitution, and the political culture of the GDR, had profound implications for the organization of the West German economy. Gramsci's perception that 'Americanization' required a particular kind of state seems particularly prophetic because the polity acquired by West Germany no less resembled an American model than did the economy. The Federal Constitution made it extremely difficult for central government to play a directive role in economic affairs. Although West Germany was a highly taxed society, the *Länder*, not the Federal Government, were the chief taxing authorities (a situation which paralleled the United States). Since there was no unified fiscal control at the centre, there was little scope for the type of macro-economic management attempted in Britain. The central government's room for manoeuvre was further restricted by a legal limitation on its borrowing powers. In this new political environment the long-serving Minister of Economics, Ludwig Erhard, advocated a 'free enterprise' ideology to which nearly all leading industrialists were committed by 1960. There was, for example, a marked antipathy among both politicians and businessmen to the sort of indicative national planning practised in France, as well as the characteristic neo-liberal preference for monetary stability over full employment.

My discussion so far has focused on Germany because, as a defeated power in the two world wars, it provides the critical case in which to explore the theme of continuity in economic history. *A priori*, defeat is far more disruptive than victory, which tends to confirm for the victorious power the basic soundness of its institutions, and this sense of satisfaction could be one factor behind the strong continuity in the development of the British economy between 1914 and the 1950s. A very brief consideration of the French and Italian economies around 1950 would, I think, confirm for you the value of placing the impact of war within a long-term perspective. My argument is not that the war had no or very little impact; on the contrary, the cumulative effects of the war years in terms of foregone investment, the inadequate maintenance of machines, the shortage of fertilizers and horses for agriculture, and the subordination of both French and Italian industry to the needs of Nazi Germany, were considerable. The best labour from France and Italy was forced to work in German factories. Material resources were similarly extorted. Germany imposed inequitable trade on both countries. 'Public finances were debilitated by the exigences of occupation, blockade, the loss of production and the contraction of the tax base. In both countries, a spiral of inflation was begun which neither managed to bring under control until about 1948. The sheer physical destruction of factory plant, railways and bridges as large tracts of Italy and France became battlefields was probably the least significant of the war's many negative economic consequences.

By 1950, the economic resurgence of both France and Italy was evident in total outputs of industrial production which exceeded pre-war levels and were grow-ing more rapidly than in Britain or America. (By the mid 1960s, French gross domestic product exceeded Britain's, despite the fact that its population was substantially smaller and its resource endowment inferior.) That this was also the case in West Germany and Japan throughout the long post-war boom has prompted the thought that there may have been positive economic advantages to military defeat, in terms of the 'shock' administered to political and economic élites and the 'purging' of collective institutions which otherwise restrict the growth process. More particularly, the French experiment in national economic planning under Jean Monnet has sometimes been interpreted as a token of a new consensus, derived from the experience of the Resistance which had been determined to make the struggle against Nazi occupation a movement of national reconstruction.

There is much to be said for the argument that the humiliation of 1940, the anguish of Vichy and the occupation, and the hyper-inflation of the post-war years, led to a real discontinuity in French attitudes to economic questions, and even more broadly to 'material life'. Up to the late 1940s, the French evinced a very strong attachment to the soil, for the ownership of land was widespread and its maintenance within families tenacious. We must disabuse ourselves of any notion that agricultural enterprise is necessarily 'traditional' (think of modern Denmark whose prosperity has been to build upon highly specialized, market-oriented farming). Many French farmers were successful businessmen whose resourceful-ness made France a major exporter of agricultural products. There was, however, an extensive peasant economy whose way of life kept it relatively insulated from the market and from the forces creating a homogeneous national culture. The prize-winning film documentary, *Farrébique*, shown at the Cannes festival in 1946, is a study of a Gascon farm, where the bread is made at home, oxen plough the land, and the farming family speak a language which a French audience required sub-titles to understand. The camera caught the final phase of something approaching a natural or closed economy which was soon to be disrupted by the attraction of a higher standard of living in the towns and the mechanization of agriculture. In 1949, only 16 per cent of France's net domestic product was accounted for by agriculture, fishing and forestry, but 36.6 per cent of its active population was still engaged in this primary sector. (The discrepancy between these two figures is a measure of the relative inefficiency of labour, and other factors of production, in agriculture.) By 1954, the proportion engaged in agri-culture had fallen to 27.4 per cent; 2.3 million people (the majority of them women) had left the land. The great *exode rural* continued throughout the 1950s, to the acute concern of many French people who feared that the disappearance of the peasantry was removing a major element of stability in political and social life.

There was another change in attitudes, probably not unconnected with the decline of the peasantry. Since the late nineteenth century a major barrier to the more rapid growth of the French economy was a *mentalité* of 'Malthusianism': a desire on the part of the small and medium-sized family enterprises which controlled most of the French economy to restrict production and limit their own expansion in the interests of maintaining familial control. The origins of this restrictive attitude lay in the peasantry: farming couples, anxious to preserve the family holding intact, had practised *coitus interruptus* after the birth of the first son, for all heirs had equal rights to property. 'Malthusianism' had diffused to the towns and even, it appeared, to family industrial enterprises which preferred to cater for small, high-quality luxury markets and eschewed mass production. They minimized risks rather than maximized profits. As in Germany, they formed producers' cartels to restrict competition among themselves and maintain prices.

The charge of 'Malthusianism' should not be overdrawn: France's economy had grown very rapidly in the period between 1896 and 1913, when new techniques in hydro-electricity and electro-metallurgy were exploited, and new products like the motor-car developed, while established industries such as steel and textiles expanded at about twice the rate in contemporary Britain. That said, evidence for a nation-wide change in fundamental attitudes to life is provided by the reversal, during the war itself, of France's secular demographic decline. In the late 1930s, the French population was not reproducing itself: for every 1,000 people there were 15.3 deaths and only 14.8 births. From about 1941 the birthrate began to rise and in the late 1940s it stood at 20.1 births per thousand, while the death rate had fallen to 13.8. The young demand investment in the future and the great revival of births was, at the basic level of 'frames of mind', linked with a resurgence of public and private investment. As one commentator put it: '. . . the wave of children has modified French attitudes towards family life and towards social, regional and occupational mobility; has led to an insistence on more housing and schools; and has reduced the resistance to economic growth of static elements in the society.' Like the French family itself, the family firm appears to have altered its attitude, outlook and hence its behaviour (Kindleberger, 'The post-war resurgence of the French economy', 1963, pp.130, 134–5).

This is, I believe, a catalogue of persuasive reasons for seeing a very considerable discontinuity in French economic history in the 1940s. It led one distinguished economist to argue in the early 1960s that 'The economic recovery of France after the war is due to the restaffing of the economy with new men and to new French attitudes . . . these new attitudes . . . seem to have their origin in the frustration of the 1930s and the war and the occupation' (Kindleberger, 1963, pp.156–7). But since this was written, the econometric study of French growth over the period 1896–1965 has called the idea of a new beginning into question. As I have pointed out several times, the French economy grew rapidly between the 1890s and the late 1920s, and if this trend of growth is extrapolated until the 1960s then we arrive at a 'counterfactual' total output very similar to the one actually achieved (Carré, Dubois and Malinvaud, *French Economic Growth*, 1975). Moreover, the rapidly expanding industries of the late 1940s and 1950s – chemicals, rubber, automobile engineering, electro-metallurgy, hydro-electricity – were precisely those in which France had made swift technological progress before 1929.

Are there broader, more deeply sedimented continuities linking the expansion of the 1920s with the 1950s? Yes: despite serious economic reverses in the 1930s, France had continued to invest in its industrial structure and, *above all*, in the education of its people. France was not unique in this: the most important resource which West European states had in rebuilding their shattered economies after 1945 was human capital – the skills, technique, scientific knowledge and practical resourcefulness embodied in an educated workforce. With these human productive resources went cultural expectations of what the 'good life' should be, and a willingness to adapt and 'rationalize' basic human drives in pursuit of it. The 'family planning' movements of post-war Europe are the tip of this iceberg of adaptivity and rationality. By its very nature, human capital is the legacy of previous generations: France in the 1940s benefited from the rapid expansion of university and secondary education between the wars. In the 1920s there were

50,000 university students; by 1938, in spite of the fact that the student-age cohort was now much smaller (partly because of the loss of births during World War I), the numbers in university education had grown to 79,000. Comparative indices of investment in human capital are extraordinarily difficult to arrive at with any certainty because of differences in educational institutions. It is worth noting, however, that in Britain, with its larger and younger population, university student numbers rose from 59,000 to only 63,000 in the same period. There are long-term continuities in under-investment in human capital, as well as in its growth. (Statistics from Mitchell, *Statistical Appendix to the Fontana Economic History of Europe*, 1976.)

Recapitulation exercise   Summarize the main continuities in the economic history of industrial, capitalist Western Europe between 1890 and 1950. ∎

Specimen answer

1   The continuity in technological evolution, particularly that associated with the industries of the Second Industrial Revolution.

2   The diffusion of modern factory processes, such as the assembly line.

3   A long-term but not steady process of capital concentration.

4   A 'managerial revolution' dating from the late nineteenth century and linked with the development of the modern corporation.

5   A multi-levelled 'Americanization' of the European economy, the origins of which reach back to the 1900s. □

Continuity may imply stability, but the terms are scarcely synonyms. Economic growth may be continuous and proceed at a stable rate (as in contemporary Japan) but the last thing it results in is stability, in the sense of little change over time. In these concluding paragraphs I want to consider Britain as the 'model case' of a society which changed very little between 1890 and 1950, just as Poland was the 'model case' of a state created, destroyed and resurrected by war. There cannot be much debate about the stability of the British *state* (as an official and juridical entity) since the constitutional crisis of 1910–1911. Tom Nairn, a Scottish nationalist Marxist, has indicted Britain as a supra-national parliamentary monarchy which concentrates political power in a central executive, has no judicial concept of 'public interest' independent of that of the government of the day, maintains a nineteenth-century principle of political representation, and has refused to inscribe the active rights of political citizenship in either a bill of rights or a written constitution. (*The Enchanted Glass*, 1987). (Even if you think the changes are overdrawn, you would have to recognize that, in these respects, the British state is different from other democracies and, furthermore, the resistance to constitutional change does itself demand explanation. Proportional representation was unanimously recommended by the Speaker's Conference which reported to Parliament on franchise reform in 1917.)

To argue, however, for the stability of British society is more controversial. Many readers will have incontrovertible evidence from their own and their parents' experience of improving real incomes, the shortening of working hours, the introduction of paid annual holidays, the spread of better health care and decent housing, widening access to secondary education, and a changing pattern of consumption associated with the retail revolution. In these, and many other ways, Britain in 1950 was *measurably* different from Britain in 1900.

Exercise But we must always ask: how big was the measure? Here are decennial indices of weekly wage earnings of manual workers and the cost of living; use them to measure the extent to which workers in 1950 were better off than they were in 1900.

Table 29.1

Weekly wage earnings		The cost of living	
1900	100.0	1900	100.0
1910	100.0	1910	105.0
1920	302.0	1920	294.0
1930	204.0	1930	172.0
1940	287.7	1940	197.0
1950	400.0	1950	310.5

(Source: recalculated from Halsey, ed., *Trends in British Society since 1900*, 1972, Tables 4.10, 4.11) ∎

Specimen answer The *answer* is the difference between the rise in money earnings and rise in the cost of living; that is, about 90 index points. Real wages had approximately doubled. This is, you will appreciate, a very coarse measure; if we wanted to pursue the matter thoroughly we would have to measure changes in the way wages were dispersed about the mean, changes in the occupational structure (which may have led to a decline in the proportion in unskilled labouring work and an increase in the numbers in more skilled, better paid jobs) and changes in the relativities between men's and women's wages. But just to take the last matter, we can easily demonstrate that within a global change certain basic *relationships* have remained very stable. The recruitment of British women to war work had, after 1918 and 1945, no effect whatsoever on their peacetime rates of participation in the labour force, and very little (if any) on the relationship between the earnings of men and women in full-time employment, as the following figures demonstrate:

Table 29.2

Rate of female participation time in the labour force (%)		Women's median full-time earnings as % of men's	
1911	35.32	1906	50.2
1921	33.71	1938	50.5
1931	34.20	1960	53.5
1951	34.73		
1961	37.49		

(Sources: Halsey, 1972, Table 4.4, Routh, *Occupation and Pay in Great Britain 1906–60*, 1965, p.58)

If you're getting a sense of *Plus ça change, plus ça reste la même chose . . .* , good, because that is where my line of argument is going to take you. Britain between 1890 and 1950 was a rapidly changing society – as indeed were all societies which had embarked on capitalist industrialization in the nineteenth century – but the more things changed, the more certain societal relationships remained, if not exactly the same, then remarkably stable.

The occupational structure, which formed the backbone of British class society, altered very little between the Edwardian period and mid-century, certainly by comparison with changes during the nineteenth century and since the mid-1960s.

Table 29.3

	1911 Males	1911 Females	1951 Males	1951 Females
Higher professionals Employers and proprietors Administrators and managers	13.1	7.6	15.3	6.9
Lower grade professional, supervisory, technical	3.2	6.0	6.3	9.0

Clerical workers, sales
   personnel and shop
   assistants
	10.1	9.7	10.0	29.9

Manual workers	73.6	76.7	68.4	54.2

(Source: Goldthorpe *et al.*, *Social Mobility and Class Structure in Modern Britain*, 1980, Table 2.3)

As you can see, the only major change was in the structure of women's employment where the proportion of 'white-blouse' workers grew three times, chiefly at the expense of women's skilled and semi-skilled manual work. Should we take this as indicating the rapid expansion of the lower-middle class relative to other classes? I think not. There are good reasons for saying that, in this period, the nuclear family – not the individual – was the basic unit of class society, and the family's class was determined by the occupation of the husband or the father. The proportion of men in middle- and lower-middle-class occupations did not change very considerably.

We have seen that wages improved over this period, but what about the rewards for manual waged work relative to those from other sources of income – from professional employment, from profits, dividends and rents? In other words, were there any changes in the way the national income was distributed? (The following figures add up to more than 100 since the individual factors sum to gross national product which includes depreciation.)

Table 29.4

	% Shares in Net National Income				
	Wages	Salaries	Self employment	Profit	Rent
1900	41.4	9.1	N/A	N/A	12.5
1911	38.6	11.1	N/A	N/A	11.8
1921	43.6	17.9	13.4	6.2	5.8
1951	45.5	25.9	12.1	23.7	4.6

(Source: Halsey, 1972, Table 3.2)

Here, the significant changes were the growth in the share of the salariat and the decline in income from rent (principally because of the introduction of rent control during World War I). Income from the profits of private companies grew considerably, but much of this may be accounted for by changes in the legal status of businesses. The share of wages was remarkably constant; it was at its highest during and immediately after World War II when the differential between manual workers' wages and professional salaries and incomes narrowed considerably, but with the outbreak of peace the 'normal' relativities quickly reasserted themselves. Of course, since the proportion of manual workers in the labour force had somewhat declined between the 1900s and the 1950s, the relative share of wages grew rather more than the figures suggest.

To what extent did Britain become a more 'open' society in these years? We can answer that quantitatively by looking at changes in rates of generational occupational mobility, and asking whether 'long-range' mobility became more frequent. To explain: if your father was a dustman and your 'final' occupation is doctor of medicine, then you have experienced 'long-range' generational occupational mobility. These are the sort of questions which interest us: what were the chances of a manual worker's child entering the professions in the 1900s and what were they in the 1950s? And how did these chances compare with the chances a professional's child had of remaining within a comparable professional status? (Don't forget that someone beginning a professional career in 1914 would have been born about 1890, and in 1951 would have been born about 1925.) A social mobility inquiry (unfortunately confined to men) published in 1954 does enable us to answer these questions and gives us some measure of the changes in the 'openness' of British society:

Table 29.5

Social status of respondent's father at respondent's birth		Respondent's final status (% of cohort)			
		1 and 2	3 and 4	5	6 and 7
Skilled manual and	Pre 1890	3.9	18.4	42.4	35.3
routine clerical	1890–99	2.3	25.6	42.9	29.2
	1900–09	5.6	22.3	45.3	26.8
	1910–19	3.2	22.2	47.8	26.8
	1920–29	1.2	11.9	56.1	30.8
Semi-skilled and	Pre-1890	0.7	8.9	32.9	57.5
unskilled manual	1890–99	0.8	12.9	34.4	51.9
	1900–09	1.8	20.7	30.5	47.0
	1910–19	1.1	12.6	39.3	47.0
	1920–29	0.9	8.1	47.5	43.5

Key
1 and 2 = professional, high administrative, managerial and executive occupations
2 and 4 = higher and lower grade inspectional, supervisory and other non-manual occupations
5 = skilled manual and routine grades of non-manual
6 and 7 = semi-skilled and unskilled manual

(Source: Glass, *Social Mobility in Britain*, 1954, Table 6, p.186)

These figures demonstrate that Britain was not (at least in our measurable terms) a significantly more 'open' society in 1951 than it was in the 1900s. There was no consistent trend for manual workers' sons to move into professional and executive occupations and there was a very high degree of self-recruitment of occupations. Short-range mobility – from a skilled manual to a supervisory or more generally 'lower-middle-class background' was quite frequent – but it does not appear to have become significantly more frequent over time. (The anomalous figures for the 1920–29 cohort – which suggest that mobility was actually becoming more restricted – are probably due to the fact that at the time of the enquiry quite a few young men had not yet reached their final occupation; some would have been promoted from skilled manual to supervisory work in the course of their careers.) □

Now that we have looked at the 'brute data' on the occupational structure and social mobility we must ask whether, in the Britain of 1950, there persisted the class mentalities of the 1900s – in particular, the fatalistic sense most workers and their families had of class being 'a life sentence', their belief that material success was a matter of luck. Had the rise in working-class incomes, the common endeavour of World War II, the resurgence of the Labour movement and the election of a majority Labour government, broken down workers' sense of their own apartness? Had workers and their families developed a belief in their capacity to shape and control their own lives? It would seem plausible. 1950 'feels' familiar to many through feature films shown on television, archive radio, personal memory and other testimony; it seems hardly possible that the popular mentalities of the 1900s would have persisted into this recent past. What, then, are we to make of these observations from a Polish sociologist who in the late 1940s collaborated with B. S. Rowntree in an extensive investigation of popular attitudes?

> When I stayed in mining villages [more than 600,000 people were still occupied in mining in 1951] I often wondered whether we did not exaggerate the impact of modern changes on our life. True, some modern inventions have entered the life of the miners, mostly cinemas and buses and to a smaller extent, wireless . . . But even when due allowance is made for these factors, the atmosphere, the style and pattern in most mining villages has not changed basically for fifty years . . . In these villages one can see . . . how great is the weight of the past, and what large areas of the community are by-passed by modern currents of thought and conduct or by modern institutions . . .
>
> Most workers do not believe they are lucky. They often say: 'If I was lucky I wouldn't be a worker. I was unlucky in one thing – I was born poor.' . . .
>
> Workers often speak of themselves as 'we' and of others as 'they'. Who are the 'we'? The average worker has only to look at a man to see whether he is one of them or not. He looks first at his hands, and when he sees strong horny hands, sometimes puffed up, and stained or greasy, he knows that he is one of 'us'. But if his hands are soft and obviously not used in his work, he belongs to the class of men from the office or shop, the men who are 'they'. (Zweig, *The British Worker*, 1952, pp.94, 146, 203)

Of course, Britain was far from a 'caste' society and social survey data can be used to demonstrate its relative 'openness' as well as its 'closure'. Of the respondents in the top occupational categories born before 1890, nearly a quarter were the sons of manual workers. But again there was no consistent movement in this figure over time and it was virtually identical for the cohort born between 1910 and 1919. If you find this apparently quite substantial recruitment of the professional stratum from the working class inconsistent with the above table then you must bear in mind that manual working families were the great majority of the population. Had their sons entered the top occupations in proportion to their numbers in the population, three-quarters of the professional stratum would have been recruited from the working class.

From the vantage point of the 1990s, we are able to see that this static picture was chiefly due to the stability of the male occupational structure. Since 1960, absolute rates of social mobility have increased considerably, but chiefly because

of the disproportionate growth of a 'service class' of professional and administrative personnel, which has been obliged by 'arithmetic' to recruit from men of
working-class background. (Women's social mobility is one of the mysteries of
empirical social science.) However, the mobility chances of working-class children *relative* to those from professional backgrounds have not improved, and the
self-recruitment of manual occupations has become even more marked.

There is, I think, a matter of great import here for students of war, peace and
social change. An earlier generation of sociologists, when speculating from the
very limited data they had to hand, argued that large-scale war, with its mass
death, the culling of élites and battlefield promotions, was a signal cause of social
mobility. It was a plausible hypothesis, but the international comparative evidence we have does not support it. Despite the 7 million German deaths in World
War II, and the upheavals of displacements and forced migrations after 1945,
post-war West Germany has been a rather more closed society than Britain
(whose war losses were, by comparison, very small) in terms of social mobility
across the manual/non-manual occupational divide and the recruitment to élite
occupations. Three Eastern bloc countries on which we have information –
Poland, Hungary and Bulgaria – have by contrast been more open than Britain,
but there the causal factors behind high mobility rates were rapid industrialization, the decline of agriculture and sweeping political change (Heath, *Social
Mobility*, 1981, ch.7; also Kaelble, 'Social mobility in Germany, 1900–1960', 1978,
and Kaelble, *Social Mobility in the Nineteenth and Twentieth Centuries*, 1986). Our
comparative evidence demonstrates conclusively that, in Western societies,
mobility rates have risen far more through peaceful processes of development
than through war.

The final aspect of British stability I want to consider was entailed by the
fundamental demographic changes that took place between 1890 and 1950.
Demographers have observed that when countries industrialize and become
'mature' industrial economies they make a 'demographic transition' from a low,
relatively stable population preceding industrialization, through a period of
extremely rapid population growth, to a new plateau of high population, but one
in which the growth rate is very low. Represented on a graph, this transition looks
like an elongated 'S'. Why this transition should have occurred as it has, and
exactly how it relates to the industrialization process, are complex questions we
cannot pursue here. The important thing to grasp is the epochal changes in the
female life-cycle which have constituted this transition. During the 1870s, the
crude birthrate (that is, live births per thousand of the population) was 35.4, and
the average number of live births per married woman was 5.8. Out of every
thousand women marrying in this decade, 611 bore five or more children. About
1880, the birthrate began to fall, particularly among the professional middle
classes. By the 1900s, the crude rate was 27.2 and women marrying between 1900
and 1909 bore, on average, 3.4 children. The birthrate fell to an all-time low of 14.8
during the 1930s and the average number of children for women marrying in
these years was fewer than two. Paradoxically, these changes were accompanied
by more frequent marriage and a lowering of the average age of marriage. If we
compare the marital condition of 1,000 women in 1901 with that of 1,000 in 1951,
then we see a very different proportion of single and married women at these
dates:

Table 29.6

| | Proportion per 1,000 females aged fifteen and over | | |
	Single	Married	Widowed and divorced
1901	395	497	108
1951	248	616	136

(Source: Carr-Saunders *et al.*, *A Survey of Social Conditions in England and Wales*, 1958, Table 1.6)

With this demographic transition, the average woman's reproductive years were greatly compressed into her first few years of married life. Her existence over time took on a new 'shape'. By comparison with the changes in everyday life experiences represented by the achievement of this new demographic stability, the social changes wrought by total war in twentieth-century Britain have been piffle in the wind.

References

Altholz, J. L. (1976) 'The warfare of conscience with theology' in *The Mind and Art of Victorian England*, University of Minnesota Press.

Arendt, H. (1951) *The Origins of Totalitarianism*, André Deutsch.

Berghahn, V. R. (1986) *The Americanisation of West German Industry 1945–1973*, Berg.

Calder, A. (1971) *The People's War: Britain 1939–1945*, Granada.

Carr-Saunders, A., Caradog Jones, D. and Moser, C. (1958) *A Survey of Social Conditions in England and Wales*, Oxford University Press.

Carré, J. J., Dubois P. and Malinvaud, E. (1975) *French Economic Growth*, Stanford University Press.

Chandler, A. D. (1980) 'The United States: seedbed of managerial capitalism' in Chandler, A. D. and Daems, H. (eds) *Managerial Hierarchies*, Harvard University Press.

Cole, G. D. H. (1947) *The Intelligent Man's Guide to the Post-war World*, Gollancz.

Davies, N. (1981) *God's Playground: A History of Poland*, vol.II, Oxford University Press.

Fejto, F. (1974) *A History of the People's Democracies*, Penguin.

Fridenson, P. (1978) 'The coming of the assembly line to Europe' in Krohn, W., Layton, E. T. and Weingart, P. (eds) *The Dynamics of Science and Technology, Sociology of the Sciences*, vol.2, Reidel.

Glass, D. V. (ed.) (1954) *Social Mobility in Britain*, Routledge.

Goldthorpe, J. H. *et al.* (1980) *Social Mobility and Class Structure in Modern Britain*, Oxford University Press.

Gramsci, A. (1971) *Selections from the Prison Notebooks*, edited by Hoare, Q. and Nowell Smith, G., Lawrence and Wishart.

Halsey, A. H. (ed.) (1972) *Trends in British Society since 1900*, Macmillan.

Hannah, L. (1976) *The Rise of the Corporate Economy*, Methuen.

Heath, A. (1981) *Social Mobility*, Fontana.

Kaelble, H. (1978) 'Social mobility in Germany, 1900–1960', *Journal of Modern History*.

Kaelble, H. (1986) *Social Mobility in the Nineteenth and Twentieth Centuries*, Berg.

Kindleberger, C. P. (1963) 'The post-war resurgence of the French economy' in Hoffmann, S. *et al.*, *France: Tradition and Change*, Gollancz.

Kocka, J. (1980) 'The rise of the modern industrial enterprise in Germany' in Chandler, A. D. and Daems, H. (eds) *Managerial Hierarchies*, Harvard University Press.

Maier, C. (1970) 'Between Taylorism and technocracy: European ideologies and the vision of industrial productivity in the 1920s', *Journal of Contemporary History*, 5 April.

Maier, C. S. (1975) *Recasting Bourgeois Europe: Stabilization in France, Germany and Italy in the Decade after World War I*, Princeton University Press.

Marwick, A. (ed.) (1988) *Total War and Social Change*, Macmillan.

Mayer, A. J. (1981) *The Persistence of the Old Regime*, Croom Helm.

Milward, A. and Saul, B. (1977) *The Development of the Economies of Continental Europe 1850–1914*, Allen and Unwin.

Mitchell, B. R. (1976) *Statistical Appendix to the Fontana Economic History of Europe*, Fontana.

Nairn, T. (1987) *The Enchanted Glass*, Verso.

Perkin, H. (1989) *The Rise of Professional Society: England since 1880*, Routledge.

Pipes, R. (1977) *Russia Under the Old Regime*, Penguin.

Routh, G. (1965) *Occupation and Pay in Great Britain 1906–60*, Cambridge University Press.

Shonfield, A. (1969) *Modern Capitalism*, Oxford University Press.
The Fontana Economic History of Europe, vol.6, pt.2, Fontana.

Zeldin, T. (1980) *France 1848–1945: Taste and Corruption*, Oxford University Press.

Zweig, F. (1952) *The British Worker*, Penguin.

UNIT 30   THE IMPACT OF TOTAL WAR

(Section 1 is written by Clive Emsley; sections 2 and 4 by John Golby; sections 3, 5 and 6 by Arthur Marwick)

1 WAR AND REVOLUTION

In discussing, in Book II, Units 11–13, the upheavals which affected the Central Powers and Russia at the close of World War I, we took as one of our starting points Hannah Arendt's 'little noticed but quite noteworthy fact' that, since the end of World War I, 'we almost automatically expect that no government, and no state or form of government, will be strong enough to survive a defeat in war' (Hannah Arendt, *On Revolution*, 1963, p.15). This, of course, does not mean that defeat in war automatically leads to revolution, except in the very broadest sense that the violent overthrow of a government or state might be defined as a 'revolution'. The experience of Turkey especially, you will remember, warns us about making the equation too simple and simplistic: Mustafa Kemal did not carry through his revolution until some time after defeat in World War I, and his successful revolution went hand in hand with a successful war against the Greeks.

Exercise   Defeat in World War I might be said to have led, or to have contributed, to a series of political events and processes that can readily be understood as revolutions in Austria-Hungary, Germany, Russia and Turkey. Each of these empires witnessed the violent overthrow of the old, existing order, mass participation in politics, and struggles between competing power blocs ending with the creation of a new state and government system. Without wishing to imply that this *should* have happened to the major powers that were defeated during World War II, can you identify any elements militating against similar revolutions occurring between 1940 and 1945? ■

Specimen answer and discussion   In the case of the French Third Republic in 1940, defeat was so rapid there was little opportunity for the kind of collapse of morale and the build-up of internal pressures of the kind that affected Germany and Austria-Hungary during World War I. You might want to argue that neither the government of Fascist Italy nor of Nazi Germany collapsed internally, that neither lost their nerve in the face of a revolutionary threat, thus denying the opportunity firstly for crowds to take to the streets, and secondly for competing power blocs to emerge and struggle for mastery. At first glance there might appear to be some mileage in such an argument. However, Fascist Italy was beginning to disintegrate from early in 1943 with collapsing morale and massive strikes in the northern industrial cities, both of which were brought about by wartime shortages and Allied bombing. 'Northern Italy', argues Martin Clark, 'was one of the few places where mass aerial bombardment proved effective in the Second World War. It disrupted production, it shattered morale, and it forced thousands of people to flee from the cities' (Martin Clark, *Modern Italy 1871–1982*, 1984, p.289). In contrast, however, in spite of the disorganization of much of the Nazi administration, of food supplies and welfare provision, the Nazi authorities remained prepared, and more importantly able, to deal ferociously with bread riots in Berlin even in the last days of the war.

You might seek to argue that both Fascist Italy and Nazi Germany were 'totalitarian' police states and that, in consequence, even up until the end, their populations were in awe and fear of the regime. I think that such an argument is less valid in explaining why there was no revolution, remembering that, until their respective revolutions, the imperial regimes of Germany and Russia employed their police fairly efficiently and often brutally against opposition. It was a palace *coup* that brought Mussolini down in the summer of 1943, and there were unsuccessful *coup* attempts against Hitler, notably the July 1944 bomb plot. These conspiracies developed in spite of the police state apparatus; so too did the food riots in the dying weeks of Nazi Germany. In Imperial Germany and Imperial Russia it was the internal collapse of the old regimes, coinciding with other problems – military defeat, food shortages, and so on – which brought revolutionary crowds successfully on to the streets and gave politicians, hitherto excluded from power, their opportunity.

What appears to me to be significantly different in World War II was that defeated major powers had large and victorious enemy armies on their territory, and virtually, if not actually, in their capitals, at the time of their defeat and surrender. Such armies – from the Germans in Paris in 1940 to the Allies in Berlin in 1945 – were unlikely to stand idly by and watch a violent and revolutionary struggle for power. Winston Churchill, you will recall from Book IV, Unit 21 (p.35), was vehemently opposed to the abolition of the Italian monarchy early in 1944 when it was proposed by the radical anti-fascist resistance committees, and later, at the end of the year, he authorized the use of British troops against the anti-monarchist rising by ELAS in Greece. Churchill was not alone in his concerns about elements of the resistance movements. The activities and the publicized programmes of the partisans in northern Italy caused anxiety among many liberal and conservative politicians, both Italian and Allied. Cardinal Schuster of Milan spoke for many when he urged the Allies to make a separate peace with the Germans in northern Italy so as to forestall a partisan uprising leading to a revolution.

To the extent that they participated in actions against the wartime governments and were forums for planning their country's future, resistance groups during World War II in general might be said to have been 'revolutionary'. But resistance groups were composed of varieties of political groupings often hostile to each other. In France, for example, while the *Front National* covered the whole country and was increasingly dominated by communists after June 1941, there were also conservative groups like the *Organisation Civile et Militaire* in the north and the Catholic *Témoinage Chrétien* in the south, and *Libération-Sud* was established in the Vichy Zone specifically to unite communists, socialists and Catholic trade unionists against the policies of Pétain's government. Divisions between resistance groups were seen at their most marked in Yugoslavia, where Tito's communist Partisans and Mihailovich's Chetniks fought each other as well as Germans, Italians and Yugoslav fascists. Tito's Partisans were able to carry out a communist revolution in Yugoslavia at the end of the war; but communist 'revolutions' elsewhere in Eastern Europe in the aftermath of World War II were not similarly the achievement of wartime resistance groups. A myth developed, especially among the communists of France and Italy, that a 'revolutionary situation' was theirs for the taking in 1945; even if the Allied victors had permitted revolutions, this myth conveniently ignores the directions given to the communist resisters by their party leaders (themselves following directions from Moscow) to lay down their arms and co-operate with the newly established central governments. □

One of the issues that has recurred throughout this course is the extent to which war has generated aspirations for change. Units 11–13 concluded by looking at the extent to which war might have been a radicalizing experience for the soldiers and sailors involved. The evidence appears to suggest that those men most troublesome, and most susceptible to revolutionary propaganda, were those who had little or nothing to do apart from the boring routine of military life in garrisons away from the front line, or in the cramped conditions of warships which scarcely put to sea, let alone saw action. A similar situation of inaction led to the creation of the Cairo Parliament by British servicemen serving in Egypt in 1944. The 'parliament' was scarcely revolutionary; its debates generally focused on those topics which were to become part of the Labour government's programme following the 1945 election, but it greatly worried the military authorities who eventually suppressed it.

Political commissars had been appointed in the Red Army from its beginning to ensure the political loyalty of the troops and to exercise Communist Party authority over the officers. The ideological elements of World War II led to political education in varying degrees in the armies of most of the major combatants. The Nazi Party had set out from the time it seized power to indoctrinate the German military; the process was stepped up on the outbreak of war using radio, film, written propaganda and the spoken word. But during the crisis of the first winter on the eastern front, the army commanders themselves concluded that there had to be an increase in the indoctrination of soldiers to prevent them breaking under the strain. This led to the creation of educational officers in the intelligence units of frontline formations. In the winter of 1943 'National Socialist Leadership Officers' were appointed to all military staffs down to divisional level. In his study of the German army on the eastern front, Omer Bartov concludes that the political and ideological indoctrination of the troops was very successful (*The Eastern Front 1941–1945: German Troops and the Barbarisation of Warfare*, 1985).

In June 1941 the British army established the Army Bureau of Current Affairs (ABCA), which prepared two regular bulletins in alternate weeks, one on the latest military events, the other on current affairs. These bulletins were designed to provide the basis for compulsory weekly discussions at platoon level. The intentions behind the scheme were the raising of morale, the improvement of relations between officers and men, and education for education's sake; but there were many critics who feared the effects of encouraging the army to discuss politics. Not the least of these critics was Churchill, who demanded to know of the Secretary of War in October 1941: 'Will not such discussions only provide opportunities for the professional grouser and the agitator with a glib tongue?' One year later, he suggested to the same minister: 'I hope you will wind up this business [the ABCA] as quickly and as decently as possible, and set the persons concerned to useful work' (both quotations from Paul Addison, *The Road to 1945: British Politics and the Second World War*, 1975, pp.148 and 151). Of course, there was a world of difference between the organizers of the ABCA and of the Cairo Parliament, but the concerns about them are both illuminating and significant.

Disaffected soldiers, sailors and policemen, crowds angry about war-induced privations, governments that had lost their nerve, are all significant ingredients of the revolutions which we have studied in the course. But perhaps what all these point to as regards the interrelation between war and revolution in twentieth-century Europe is the way that total war has tested regimes to the utmost. The unconditional surrender demanded by the combatants in such war has meant that defeated regimes were bound to be swept away leaving a governmental vacuum; but the pressures of such war have also led to some regimes collapsing from within even before total military defeat and unconditional surrender. In both cases there has been political change, but it is in the latter instance that the change is most obviously revolutionary. The men with the revolutionary ideologies have played little part in bringing down the old regimes; it is their own political acumen, their ruthlessness, their luck, and sometimes the support of a major external power, which has enabled a few of such revolutionaries to seize power and hold on to it.

2 THE DEBATE OVER THE SOCIAL CONSEQUENCES OF WORLD WAR I

By now you must be fully aware that in discussing the extent to which wars effect social changes it is not enough, as Arthur Marwick points out in his introduction to Book II, Units 8–10, to 'list social changes during, at the end of, or after the war' (p.41). It is essential to establish what developments were already taking place before 1914 and to keep any longer term forces in mind when studying the changes that occurred during the war. Even then, as Marwick states, 'those who wish to argue that the war did bring social changes have . . . to show how they are related to the actual war experience' (Units 8–10, p.41). So, although I hope you find the debate over the social consequences of World War I fascinating and thought-provoking, it is by no means straightforward.

When it comes to revising for the examination, although it is vital to read through Units 8–10 which address this topic directly, it is important not to ignore Book I of the course which surveys the condition of Europe in 1914, and Unit 1, especially Aims 1 and 4, where Arthur Marwick first introduces the topic of the place of total war in historical change. So, before I examine Units 8–10 in some detail, I want to refresh your memory by looking at a few sections from other parts of the course material.

As you will appreciate by now, the debate over the social consequences of World War I is just part of a much wider debate that has taken place between historians for the past three decades, concerning the extent of the impact of total war upon states, societies and individuals. In the first section of his article 'Total War' in the Course Reader (pp.26–8), Ian F. W. Beckett gives a brief summary of the historiography of this debate. Beckett acknowledges the seminal and leading role that Arthur Marwick has taken in this controversy, not only through his books, particularly *Britain in the Century of Total War* (1968) and *War and Social Change in the Twentieth Century* (1974), but also with the production of the Open University course A301 *War and Society*. Beckett acknowledges that Marwick's thesis of 'war as a determinant of major change has had a profound impact during the past decade'. But he concludes his section on 'The historiography of total war' by stating that, 'while the debate had continued to be waged within the context of parameters laid down by Marwick, recent and current research has done much to suggest that the social impact of total war in the twentieth century should not be overstated'.

While an important aspect of this course is concerned with discussing much of the recent research carried out in this area, Arthur Marwick has been at pains to point out, both in the opening unit of the course and again at the start of this book, that this course does not attempt to assert the primacy of war as a major factor in social change. In section 2.4 of Unit 1, a key section because it is the first time that the issue of the social consequences of World War I is discussed, Arthur Marwick states that, 'Nowhere in this course is it argued that war is the most important, still less the only, cause of major social change: the task is to evaluate the significance of war as against all other possible factors' (p.21). These 'other possible factors' he lists under the headings 'structural', 'ideological' and 'political'. Arthur Marwick then, in an exercise beginning on page 22, quotes from and evaluates six secondary sources all of which reveal the particular positions taken up by the writers in relation to their views concerning the significance or otherwise of World War I in bringing about historical change. It is well worth turning back to this section, because it not only discusses important issues relating to this topic, but it is also an exercise in what Arthur Marwick calls, in the Introduction to the Course Reader, 'Knowing your historian'. I am only going to refer to two of the extracts at present, both of which raise important considerations.

In extract (e), Wolfgang J. Mommsen argues that although 'World War I had a far-reaching impact on the social fabric of Germany', in 'socio-economic terms the exigencies of the war appear not to have initiated anything altogether new; rather they resulted in a considerable acceleration of those processes of change in economy and society which had already been under way for a considerable time'. Marwick points out that by emphasizing long-term forces, Mommsen is pointing to structural factors as being of prime importance. But Marwick quite rightly takes issue with Mommsen's use of the word 'acceleration'. It is a word that all of us at some point in the course have been tempted to use when discussing the impact of wars on society but, as Marwick points out, although 'accelerate' may *describe* what took place, what is essential is to discover *why* this acceleration occurred.

Extract (h) is from an article by Alastair Reid in which he argues that the war did have important consequences and although 'the quality of social relationships' did not alter radically, by their very participation in the war effort, underprivileged groups improved their social position. Here Reid refers to Andreski's concept of a 'military participation ratio', which Arthur Marwick also employs, although he states on page 26 that he prefers 'to talk simply of "participation"'. Marwick discusses Andreski's formulation in more detail in the introduction to Units 8–10, p.42, when he states that the formulation basically posited that 'in "society at war" those whose participation in the war effort is vital (for example, certain skilled workers, or women replacing men in certain jobs) will tend to make gains in wages, social benefits, etc., other things being equal – which of course they are not, the very destructiveness of war always being a counter-valent negative force'.

You may wish to reflect on Arthur Marwick's concluding remarks to the whole exercise, where he states that on close examination these six accounts 'do not clash as much as they may seem to do at first sight' (p.27). He argues that there is agreement on the main developments and the disagreements occur over the differences of emphases which are given to 'the complex of forces which bring about social change'. However, there is no doubt that the differences of emphases are sometimes very marked indeed and what is interesting is to investigate how and why. For example, Sandra Stanley Holton's interpretation of how women in Britain came to obtain the vote in 1918, is virtually diametrically opposed to Arthur Marwick's. One reason for this is that they differ in their interpretations of the extent to which attitudes towards votes for women were changing in pre-war Britain.

Clearly, in any discussion of the impact of war on historical change, it is essential to determine what structural (demographic, industrial and economic) and 'guided' or 'political' changes were already taking place before the outbreak of the war, and what further changes would have occurred if war had not broken out. This is the central theme of Unit 5, and it is here that Arthur Marwick introduces you to the ten areas of social change with which the course is concerned. If you have completed the exercises in this unit you should have an exercise chart which details/the state of the major European powers in 1914 in relation to these ten issues. Have this chart beside you, together with Arthur Marwick's chart on pages 183–201 of Unit 5, as I now survey the detailed discussion of these points that took place in Units 8–10.

Social geography

As Bill Purdue remarks on page 62 of Units 8–10, 'To the majority of contemporaries in 1919, the most obvious effects of the war must have been the enormous loss of population and the tremendous physical damage'. But although the war resulted in vast loss of life (and one of the problems, as Purdue points out in Units 8–10, p.54, is the extreme difficulty in estimating accurately the numbers killed), there was no overall drop in the population of Europe. Rather, the effects of the war were to:

1   'cut back the rate of growth of the European population';

2   'cut across long-term patterns of growth';

3   '[alter] the balance between the sexes and between different age groups'. For example, in Germany in 1911, in the age group twenty to forty-four, there were 100 men to every 101 women, whereas the 1925 census revealed that, as a result of the war, there were only 100 men to every 113 women in the same age group.

Your exercise chart should show that population growth before 1914 was higher in the poorer countries of Southern and Eastern Europe and lower in the richer Northern and Western countries. In Russia, population growth was such that, even with the large losses of life among the armed forces and civilians, these losses were not, as Purdue states on page 58 of Units 8–10: 'sufficient to prevent the continued growth of its population'. France's population, on the other hand, even with the addition of Alsace and Lorraine in 1919, was lower by 395,000 than it had been before the war (Dyer, *Population and Society in Twentieth Century France*, 1978, p.63). This was largely because of France's extremely low birthrate, but account must also be taken of the fact that, apart from Serbia, France's losses in the armed forces were relatively higher than its Western counterparts, that is, 10.5 killed out of 100 active men, as compared with 9.8 for Germany and 5.1 for Britain (Bernard and Dubief, *The Decline of the Third Republic 1914–1938*, 1988, p.78). The implications of these demographic changes to the countries of Europe are fundamental when discussing the nine other areas of social change.

Economic performance and theory

Purdue opens this section in Units 8–10 by stating that 'The effects of World War I on the European economy were almost all disagreeable' (p.62). For France, Belgium and Serbia there was vast destruction of property, but for all the European countries the financial costs of the war inflicted heavy burdens which had long-term consequences. 'Even though taxation was increased in every country, no country financed more than 25 per cent of its wartime expenditure from revenue, with the balance being raised from credit of one sort or another' (p.64). Consequently all countries experienced major economic problems. This, together with the fact that during the war the economies of the European countries were diverted from their traditional areas of production towards wartime economies, meant export markets were lost, many permanently, and that overall, Europe's trading and financial position declined markedly. The major beneficiaries were Japan and, in particular, the United States, which, as Ian Beckett points out, 'moved from being an international debtor before 1914 to an international creditor on a large scale' (Course Reader, p.34). Certainly, 'The balance of economic power swung away from Europe' (Units 8–10, p.71).

Bill Purdue also raises the question of whether the war really did have a permanent impact on the international economy. He uses the introduction of *From Versailles to Wall Street* by D. H. Aldcroft to illustrate alternative interpretations. In *Europe 1880–1945*, Roberts concludes that important changes were evident immediately after the ending of the war, and he writes of 'The fragmentation of the old economic system' (p.359) and a change of mood which existed after the war which led to a 'new wave of protectionist thinking' (p.360). However much some Europeans would have 'wished to return to the prewar economic system, they were psychologically inhibited from doing so, even if the possibility had existed' (p.362). But Purdue concludes, in his section on 'Corporatism and the challenge to the market economy' (a discussion which is developed in Unit 14), 'There *was* a challenge to the principles of the market economy in most post-war Western societies – a challenge based on the growth of government powers during the war, the problems of reconstruction and demobilization, and the increased strength of socialist parties and trades unions. Greater governmental responsibility for economic and social matters and a more influential position for trades unions were to remain features of most Western societies during the 1920s, but within a few years of the war Britain, France and even Germany were demonstrably once more free market economies' (p.71).

Social structure

Perhaps this is the most complex issue to assess in determining the impact of World War I on social change. Bill Purdue admits that assessment is difficult because of the 'sweeping and widely differing views as to the nature of the pre-war society' (Units 8–10, p.71). For example, if you turn to Arthur Marwick's exercise chart in Book I, Unit 5, page 184, you will see that in relation to Britain, Marwick concludes that 'the upper class was still strongly coloured by aristocratic elements, while incorporating the more successful bourgeois elements', while, on the other hand Roberts argues that by 1914 the bourgeoisie were the dominant class in Britain.

Bill Purdue illustrates well the two extremes of the argument concerning the nature of European society in 1914 by noting the titles of two books which are discussed at some length in the course – Arno J. Mayer's *The Persistence of the Old Regime*, and Charles S. Maier's *Recasting Bourgeois Europe*. As Purdue says, 'if an aristocratic *ancien régime* persisted up until 1914, then a "bourgeois" Europe could not have been *recast* after the war' (Units 8–10, p.71).

Another problem in discussing this topic, as Purdue points out, is that it is impossible to generalize about 'a European society'. The social structures of countries varied enormously. But Purdue does conclude:

1   Aristocracies (defined as families who own great landed estates, are usually titled and may include members of royal families) suffered as a result of the war. Partly this was because many of the monarchies were on the losing side and the power of the aristocracy was closely allied to the monarchies and their governments. Another reason was that as new nation states were created after the war, so aristocratic families who were often not of those nationalities lost their estates. Also, the land reforms, which took place in East and Central Europe, resulted in many great estates being transferred to the peasantry. Finally, the number of men from aristocratic families killed in the war was relatively higher than from any other section of the population.

2   It is more difficult to make generalizations about the middle classes. Many manufacturers involved in war production made fortunes. But overall, it is Purdue's belief that the middle classes in the West did not benefit from the war, at least not immediately. Increased taxation, a fall in rental and fixed incomes, the tendency for salaries to lag behind wage and price increases, and the inflation during and immediately after the war, especially in Central Europe, seriously affected middle-class savings. However, these sorts of generalizations cannot be applied so easily to Eastern Europe where the social structure was so markedly different.

3   In discussing the working classes in this respect, we return to Andreski's formulation of participation and to the crucial role played in the war by the working classes. Purdue argues that the groups who gained most from the war were the industrial working classes in the West and the peasantry in parts of Central and Eastern Europe. But by the mid 1920s, a time of high unemployment and deflation, Purdue concludes: 'the erosion of different standards of living between middle classes and working classes appears to have been halted and perhaps reversed' (p.81); and 'the social structure of West European society reasserted the social pattern and the process of change discernible before 1914' (p.82). Here Purdue is arguing that structural forces were paramount. Even in the East, where there were greater changes, Purdue states that these changes 'owed more to the force of nationalism and to the national/political, geopolitical changes consequent upon the post-war settlement than to social forces' (p.82).

National cohesion

Before 1914 monarchism and nationalism were the major forces for national cohesion, but while the former was on the wane, the latter was increasing in importance. As a result of the war and the Versailles Settlement, the principle of legitimacy was dealt a death blow and the concept of national self-determination, in Roberts's words, 'won its greatest triumph at Versailles' (p.328). However, as Purdue comments, 'the post-war settlement created as many new minorities as it satisfied old ones' (p.84) and the nationalism of minorities within the new national states was now to become a major threat to national cohesion. Whereas the major Western powers were nationally cohesive, the situation in Central and Eastern Europe where the states were 'not nationally homogeneous or cohesive, but territorial disputes and conflicting ambitions between neighbours ensured that national minorities and their treatment would become the pawns of national rivalries' (p.89).

Social reform and welfare policies

In an exercise on page 91 of Units 8–10, Arthur Marwick draws up a league table of countries which benefited most from social welfare legislation during the war. The critical factors taken into account in coming to his conclusions were: the economic strengths of the individual countries in 1914; the degree of social welfare legislation which had taken place before 1914; and the extent to which the countries had been affected by the war through 'occupation, invasion and direct damage'. Marwick concludes (p.96) that it was in Britain that the most significant amount of social reform took place, and he gives as his reasons the fact that:

1   Britain was the wealthiest country;

2   Britain had the most developed labour movement;

3   Britain did not undergo the deprivation experienced in Germany, nor the devastation and destruction that occurred in France;

4   Britain was a more 'open' and unified society.

It is noticeable that overall the greatest degree of social welfare legislation occurred in the countries of Western Europe and the least in Eastern Europe.

The table on pages 98–100 shows that in most European countries there was a flurry of social legislation in the immediate post-war years. Arthur Marwick stresses that before arguing that these reforms were primarily associated with the effects of the war, it must be demonstrated that they did not have more to do with developments already taking place before the war (structural changes); the efforts of particular politicians or political parties (guided or political changes); or developments primarily related to the events of the post-war years and unconnected with the war. Finally, you should consider whether the social reforms really were substantial in nature or whether 'they are so trivial as not to count in any general argument about the war being related to significant social change' (p.101).

Material conditions

Here Arthur Marwick demonstrates that for most European countries material conditions worsened during the war. For some countries (for example, Serbia) this was largely because of invasion and destruction; for others (for example, Germany and Austria-Hungary) it was because they were successfully blockaded and deprived of resources from overseas. Conversely, Britain was comparatively better off because it did not experience invasion or physical devastation. Britain also possessed vast overseas possessions and a large merchant fleet and navy which enabled it to continue importing resources from abroad. Marwick notes that Jay Winter, Bernard Waites and Alastair Reid all agree that, in Britain, 'for the working class as a whole living standards rose during World War I, and that the rise was particularly significant for those at the bottom end – those who fell into the residuum of pre-war times' (p.107).

Customs and behaviour

Arthur Marwick's thesis is that in all the countries of Europe there were 'long-term forces making for change in customs and behaviour, but that such forces are more apparent in the advanced countries; that within the context of long-term change, the war did indeed have identifiable effects in both sorts of country; that limited but important changes, which can be related to the war experience, are apparent in the developed countries, but that, given their relative level of backwardness, the really striking shake-up, as it were, comes in the less developed countries, where the cataclysmic effect of war was felt most strongly' (p.108).

Women and the family

As Arthur Marwick states at the start of this section, 'This is the area in which the debates over the effects of war on society have raged most furiously' (p.113). With regard to whether women's participation in wartime was an important factor in winning them the vote or improving their employment opportunities, it is worth turning back to Book I, Unit 1, section 2.4, and re-reading extracts (f), (g) and (j). Sandra Stanley Holton's interpretation of the achievement of women's suffrage in Britain denies that wartime participation was a factor. She stresses political and ideological forces, and even suggests that the war 'postponed such a victory' (p.22). James F. McMillan, in discussing the French experience, stresses structural forces and rejects any view that the war improved employment opportunities for women in France. On the other hand, in extract (j) Arthur Marwick, while discussing a range of factors, argues clearly that the war was a significant factor and that 'participation' in the war did lead to an improvement in the position of women.

A further wide range of sources is considered in section 2.8 of Units 8–10. With regard to employment opportunities for women, Marwick concedes that while there was a large expansion in the employment of women during the war years, generally speaking, statistics reveal that after the war employment figures drop to around the pre-war numbers. However, he does point out that, although small in number, 'in certain important professional occupations, from which women had very largely been excluded before the war, there were long-term changes, particularly in the legal profession, accountancy, and medicine' (p.113).

The arguments concerning the acquisition of the vote and employment opportunities still go on, but perhaps what can be discerned in relation to women and the war, at least in Western Europe, 'is the new assertiveness and self-confidence which women showed in the *post-war* years, but which were derived from the new experiences of war' (p.120), and which is highlighted in the newspaper report on British servants. Although employment opportunities for women after the war were limited, the fact that during the war they became involved in men's work for the first time gave them, as Roberts states on page 485, a confidence 'so that it was impossible later to believe they could ever have been thought unable to do it'.

High and popular culture

Arthur Marwick recommends a re-reading of the article by Josipovici printed in the Course Reader, the thesis of which is that, 'Although the First World War effectively marks the break between the world of the nineteenth century and our own – both in the minds of those who lived through it and those who read about it in the history books – the modern revolution in the arts did not take place during the war or immediately after it, but a decade or so before it' (p.73).

Nevertheless, Arthur Marwick argues, from the material he presents in this section, that many writers, painters and composers turned to 'modern' styles in order to convey the horrors, irony and hopelessness of the war, and that this in turn helped to make modernism in the arts more acceptable. He also uses an extract from Paul Fussell's book, *The Great War and Modern Memory*, in which Fussell argues that not only did the war, and in particular the irony of the war, become part of a literary consciousness, but it also played a major part in bringing to an end an optimism and belief in progress which still, in Marwick's words, 'characterized much high culture' (Units 8–10, p.121).

With regard to popular culture, the war did not see the introduction of new forms but it brought about an enormous expansion in the reading of newspapers, it made film a more respectable medium and it 'legitimized public dancing' (p.131). There was a large increase in the number of public dance halls and an expansion in the gramophone and record industries.

Political institutions and values

In this section of Units 8–10, Arthur Marwick, in the brief space of three pages (131–3) indicates the major changes, country by country, which took place between 1914 and 1918. For the purposes of revision I can do no more than urge you to re-read these pages.

In conclusion, although after reviewing all the evidence you may wish to argue that the war was not a fundamental factor in bringing about significant social changes, nevertheless, I find it difficult to believe that European societies in 1919 were not different from those in 1914, even if only in the sense of what Paul Fussell calls 'the texture' of life having changed. Fussell argues in relation to Britain that these changes of 'texture' brought about by the war, some of which were trivial, others much less so, could still be discerned in a variety of ways at the time he was writing his book, *The Great War and Modern Memory* (1975). These changes included:

> . . . the odd pub-closing hours, one of the fruits of the Defence of the Realm Act; that afternoon closing was originally designed it was said, to discourage the munitions workers of 1915 from idling away their afternoons over beer. The Great War persists in many of the laws controlling aliens and repressing sedition and espionage. 'D'-notices to newspapers, warning them off 'national-security matters', are another legacy. So is Summer Time. So are such apparent universals as cigarette-smoking, the use of wristwatches (originally a trench fad), the cultivation of garden 'allotments' ('Food Will Win the War'). So is the use of paper banknotes, entirely replacing gold coins. The playing of 'God Save the King' in theatres began in 1914 and persisted until the 1970s, whose flagrant cynicisms finally brought an end to the custom . . .
>
> Even cuisine commemorates the war. Eggs and chips became popular during the war because bacon and steak were scarce and costly. It became the favourite soldiers' dish off duty, and to this day remains a staple of public menus not just in England but in France and Belgium as well. Stephen Spender's thrifty grandmother was not the only user 'right up to the Second World War' of the 'little squares of sweetened paper' popularized during the Great War as a sugar substitute . . .
>
> A lifelong suspicion of the press was one lasting result of the ordinary man's experience of the war. It might even be said that the current devaluation of letterpress and even of language dates from the Great War.
> (pp.315–16)

3 THE PLACE OF THE INTER-WAR YEARS IN THE STUDY OF WAR, PEACE AND SOCIAL CHANGE

Within the course team there has at times been argument over what the title 'War, Peace and Social Change' really means. One could interpret war as being the periods 1914 to 1918 and 1939 to 1945, with peace referring to 1918 to 1939, 1945 to 1955, and perhaps also 1900 to 1914. But that would, in effect, be to see the course as simply presenting a conventional treatment of European history, exactly in the manner of J. M. Roberts, and I have already, at the beginning of Book I, Unit 1, explained how our course differs from the kind of textbook approach offered by Roberts. It is, however, a striking fact that while we have spent some time on the different kinds of war (total, internal, civil, and so on) we have never offered a definition of peace.

Europe has now (1990) been at peace for nearly half a century; and, apart from a few generally short wars, none involving the entire continent, there had been peace for very nearly a century before 1914. So is peace the normal condition? But then, we most usually refer to the period 1918 to 1939 as 'the inter-war years' rather than 'the years of peace'; and in Unit 28 you were encouraged to discuss the notion of there having been a 'Thirty Years' War' in the twentieth century. Then we have to take account of such concepts as the 'Cold War', 'internal war', and all the other conflicts (not necessarily *class* conflicts, in my personal view) in societies. My view is that there is a common-sense distinction between 'war', when practically all the nations of Europe are tearing each other apart, and 'peace', when this is not so. But certainly there are respectable arguments that the distinction is not as rigid as might at first sight appear. Beyond that, as with so many of the words used by historians, 'peace' is used, and perfectly legitimately, with different shades of meaning: it can, for instance, be used in the limited sense of a peace settlement or treaty.

The phrase 'war, peace and social change' originated as the sub-title of the first book in which I put forward my theories about the interrelationship between war and social change (*Britain in the Century of Total War: War, Peace and Social Change 1900–1966*, 1968). Personally, though some time has been spent on discussing what is meant by 'social change' (correctly I believe), I see the whole phrase as a unity, the parts of which should not be defined separately. The important word is the first word, so that, in my view, what one is concentrating on is how far times of 'peace' are, or are not, affected by the legacies of a previous war, or premonitions of the next war, and how far, if at all, social change is related to war.

I say this to show that I would not be surprised to find that you were uncertain about how you should treat the material contained in Book III of the course. To help you I am going to list five key considerations, and these should inform your revision of Book III:

1   This is the most important consideration, relating to the central question addressed by the course. That question is this: looking at the major events, developments and changes in Europe between 1900 and 1955, how far were these events, developments and changes affected by war, and how far did they arise from forces operating entirely independently of war? In answering this question clearly there is an important place for studying the happenings, developments

and changes of the years 1918 to 1939. So essentially what you have to do with respect to that period is to identify the most important happenings, developments and changes; then, having identified them, to ask whether or not, or in what degree, they were affected by war, bringing out in so doing the other forces lying behind the happenings, developments and changes.

2   This is also an important consideration, but a more precise one, concerning our major topic of the relationship between war and revolution. We have seen in the inter-war years the rise (Italy, Germany) and continuance (Russia) of revolutionary regimes. Nowhere in the course has it been asserted that World War I 'caused' Mussolini or 'caused' Hitler; but there are complex interrelationships, and these are what you should be concentrating on in your revision.

3   Another of our major considerations is the causes of war. Obviously Book III, and particularly Unit 20, but also Units 17 and 18, have primary importance in helping you to assess the origins of World War II.

4   The big question involved in key consideration (1) was the working out of the relationship of war to all the other potential forces of change. However, we do also have to have a specific interest in pinning down such consequences as there are of war. Book II, Units 8–10, 'The debate over the consequences of World War I' did necessarily extend into the post-war years. But obviously for further material relating to the long-term consequences of World War I, Book III is an invaluable resource.

5   Finally, I come to a point I have repeated two or three times throughout the course. If we are to make a valid assessment of the consequences of any particular war, we have to be clear about the state of society, and the processes of change already in operation, before the war broke out. Thus, Book III contributes towards a 'base line' upon which we can subsequently work out the consequences of World War II.

With these five considerations in mind, I am now going to take you on a revision tour through the separate units of Book III.

3.1   Units 14 and 15 *The Western democracies* (by John Golby)

I'd like you to re-read the first of the five considerations which I have just set out. Whatever questions we choose to address in a history course we must ensure that the information provided is accurate, balanced, and – within the limits of time, space and relevance – comprehensive. Thus, although I have stressed, and shall continue to stress, the importance of thinking, of addressing problems and issues, I would never wish it to be forgotten that there is a fundamental obligation upon our teaching material to *get it right* (to the extent that that is possible, given the difficulties of interpreting historical evidence). It is all very well discussing theories about corporatism, or war and social change, but such theories must always be based on correct information. We, of course, wrote our course books after the publication of such major secondary works as those by Roberts and Maier: now the onus is on us to convey to you the results of any important recent research. It is by no means inevitably true that a newer research article will always be 'more correct' than older interpretations, but it is important to be on guard against versions of events that often become entrenched in the older textbooks, which are not really sustainable in the light of more recent research. In offering guidance for the revision of Units 14 and 15, I am going to start by drawing attention to the references John Golby makes to the conclusions of recent research casting doubt on traditionally held views, which must now be considered open to question. My other two topics will then be the Maier thesis, and the relationship or otherwise to war of some of the main economic and social developments discussed by John Golby.

Some recent research conclusions

How close was revolution?

Probably the biggest issue of all is that of how close the various societies were at different times to revolution (this question is, of course, very closely related to the Maier thesis). First, there is the question of the December 1918 'uprising' in Berlin (Unit 14, p.14). While Roberts speaks of a 'minor civil war', Martin Kitchen, as Golby points out, has more recently declared that: 'Far from being a determined effort by unscrupulous Bolsheviks to overthrow the régime, it was an ill-considered and chaotic demonstration' organized by those who were concerned by the apparent right-wing course that the provisional government was taking (Kitchen, *Europe between the Wars*, 1988, p.162).

A couple of pages later, referring to Britain in February 1919, Golby offers a memorable quotation from Winston Churchill, whose implication is that trade unions in Britain were an anti-revolutionary force: 'the curse of trade unionism was that *there was not enough of it*, and it was not highly enough developed to make its branch secretaries (let alone its rank and file) fall into line with the head office' (p.16).

That there was conflict and violence, particularly in Germany, is not to be denied. The question is what interpretation should be put on it. Note that on page 18 Golby gives the figure of 1,200 people killed in the reprisals carried out by the *Freikorps* following the breaking up of the Bavarian Soviet Republic in 1919. It may be reasonable to conclude that much violence was repressive violence initiated from above, rather than, as one would expect in a revolutionary situation, violence initiated from below.

A further very important point about Germany at the end of the war is made in the reference to research by Wolfgang Mommsen on pages 20–1. In the words of Golby, Mommsen:

> pointed out that in many respects the political parties of the Left did not reflect the feelings of much of the working-class discontent during this period. From his research in the industrial Ruhr, Mommsen concluded that the major desire of most working men was not to embrace a political ideology which demanded revolution, but rather they wanted immediate improvements in their working conditions and they desired nationalization, especially of the coal industry. These demands were not necessarily in line with the political programmes of the left-wing parties. So theirs was much more a social protest movement than a wish to achieve major political and other structural changes. (Mommsen, 'The German Revolution 1918–1920', 1981)

Golby's summing up is worthy of very careful consideration:

> On reflection, it is clear that the belief in the existence of popular support for further radical changes, let alone further revolution in Germany, was

exaggerated by the government and also by later commentators. After the ending of the worst and most damaging war imaginable, it is questionable whether vast sections of the population had the appetite for renewed strife and civil war. Perhaps it is understandable that the government, when faced with having to demobilize some 6 million servicemen rapidly in late 1918 and early 1919, was anxious about how these men would react after the defeat of Germany. But, in fact, most of those who had been on active service only wished to return to their homes. Indeed, research has shown that comparatively few German soldiers who had fought on the Western or Eastern fronts were involved in the revolutionary unrest immediately after the war, and that the leaders of the revolts came from sections of the navy and workers who had spent most of their war years in Germany itself. (p.21)

Golby then goes on to cite Richard Bessel's arguments that by authorizing the activities of the *Freikorps* in putting down revolts, and thereby tacitly approving of the brutal manner in which the *Freikorps* went about its business, the government helped 'to create that very radicalism which its leaders had been determined to combat . . . Seen in this light, the radicalism of the workers in 1918–1920 appears largely defensive – motivated by growing distrust of the new government, and fear and hatred of the *Freikorps* and the *Reichswehr*. It was not necessarily a movement of workers striving consciously for a particular (Marxist or otherwise) party-political programme of working-class emancipation' (Open University, 1987, A323 *Weimar Germany*, Study Guide, p.26). 'If,' says Golby, 'with the luxury of the hindsight of seventy years, we can conclude that the threat of a socialist revolution largely reflected the fears of the government rather than the intentions of the vast majority of the governed in Germany, the same can certainly be said for Britain and France' (p.21). On page 22, Golby once again quotes Martin Kitchen with regard to the British Communist Party, which in 1921 had a membership of around 5,000: it 'was no more a threat to the established order than were the Jehovah's Witnesses to the established church or the Mormons to the institution of marriage' (1988, p.187).

French industrial growth in the inter-war years
On page 30 Golby effectively cites two experts, Peter Fearon and François Caron, in support of the now widely agreed view that France in the inter-war years enjoyed higher industrial growth rates than any other European country. (France, of course, was less fully developed industrially than Germany or Britain, but any notion of economic stagnation simply has to be abandoned.)

Stability in Britain in the 1930s
On page 67 Golby asks you to read the final chapter entitled 'The Revolution that Never Was' from the book by Stevenson and Cook, *The Slump*. You may like to re-read that chapter now. Certainly, the authors make it very difficult to continue to sustain the view that there was a potentially revolutionary situation, or even extreme class conflict, in Britain in the 1930s.

France in the 1930s
On page 57 Golby comments that 'a number of historians' have doubted whether the right-wing demonstration of 6 February 1934 was intended to carry through a *coup d'état*. To what Golby says I'd be inclined to add that this kind of street demonstration was rather usual in Paris – aiming to influence votes within the French parliament, but usually not to overthrow the system of government. On

page 57 Golby refers you to the table in *Documents 2* (document I.2) giving the general election statistics for 1936. These make it clear that the swing to the Left, often represented as being overwhelming, amounted to 3.8 per cent. Just how unstable France was in this period (throughout the inter-war era there were about 2,000 civilian deaths resulting from clashes with the police) remains a matter of legitimate debate. It is worth noting that, in the very last words of Unit 15 (quoting from Roberts), the failings of French political institutions are attributed, not to deep structural factors (conflict between classes, for instance) but to the faults of politicians.

The Maier thesis

When it was published in the 1970s, Charles Maier's book, *Recasting Bourgeois Europe: Stabilization in France, Germany and Italy in the Decade after World War I*, was immediately recognized as a work of great originality and significance, and it has continued to hold its place ever since, with Maier emerging as a major American expert on the history of twentieth-century Europe. Manifestly, the book engages directly with several of the central concerns of our course. Furthermore it is a very striking example of a particular approach to historical study, and of the way in which the approach adopted influences the conclusions. No apology, therefore, is needed for calling upon you to engage with Maier's ideas, even if only through the rather unsatisfactory means of providing you with, in the Course Reader, the Introduction and Conclusion to his book.

Maier believes that the term 'bourgeois Europe' is, with reference at least to France, Germany and Italy, the appropriate one for Europe as it was in 1914. World War I brought changes and upheavals, and a potential for revolutionary transformations in the aftermath of the war. In fact, through a process of 'stabilization', 'bourgeois Europe' was preserved, though in 'recast' (or 'altered') form. John Golby's sympathetic but critical analysis of the essence of Maier's arguments contained in the two chapters printed in the Course Reader may be taken in conjunction with the commentary offered in the Course Reader Introduction. Two issues should be firmly in the forefront of your mind at this stage in your studies.

First of all, if we are to make an assessment of how World War I affected the power structure and social order in the European countries, we have to have a clear idea about the power structure and social order on the eve of the war. John Golby, echoing Bill Purdue, points out that Maier's concept of a bourgeoisie ruling pre-1914 Europe is in conflict with Mayer's concept of the 'old regime' (that is, the landed aristocracy) still being in power then. Maier does recognize that the bourgeoisie had formed close associations with the old élites (as Golby points out on page 10), while Mayer, of course, had recognized that successful elements of the bourgeoisie were happy to support the old regime. For my part, I suggested in Book I, Unit 4, that rather than use either of the terms 'bourgeoisie' or 'old regime', it is better to think of an 'upper class' consisting of the still powerful landed aristocracy amalgamated with successful business and professional elements: the precise 'mix' differed from country to country. The advice here is that, before going into the exam, do have worked out in your own mind how you see class structure (a) before 1914, and (b) during the inter-war years. The usage of Maier, it must be said, is consistent and persuasive (though, obviously, open to question).

Secondly, Maier has a conflict model of society: he expects clashes as different groups compete for power, and he regards stabilization as something that needs explaining. Although Maier is concerned with the peculiarly intense crisis (as he perceives it) induced by the dislocation of World War I, in his view of history the war is by no means in itself the unique cause of crises – the potential for revolutionary upheaval already being inherent in society before 1914. Now, whatever the merits or demerits of the general approach to history, we have just seen that John Golby draws our attention to recent works suggesting that notions of the likelihood of revolutionary upheaval (to be averted by 'recasting' the social order, though with the bourgeoisie still in charge) are not securely based.

However, enough of criticism. John Golby (pages 12–13) provides you with a most helpful breakdown of Maier's thesis about the recasting of 'bourgeois' Europe into a more 'corporatist' Europe, which falls into four key chronological sections:

1   1918 to the end of 1919: a period of great turmoil during which industrial discontent and the threat of possible revolutions were stifled and contained by the élites and the middle classes uniting and combining against the claims of the militant Left.

2   1920 to 1921: a period in which the Left was largely defeated and which resulted in crises within the ranks of the socialist parties. This in turn produced schisms and the formation of communist parties. Meanwhile, governments were unable to maintain stability primarily because of both domestic and international economic problems. The problems of reparations, inflation and revaluation seemed at times insurmountable.

3   1922 to 1923: years which Maier interprets as ones where nationalist or, on occasions, authoritarian remedies were attempted and which replaced the efforts of the Left.

4   Finally, the middle years of the 1920s to 1929 are, in Maier's terms, ones of 'corporatist settlement', when the hopes of returning to a pre-1914 system had to be jettisoned, and when social and economic stability was achieved by governments, but only as a result of considerable influence and power being transferred to various interest groups.

Now let us note briefly other comments made by Golby on the Maier thesis, ones of particular relevance to our own general concerns. Maier puts great emphasis on the growth of organized labour during the war, but at the same time he does recognize that this power had been growing *before* the war (Unit 14, p.11). Similarly, Maier recognizes that the growth of pressure groups, an important element in corporatism, goes back to the late nineteenth century. An important item in the argument about the growth of corporatism in Germany is the Stinnes-Legien Agreement of November 1918 (also stressed by Feldman). Golby gives important support to Maier's arguments (and also, in this case, to the significance of the war) by quoting Richard Bessel's words that this pact, signed on 15 November 1918, was 'one of the most important compromises on which the economic and, ultimately, political order of Weimar Germany was based' (p.22). Lastly, Golby uses the evidence of the multiplicity of parties existing in Germany to 'help to support another strand of Maier's thesis in which he argues that one reason for a transition towards corporatism in Germany, as he sees it, was the inability of successive German governments to deal competently with an increasing number of issues, and that the interest of influential groups became more powerful at the expense of parliament' (p.25). (Here we are clearly *not* discussing the *direct* influence of war.)

Economic and social developments and their relationship, if any, to the war

I want to start with the question of political reform, dealt with by Golby on pages 22–3. Golby echoes Clive Emsley in pointing out that the powers of the *Reichstag* were increasing before 1914. But can one really say that Germany was genuinely on the road to representative government? I doubt it. I think we can say that the Weimar Republic was a consequence of the war in that it was the war that created the necessary 'clean break' or, if you prefer, 'power vacuum'. But how different was it in reality? Golby suggests that the 'key point' is that the bureaucratic and judicial structure was maintained by the old order and, in one sense, the form that the constitution took was of less importance. Citing Maier he notes that the head of the *Junker*-dominated Agrarian League had written only two days after the resignation of the Kaiser that the essential factor was to ensure the continuation of 'the bourgeois social order. Whether we wish to republican or monarchical forms is not an issue for today' (Maier, 1975, p.54). Golby adds that despite the various constitutional and electoral changes there was remarkably little change in the composition of the political parties or even political voting habits. Golby writes that 'it is important not to over-emphasize the changes'; for myself, I can't help beginning to wonder if there isn't a slight danger here of under-emphasizing them.

Golby cites Ross McKibbin in support of the view that the British Labour Party did not change at all between the pre-war and the post-war years: 'Everything points to Labour's enduring *ante-bellum* character: continuity of leadership and personnel at all levels, effective continuity of policy and, above all, continuity of organization' (McKibbin, *The Evolution of the Labour Party, 1910–1924*, 1974, p.240). My view (which McKibbin is, in fact, attacking here) is that the Labour Party was totally transformed (largely by virtue of the *participation* of Labour leaders in government), and that McKibbin has mistaken the trivial for the significant – but again that is a personal opinion. In France, Golby continues, there were very few political changes between 1914 and 1919. He raises an important general issue in mentioning the 'seemingly minor electoral change made in 1919' which replaced the old single member constituencies with large multi-member districts – a change that, as Golby explains, disadvantaged the parties of the Left. Is this a case of an independent political action influencing history, or is it perhaps again the case that it was because of the 'clean-break' notion at the end of the war that this electoral change was carried out in the first place?

As part of his attempt to analyse the effects of war as against other influences (beginning on page 25) Golby selects two fundamental economic developments: first of all, inflation, which he sees as 'primarily an inheritance from the war' (p.26); secondly, the process of getting industry back to peacetime conditions. Golby notes a permanent interruption to the overseas trade of Britain, France and Germany. He quotes Peter Fearon in support of the contention that the industry most severely hit by the war was agriculture. Industrial growth, it is suggested, was set back eight years by the war. But Fearon's warning is quoted: 'It would be a grave mistake to assume, however, that all economic events of the 1920s can be traced back to the war.' We have already encountered the new view that the French economy was growing strikingly in the inter-war years. François Caron is quoted (p.30) as saying that this 'was as much a continuation of the growth of the immediate pre-war years as of the industrialist spirit of the First World War'. Note that this is not denying influence to World War I, but is pointing also to a pre-war trend. I would certainly wish to stress the part played by the development of metallurgical industries in Paris to meet the needs of war.

Unit 15 discusses social change under seven headings, which are similar, but not identical, to the ten areas of social change that I have been using throughout the course. The reason for the slight discrepancy is that Golby has derived his headings from chapter 14 of Roberts. As we now know very well indeed, the question of the changing role and status of women and its relationship to war is very vexed. The Margaret Bondfield gramophone recording of 'The Woman's Opportunity' which is included on audio-cassette 3, item 2, is well worth playing again, in conjunction with Golby's comments on it. Note in particular Golby's remark about not falling 'into the trap of applying the values of the early 1990s to the late 1920s' (p.43). In other words, what may not seem to us like much in the way of emancipation may well have been perceived as quite a significant emancipation by women of the time.

With respect to Golby's discussion of 'The Great Depression', I would particularly like to remind you of his reference to the concept of the 'analogue of war' originally put forward by the American historian W. E. Leuchtenburg. This refers to the way in which many politicians thought they should try to solve the problems of peacetime by applying the remedies of war (pp.49, 58). This is a good way of summarizing the confusing legacy of war. In so far as the example of war called for positive state action, the example was on the whole a good one; in so far as the problems of peace were rather different from those of war, the example was a less good one.

I would very strongly recommend you to re-read the final parts of Unit 15, starting on page 58, and covering the topics of social reform, material change, leisure, and social cohesion. Clearly these are related more to long-term social and economic trends than directly to the war, though you really do have to take what is said here in conjunction with Units 8–10. I would be inclined to single out the higher living standards, and the raised expectations, of at least some sections of the various populations during the war. But these parts of Unit 15 are really, apart from providing general information in the spirit of key consideration (1) (see pp.108–9), most directly related to my fifth consideration: the need to provide a basis of what Europe was like in 1939, in order to assess what changes, if any, came with World War II.

3.2   Unit 16 *Internal war and the development of the Soviet Union* (by Bernard Waites)

It is useful, I think, to start by referring back to the first of Bernard Waites's two conclusions at the end of Unit 16, sub-section 5.1 'State violence and social development'.

> In this unit we have charted enormous changes which were not simply social but societal. Clearly the historical context of these changes was not 'peace', such as Britain and France were enjoying during the 1920s and 1930s. Though we might talk of these societies as experiencing 'class war', this is hyperbole. Despite profound conflicts of interest between them, the classes in these societies did not engage in armed struggle and the violence

that occurred during social conflict arose almost invariably from the attempts of the police to enforce law and order. The capitalist economy in these societies was relatively insulated from the polity. The state's monopoly of force was not placed directly at the disposal of any class or group in society and it was not brought to bear on processes of economic and social development. By contrast, internal war is not a hyperbole to describe the context of societal change in Soviet Russia. There, the state's monopoly of violence was brought to bear upon development; the great mass of people were coerced into changing their ways of living by the police, the militia, party cadres and the army. To be sure, coercion was complemented by exhortation and state-directed cultural change, but even these non-coercive aspects of 'social revolution from above' were scarcely irenic for they often propagated a psychosis of internal war: *kulaks*, hoarders, NEPmen, bourgeois specialists, Trotskyists, wreckers . . . the list of internal enemies was seemingly endless. Whether state violence had a comparable role in effecting socio-economic change in fascist states is a question we will examine in later units. (Unit 16, pp.104–5)

That is an excellent summary of how the place occupied by a study of Russia in our discussions of war, peace and social change differs from that occupied by the study we have just been revising of France and Britain (and 'democratic' Germany). The phrase 'societal change', incidentally, is not generally used elsewhere in our course: it has the force of 'social change amounting to complete social transformation'; it refers to the kind of change that historians like Maier suggest ought to be expected after the upheavals of war but which, for the sorts of reasons given by Maier, do not eventuate.

In introducing the concept of 'internal war', Bernard Waites is making the point that in Britain we have a tendency to concentrate too exclusively on the two total wars, and that any course focusing on war really must include internal war, particularly since that in the Soviet Union resulted in loss of life almost certainly exceeding that of World War I, and perhaps even exceeding that of World War II. 'There is,' he says, 'good reason for believing, however, that this "internal war" had destructive consequences of the same order of magnitude as the world wars' (Unit 16, p.75). In his 'final word of introductory clarification', he writes:

Those brought up in Britain will, understandably, tend to think of war as armed conflict between sovereign states, officially declared and, in twentieth-century Europe, fought until military defeat brought about a change of regime for the vanquished. The arena for wars of this type is the system of nation states and, arguably, it is in the international system that such wars have had their most profound consequences. People from other societies can perhaps more readily appreciate that war is a highly differentiated phenomenon: not only may the arena of war differ (with conflicts erupting within a society and assuming a bitter struggle over its political form and social system – as in Spain or Greece) but the modes of warfare have varied greatly too. 'Irregular' warfare has been a feature of peasant societies undergoing revolutionary upheavals, as in much of Russia between 1918 and 1921. From the perspective afforded by international war there is a clear demarcation between war and peace. Diplomatic and legal conventions recognize belligerent status and define, in theory, the conduct of belligerent powers towards neutrals and enemy prisoners. There is no such clear demarcation between internal war and social peace, for internal wars arise from conflicts endemic to the society and their modes of warfare are frequently intensified forms of chronic violence. 'Irregular' warfare, for example, is often barely distinguishable from banditry and other forms of lawlessness. *Furthermore, the relationship between internal war and social change is not always a straightforward one of cause and effect.* [My emphasis.] Many Soviet leaders in the late 1920s and early 1930s, for example, saw the massive violence inflicted on the Russian peasantry as a *necessary precondition* for the rapid industrialization of the country and the inauguration of socialism. Interestingly, Western historians have echoed this view by debating whether Stalin's violent coercion of the peasantry was really 'necessary' to provide the economic surplus needed for capital investment (Millar and Nove, 'Was Stalin really necessary?', 1976). There is a not dissimilar question as to whether the purges of the Soviet Communist Party in the 1930s were 'necessary' in order to renew the ruling élite. *What these arguments are implying is a functional, rather than a causal relationship between internal war and social change.* [My emphasis]

As I understand it, what is being said here is that internal war is a deliberate instrument in a 'guided' or intentional attempt to bring about social change or social transformation; such internal social consequences as the international total wars may have had were much more unintentional. (Waites actually argues that the international consequences of such wars are the most important ones: these are usually partly intentional, partly unintentional.) At any rate, there can be no doubt that, as a matter of objective fact, internal war has been extremely important in the period which we are studying. It would seem to be a phenomenon most likely to appear in less developed societies, and less likely to appear in more fully modernized societies such as Britain and France. If we were to take into consideration the period since 1955 I think it would be reasonable to say that internal war has not been a marked or sustained feature in European society as modernization has spread. In that perspective, the two total wars do perhaps again regain much of their significance. However, you will recall that my first consideration in relating the inter-war material studied in this course to the course as a whole was that, putting war aside temporarily, it is absolutely essential that we *get it right*: we can't begin to understand what was happening in Soviet Russia without exploring the question of internal war (and, of course, that of totalitarianism).

Bringing war back into focus, the major problem we have to address is that of whether internal war and the modernization of Soviet life is in itself connected to World War I. Waites refers to the years 1914–1921/22 as 'the multi-faceted seven-year crisis', and I think it would probably be futile in connection with this particular problem to separate out the period of international war: certainly the intensification of brutalization came in the period of atrocity and counter-atrocity in the civil war between Whites and Reds.

Bernard Waites uses a number of different phrases to describe one of his major concerns in Unit 16: 'development', 'social development', 'social change', 'societal change'. (Remember the first key consideration I set out: we have to be clear what was happening in the Soviet Union, as elsewhere, before we can even begin to bring in questions about war's possible influence.) Three areas of highly significant social change are particularly worth recalling.

The first change is in class and social structure. The regime 'created a new élite political stratum' (p.97), and we are given the example of the twenty-nine-year old

Kravchenko who finds himself 'overnight, transformed into one of the élite . . . one of the million or so top Party officials, industrial managers and police functionaries who were, taken together, the new aristòcracy of Russia'. Kravchenko found it difficult to establish friendly relations with the workers, finding that 'for an engineer in my position to mix with [them] might offend their pride; it smacks of patronage. In theory we represented the "workers' power" but in practice we were a class apart' (these quotations are taken by Waites from Kravchenko's memoirs, *I Chose Freedom*, 1947, pp.174–5).

Secondly, there is the position of women (referred to, you may remember, in the extracts from Simone de Beauvoir's book *The Second Sex*, which we studied in Unit 27). 'Not the least of the social consequences of industrialization was a veritable revolution in the position of women in the workforce' (p.96). The Soviet regime, it is pointed out, recognized that if it was to attract women into production, then it would have to provide crêche and childcare facilities, and public amenities (such as laundries and public catering) which would lessen the burden of housework.

> Although women's share in industrial labour as a whole rose by only about a quarter, they entered industries and trades that before intense industrialization had been virtually closed to them. In January 1929 women were 28.5 per cent of workers in large-scale industry, but they predominated in trades (such as textiles and clothing) where women's work was well established. By July 1935 women were 39.8 per cent of workers in large-scale industry, and it is clear that the huge expansion of the extractive and capital goods industries could not have taken place without their labour. They had risen from under 8 per cent to 24.1 per cent of those in coal mining and from 8.9 per cent to 26.2 per cent of the engineering and metalworking labour force. Clerical employment had witnessed a great influx of women workers; they rose from 12.4 per cent to 44.3 per cent of the clerical labour force. Despite concerted efforts to attract women into factory training schools, they were generally confined to the lowest-skilled and worst-paid jobs, where they had little prospects for promotion. Those who tried to improve their industrial status often encountered considerable male resistance and harassment. (Unit 16, p.97)

Thirdly, Waites refers to the rejuvenation (that is to say, the bringing in of new talented young blood in place of the old party members) of the Communist Party which was a result, though possibly an unintended one, of the political purges of the *Ezhovshchina*.

Now, go back and re-read the two sentences I emphasize in the passage on internal war I quoted from Unit 16. Waites is not drawing a direct line between internal war and these areas of social change. Change in the status of women and, in part at least, in the class structure, are due to industrialization. What Waites is arguing is that to achieve this industrialization internal war against the peasantry was necessary. As with international total war, internal war could have unintended consequences as well – perhaps, for instance, the rejuvenation of the party just mentioned. However, the fundamental distinction remains valid. Internal war was waged in Russia to achieve certain definite purposes, specifically industrialization and modernization. International total war is waged overtly for international objectives. Whatever social changes there may be are essentially unintended. I would personally take the comparison a little further. As Waites makes clear, internal war in Russia was every bit as devastating and destructive as international war. In international total war, I have suggested, destruction can lead to significant reconstruction – this does not seem to be the case in internal war. Participation in international total war, I have said more than once, can lead to social gains. There is little of that effect in internal war which, of course, is really a one-sided war: all the might of the Stalinist state on one side, ill-equipped families and individuals of various categories on the other. Since this course is concerned with questions of historical explanation, I want finally, in this discussion of internal war, to draw your attention to a sentence on page 78 of Unit 16: 'Stalin did more to shape twentieth-century Europe than any other single individual . . .' Do we here have an example of an individual being more important than structural or ideological forces, or than the forces of war? Or should we think of Stalin as analogous to Napoleon – Napoleon waging an international war, Stalin an internal war?

Unit 16 plays its part with respect to consideration (4) on page 109, that is to say setting the base line against which we can measure the effects of World War II. Bernard Waites makes clear the levels of industrialization, collectivization of agriculture and urbanization attained by the time of Hitler's invasion in June 1941. These, he points out, 'laid the basis for, among other things, Soviet military might (*before* Hitler's attack Russia had the world's largest tank park)'. Remarking that the launching of the First Five-Year Plan 'began the transformation of Soviet Russia from an underdeveloped rural society to an industrial, urbanized superpower', Waites draws your attention to the major question you should now be in a good position to answer, that of whether World War II 'simply pushed Russian society further along the lines laid down by Stalinist modernization, or whether it deflected development in specific ways' (p.92).

Now let us turn to the issue of totalitarianism. It is important, I have said several times, to get things right, and to get right comparisons and contrasts between the Russian dictatorship, the dictatorships of Mussolini and Hitler, and, of course, the Western liberal democratic powers. Then there is the simple-sounding, but really rather complex, conundrum of whether total war leads to totalitarianism, with totalitarianism in turn leading to further total war. Clearly there are parallels between the state control established in Russia and the kind of state control developed for the purposes of waging war; but parallels do not necessarily imply connections. Perhaps it is more fruitful to turn to the concept of the Analogue of War mentioned by John Golby in his discussion of the Western countries. Waites talks (p.86) of the Russian 'state's need to mobilize society for the great industrialization drive of the First Five-Year Plan (operated from October 1928) by creating a siege mentality' (p.86). Here perhaps there is some reflection of the experience (or 'analogue') of war, where something of the same kind of siege mentality had had to be created. Waites also speaks of the technology of totalitarian control, especially 'rapid, mass communication and transportation', and I think it could reasonably be said that the first effective development and exploitation of these technologies in this way did occur during World War I. But let us remember that for many countries World War I issued in democracy and national self-determination: at the very least, there is no automatic link between war and totalitarianism, and it would probably be right to say that the real key lies in particular political ideologies.

The main point made in Unit 16 with regard to totalitarianism (one of the major points in the unit as a whole) is that Soviet Russia under Stalin did not conform fully to the political science definition of totalitarianism, and that, in the words of the very last sentence of the unit, there is reason to doubt that Fascist Italy and Nazi Germany 'can be lumped with the Soviet Union as "three of a kind"'. Bernard Waites makes the point of the lack of continuity between earlier policies and the really horrific and vicious purges breaking out in 1935 when 'revisionist writers see a distinct break' (p.101). Waites also argues that there was a 'chaotic situation, in which Stalin was responsive to pressures "from below" and often acted as the mediator between "radical" and more "moderate" factions' (p.101). I have no reason, nor have I have the knowledge, to challenge the general conclusion, which on the whole seems persuasive enough. I shall confine myself to two comments:

1   I believe the political science model of what constitutes totalitarianism has to be considered very carefully. It strikes me as being such a rigid and 'unreal' model that there is little difficulty in showing that a regime, such as Stalin's, does not conform to it. Personally I prefer to start with the regime rather than with a model: looking at the regime it was, as Bernard Waites makes abundantly clear, a pretty obnoxious one: certainly dictatorial and, at least in a broad general sense, 'totalitarian'.

2   I fancy that it is a characteristic of all personal autocratic dictatorships to be 'chaotic'. Hitler's regime, as I see it, was in many ways 'chaotic', as are the shabby Latin American dictatorships of today. So, without contesting the general point, I'm not sure that these particular arguments are overwhelmingly convincing.

3.3   Unit 17 *Italy 1918–1940* (by Geoffrey Warner)

The relationship of this unit to the general topic of war, peace and social change emerges very clearly from the five questions set out on page 111, which Geoffrey Warner says you should be able to answer when you have finished the unit. They make very good questions on which to base your revision (the first two questions are clearly central to the aims of the course as a whole):

1   What were the consequences of World War I for Italian politics and society?

2   What was the nature of Fascism and to what extent was it a product of World War I?

3   How and why did Fascism come to power in Italy in 1922? To what extent was this 'inevitable'? (This reaffirms our need to get the facts right: only by doing so will we be able to answer fully question 2.)

4   What was the nature of the Fascist regime? How much support did it enjoy and how does it fit into the so-called 'totalitarian model'? (Refer once again to consideration (1) on pages 108–9.)

5   How far was war basic not only to Fascist philosophy but also to Fascist practice? (This is a version of part of the overall course aim concerned with the relationship between war and revolution, taking Fascism as a revolutionary, or, if you prefer, counter-revolutionary philosophy.)

In discussing Italian politics and society at the end of World War I, Warner reminds us that, as you saw in Book I, Units 2–5, 'pre-war Italy's constitutional and parliamentary foundations were weak', explaining, however, that World War I further undermined them, and this for two main reasons.

The first was that Italy's economy, being less strong than those of its allies, suffered proportionately more from the economic consequences of the war, such as inflation and unemployment. The second reason was political. First of all the war, in Roberts's words, 'accentuated the divorce between patriotism and the left which had lain in the teaching of prewar Socialism'. This led to increasing polarization between the Left and the nationalist Right. Furthermore, successive Italian governments seemed unable to cope with either the economic or political situation. This was because the political system in which they were accustomed to operate depended upon the absence of mass parties and, unfortunately for them, the aftermath of World War I saw not only an increase in the strength of the Socialists, but also the emergence of a second mass party, the Roman Catholic *Partito Popolare* or 'People's Party'. (Unit 17, pp.111–12)

Geoffrey Warner then comes down in favour of the view that in Italy's post-war crisis political factors were more important than economic ones. But, he clarifies, 'the war did not create Italy's problems; it merely exacerbated them.'

An important element in Unit 17 (all a part of our first key consideration) is the manner in which Geoffrey Warner uses the latest research to criticize some of the points made by Roberts. For instance, he uses a statistical analysis to demonstrate that the economic strain of the war on Italy was not so much greater than that on other countries as Roberts suggests. On the other hand, he suggests that the fall in real wages for workers was greater than indicated by Roberts.

The unit next draws our attention to the three main developments of the Italian political scene in the aftermath of World War I:

the growth and increased combativeness of the socialist trade-union movement and of the PSI (Italian Socialist Party);

the birth and rapid development of the Catholic People's Party and of the Catholic trade-union movement;

the ferment of nationalist forces, which were hostile to both socialism and the liberal parliamentary system.

With regard to Italian labour unrest after the war, Warner draws attention to two particular features. The first was that the industrial unrest culminated, in September 1920, in large-scale factory occupations in such northern cities as Turin, Genoa and Milan, where Italian industry was concentrated. Giolitti, prime minister at the time, did not (probably rightly) take these occupations too seriously, but his alleged passivity in the face of what *looked like* revolutionary activity and his pressure upon the bosses to grant concessions antagonized the employers and the middle classes generally.

The second special feature of post-war Italian labour unrest was that it extended into agriculture – during the *biennio rosso* (two red years), four out of ten Italian strikers were in the agricultural sector.

On page 117 Geoffrey Warner gives a most effective summing up of the relationship of the three main political developments to the war:

Both the growth of the PSI and the emergence of the PPI were a direct result of World War I. One should not posit too much of a connection between death and deprivation, whether in the trenches or on the home front, and political radicalization, but it is surely significant that increased unionization of labour, greater industrial militancy, and heightened demands for political, economic and social reform were well-nigh universal phenomena in all belligerent countries. The old order had failed. Indeed, the war itself had underlined the failure. It was time for a better tomorrow and ordinary men and women seemed more inclined to organize and agitate for it. [These last two points, if you care to look at it that way, fit into my notions of war as 'test' and war as 'psychological experience'.]

The ferment of right-wing nationalism, which was the third major development of post-war Italian politics, also grew directly out of the war, but in a different way. Although 1918 had witnessed the disintegration of Italy's traditional enemy, the Austro-Hungarian Empire, and although the subsequent peace settlement awarded Italy much additional territory at its expense . . . the nationalists who had propelled the country into war in 1915 were still not satisfied.

Geoffrey Warner goes on to take up the question of the extreme nationalists, mentioning in particular the nationalist poet, Gabriele d'Annunzio. He is critical of Roberts's description of d'Annunzio's intervention at Fiume as 'almost comical', for, in fact:

. . . it illustrated not only the strength of nationalist feeling, but also the connivance of some sections of the armed forces – the local Italian commander allowed d'Annunzio to take over – and the relative impotence of the Italian government, which was unable to retrieve control of the situation for more than a year. This connivance at right-wing defiance of the government on the part of sections of the state apparatus, and the apparent inability of the government to deal with either the defiance or the connivance, was to be a feature of the rise of Fascism.

At a more symbolic level, d'Annunzio's occupation of Fiume provided a foretaste of Fascist theatricality. (p.118)

However, Warner makes the most important point that Fascism was not of great importance at this stage, and that Roberts gives a wrong impression here: in the words of Warner, Fascism's 'size and influence was minimal until the end of 1920'. Immediately following (p.118) we get another indication of the influence of war, this time on Mussolini himself: very early in the war he had broken with his socialist comrades over the issue of Italian participation in the war, 'believing that this was essential in order to create the necessary conditions for a socialist revolution'.

Three developments in the last quarter of 1920 rescued Fascism from the doldrums and transformed it from the status of an irrelevant sect to that of a mass movement contending for power. These were: (a) the factory occupations of September and the parallel agrarian unrest; (b) the local elections of September/October, as a result of which the PSI gained control of 2,022 communal and 26 provincial governments compared with 400 and 4 in the previous elections in 1914; and (c) the Treaty of Rapallo between Italy and Yugoslavia in November, by which the former renounced its claims to Dalmatia, Fiume was declared a free city, and d'Annunzio and his supporters subsequently driven out by the Italian armed forces. For the Right, the first two developments constituted a major challenge to the existing structure of property relations and political power, while the third was regarded as an act of treachery on the part of the government. (p.119)

Geoffrey Warner is at great pains to stress how much the rise of Fascism owed to the complicity of state authorities. In support of this point there is a valuable quotation from the leading historian Christopher Seton-Watson, which you should be sure to give careful attention to in revising this unit.

From being an unimportant sect, Fascism was now growing rapidly. Originally it was heavily concentrated in the north of the country, but in later 1921 it began to extend its influence to central and southern Italy. Still, says Warner, 'Fascism was essentially a northern phenomenon'. He adds: 'It must be stressed that the Fascist surge was a counter-revolution and not, as it was so often portrayed by apologists at the time and since, a defensive action against the threat of "Bolshevism".' This is absolutely true, though personally I see no objection to calling Fascism 'revolutionary' (as I would similarly regard Nazism), since I believe that there can be revolutions of the radical Right just as much as there can be revolutions of the Left – the only kind recognized by traditionalist Marxists. Using some important statistical material, Geoffrey Warner brings out that, although not greatly supported by industrial workers, the Fascist party did draw its membership fairly equally from all sections of society; above all, it was a party of young people.

Already split between communists and socialists, the Left was further weakened when a moderate socialist party, the PSU, split from the main party in October 1922. This, of course, made things still easier for Fascism. The feeling was growing that, sooner or later, Mussolini and the Fascists would have to be taken into the government. As Warner puts it, this time echoing Roberts: 'Mussolini's accession to power did not at first seem to signify a fundamental change in the governmental system. His was a coalition government; it contained only four Fascists and the special powers it took were only for a limited period' (p.123).

But Warner is critical of Roberts's attempt to explain why Mussolini became a fully-fledged dictator, and how or why his government became a regime. Warner feels that Roberts fails to recognize the full importance of the 1924 elections, the Matteotti murder and the so-called 'Aventine secession'.

> It was not just the electoral law that enabled Mussolini's supporters to win the 1924 elections, but also the widespread fraud and intimidation which accompanied its implementation. It was this that was denounced by the PSU's secretary-general, Giacomo Matteotti, in the Chamber on 30 May 1924, and it was his denunciation which led to his disappearance on 10 June. Although Matteotti's body was not discovered for some weeks, it was widely and correctly assumed that he had been murdered by the Fascists on account of his accusations.
>
> While the 'Aventine secession' (named after an incident in the history of Ancient Rome) was an unfortunate tactic on the part of the opposition parties, it might have achieved more if they could have agreed on something else as well. As it was, the PCI soon returned to the Chamber [following the 'secession' by the left-wing parties], while Pius XI vetoed a promising initiative for an alliance between the PPI and the PSU. Even then Mussolini's position remained weak, especially as evidence of Fascist complicity in Matteotti's abduction and murder mounted. Once again, however, the king failed to act; the general and admiral serving as war and navy ministers refused to join some of their civilian colleagues in resigning, thus in effect pledging the support of the armed forces for Mussolini; and Italian business, enjoying the effects of a mini-boom and good labour relations, came out in favour of the government. (p.124)

What was most decisive of all, Warner says, is that the Fascist leadership urged Mussolini to take the offensive. This he did in the speech to the Chamber of 3 January 1925, when he accepted 'full political, moral, and historical responsibility for all that has happened' and warned that 'when two irreducible elements [i.e. Fascism and anti-Fascism] are locked in a struggle, the solution is force'. But it was not until December 1925 that the Decree on the Powers of the Head of the Government made Mussolini responsible only to the king and not to the Chamber; elected local governments were abolished in two stages in February and September 1926. And it was not until November 1926 that all opposition political parties were banned, though the rights of opposition trade unions had already been effectively suppressed in October 1925. Warner indicates that there was nothing 'inevitable' about the rise of Fascism. Again, he agrees with Roberts that too many politicians thought they could 'use' the Fascists when the Fascists were in fact 'using' them.

Summing up with regard to the principal theme of the effects of World War I, Warner writes of the war:

> . . . while Italy was not destabilized economically by the conflict, it was destabilized politically. The emergence and/or growth of the PSI, the PPI and the Fascist movement itself, all of which were attributable in large measure to the war, posed a powerful threat to the pre-war liberal regime which the latter was, in the end, incapable of surmounting. However, this is not the same thing as saying that World War I led to the accession of Fascism to power. The weakness of the Italian political system was due, not so much to the war, as to the way in which Italy had been united and the way in which it had been ruled since unification. There had been neither the time nor the inclination to lay the foundations of a stable democratic tradition. Fascism proved more able to profit from this state of affairs than its rivals. (pp.124–5)

Next Warner turns to the question of totalitarianism. He makes use of the political science model of totalitarianism introduced by Bernard Waites in the previous unit, but perhaps with less conviction. He also seems to perceive Stalinist Russia as more totalitarian than Waites was prepared to concede. He quarrels with Roberts's statement that as 'a totalitarian system Fascism was far less impressive than Bolshevism'. His own formulation is that though Fascism was less totalitarian than Stalinist communism, it still was very totalitarian, adding that it should also be compared with Nazi Germany. You may recall that I was slightly sceptical about the political science model of totalitarianism: Warner suggests that rather than being characterized by this descriptive list of features, it is better characterized 'by its purpose: the progressive annihilation of the boundaries between state and society' (p.126). The important comparative point is that the influence of the Italian Fascists 'was not on a par with' that of the German Nazis or the Russian Communists. Examining the Italian mass media under Fascism, Warner concludes that 'while government influence was considerable, it would be a gross exaggeration to claim that the regime possessed anything approaching a monopoly of them'. Ostensibly, Fascist economic policy was adopted on the basis of 'corporatism', a word you have now met many times. It would be a good idea to refresh your memory of the excellent definition of corporatism cited on page 130 of Unit 17. Warner concludes that 'Roberts's scepticism about the role of corporatism in Italy's economic life is justified' (p.131).

Returning to his point about totalitarianism being essentially concerned with the annihilation of the boundaries between state and society, Warner points out that Italian Fascism was the first regime to institute totalitarian educational, youth and leisure policies (subsequently taken up by Nazi Germany and the Soviet Union). But for all that there remained many important political forces which were largely independent of Fascism: some are mentioned by Roberts, though he omits to mention the armed forces. Geoffrey Warner draws particular attention to Catholic Action, a network of lay organizations controlled by the Church set up well before World War I, and not in 1931 as stated by Roberts.

The final topic discussed in Unit 17 is that of 'Fascism and war'. Warner summarizes as follows:

> Mussolini's underlying assumption was that life was a perpetual struggle. This was linked with two myths: the idea of revolution, which he took partly from Marx and partly from Sorel; and the idea of the nation, which he took partly from Mazzini and other Italian nationalist thinkers. World War I removed the contradiction between these two myths and indeed permitted their fusion. If Italy's participation in the war was motivated by nationalist considerations, it would also lead to revolution.
>
> Mussolini wanted, in his own words, 'to fascistize the nation, so that tomorrow Italian and Fascist, more or less like Italian and Catholic, will be the same thing'. This new Italy would reject old stereotypes – 'mandolin players' and 'exquisite manners' – in favour of a tough, ruthless image. Expansion and war would be the means of achieving this objective. (p.138)

There follows a splendidly concise summing-up of the entire unit, which you should certainly read carefully in your revision. Geoffrey Warner's final sentence may be compared with the idea expressed by Martin Clark that Fascism was created by World War I and destroyed by World War II. Warner's sentence is 'The fact that war brought about Fascism's collapse was in a sense paradoxical, since war and foreign conquest were essential both to Fascist theory and practice.'

3.4   Unit 18 *State, economy and society in Nazi Germany 1933–1939* (by Bernard Waites)

Very obviously, the subject matter of Unit 18 would seem to be most relevant to the second overall course aim, that part relating to the relationship between war and revolution (accepting Nazism as a revolution of the Right), and the third course aim, the causes of wars, in so far as Nazism was obviously orientated towards aggressive military expansionism. In fact, perhaps of all units in the course this one most persuasively makes the case that factors other than those arising directly from war are the important ones in historical development. As an up-to-date survey of all the most recent research, Unit 18, then, relates most directly to the first of the considerations I identified in the introduction to this section. Unit 18 provides you with the necessary information and detail on the main historiographical debates to enable you to reach informed conclusions about how far, if at all, developments in Nazi Germany are related to war.

Unit 18 opens by discussing various theories about the rise and nature of Nazi Germany and, in particular, examines two interpretations – the 'intentionalist' and the 'functionalist' – of how Nazi Germany came to be a state driving forward towards war. The first interpretation, associated with, among others, Eberhard

Jäckel, argues that Hitler had a clearly enunciated programme of aggrandize-
ment and aggression (even if, of course, he often had to adapt to the unexpected).
The second interpretation speaks of 'polyocratic' instability: it was the anarchic
competition between rival centres of power which caused the uncontrollable
drive towards external aggression, a view particularly associated with another
German scholar, Hans Mommsen.

The other four questions spelt out at the beginning of the unit are much further
away from any direct connection with war:

> What was the relationship between Nazism and capitalist interests before and
> after Hitler's accession to power?

> How was it that a man with the declared intention of destroying the Weimar
> Republic came to be appointed its Chancellor?

> How far did he have a blueprint for aggression and to what extent were
> economic and social policies dictated by the purposes of foreign conquests?

> How are we to best explain the apparently uncontrollable dynamism of
> Hitler's Germany: by reference to a totalitarian dynamic or to its 'polyocratic'
> instability?

In next discussing the early days of the National Socialist movement, Waites
mentions the associated military detachments many of whose members, of
course, though Waites does not mention this, were ex-officers or ex-soldiers. The
most important item in the twenty-five-point programme of the new National
Socialist German Worker's Party, founded in February 1920, was opposition to
the Versailles Settlement (itself, of course, in no uncertain way intimately related
to World War I). In discussing the growing support for the Nazis at the end of the
1920s and the beginning of the 1930s, Bernard Waites corrects a deeply held
assumption about the connection between the economic slump and the growth of
Nazi electoral support.

> . . . the Nazis did not make their gains among those groups most affected
> by mass unemployment (chiefly the industrial working class) and the
> connections between Hitler's rise to power and the economic crisis were
> more indirect than is often assumed. Before the collapse of the industrial
> economy, major gains were made among the stricken farming
> communities of Protestant northern Germany. Because of falling prices,
> greater foreign competition and higher tax bills, many farmers faced
> bankruptcy and foreclosure; the Nazi party was able to mobilize their
> discontent and that of the independent artisans, shopkeepers and
> merchants of small-town Germany. The NSDAP thrived on the
> disappointments of all classes, but the most solidly pro-Nazi sector of the
> electorate was to be found among Germany's large self-employed labour
> force, whether in agriculture or handicrafts. (pp.151–2)

Section 3 of Unit 18, 'The NSDAP and business interests before 1933', is a most
thorough exposition of this issue, stating quite categorically that 'no historian
now seriously contends that Hitler was the puppet of monopoly capitalism'. If
you are in any doubt over this, you must re-read this important section.

As with Mussolini, the actual gaining of total power came in stages; Bernard
Waites speaks of 'the accession of power' and then 'the Nazi seizure of power'. He
shows how (again as with Mussolini) powerful people thought that they could
'use' Hitler:

Like Papen, who acted as the President's agent in the final political crisis, Hugenberg deluded himself that Hitler could be constrained within a coalition. After Schleicher's entire ministry had resigned, Hindenburg appointed Hitler Chancellor in a Cabinet numerically dominated by Nationalists and with Papen enjoying, on paper, wide powers as Vice-Chancellor. Hitler had only two National Socialist colleagues in the Cabinet, Hermann Goering and Wilhelm Frick, but since Goering was appointed to the Prussian Ministry of the Interior, formidable police powers fell into National Socialist hands throughout the greater part of Germany.

Though he had never disguised his intention of destroying the parliamentary republic, Hitler's accession to power was formally constitutional. He had calculated that his revolutionary purpose would be more effectively achieved by observing legal formalities; even when he became Chancellor he preferred to postpone a ban on the KPD until he had secured a *Reichstag* majority to enact a draconic Enabling Law. To many on the Left it appeared that the real beneficiaries of 30 January were the reactionary Nationalists who, it seemed, had made a 'prisoner' of Hitler. (p.156)

In discussing the Nazi seizure of power, Bernard Waites points out that Hitler consolidated a one-party regime in two stages:

During February, March and April of 1933 he used the police and the SA to crush the left-wing parties and the trade unions.

Then he compelled the middle class and Nationalist parties to renounce their political independence.

The way in which the Nazis followed the established tactic of legality is stressed: fresh elections were held to provide the majority which would make it possible to enact the legal instruments of National Socialist *Gleichschaltung*.

Next, the unit moves on to sub-section 4.2, 'Liquidating the revolution'. There is a quotation from an important speech made by Hitler on 6 July 1933: 'Revolution is not a permanent condition . . . The ideas in our programme do not commit us to behaving like fools and destroying everything, but to realising our conceptions wisely and carefully . . .' Bernard Waites suggests that revolution had to be liquidated in order that the intimately connected goals of rearmament and economic recovery, and probably too of aggressive foreign policy, could be efficiently pursued. These goals were threatened by the 'unguided', spontaneous 'revolution from below' – that is, the outbreak of disorderly Nazi enthusiasm, to which our attention has been drawn. On 30 June/1 July a purge of old comrades was carried out. Note the important point that is brought out: the purge

> . . . quickened the process by which Hitler's public image and popularity were dissociated from that of the Nazi Party. The Führer's personal standing in the eyes of the great majority of Germans was, all the evidence suggests, greatly enhanced by his sanctioning of the state murders. These met the traditional bourgeois demands for 'peace and quiet' and 'law and order' which the unruliness, arbitrary violence, and public outrages of the SA had threatened. (p.161)

There follows a brief sub-section on 'The reversion to legality and the "dualism" of the police and SS'. The regime, we learn, 'preferred to pursue its internal opponents (of whom very few were from the political or social élites) by legal procedures and through the judicial system which it had inherited'. 'Dualism' refers to the way in which alongside this inherited system there grew up an improvised system uncontrolled by the regular organs of state government and justice, run by the Gestapo, and dependent for its dubious legality upon a series of emergency decrees.

The section that follows links up in part with something Bernard Waites had previously said about the Soviet system which, he argued in Unit 16, had established a durable institutional basis, not dependent on the whims of Stalin. He argues that the Nazi system lacked durability because it depended so much on Hitler.

The long-term objective of Nazi economic policies (discussed in section 6 of the unit) was the establishment of a *Wehrwirtschaft* or 'military economy'. The economic recovery of Germany fell into two phases: 1933 to 1936, and 1936 to 1939. In both phases, state expenditure and investment were basic instruments of the economic policy, but between 1933 and 1936 spending on the military represented a relatively modest proportion of government outlays, whereas during 1936 to 1939 spending on rearmament, and on projects intended to ensure Germany's strategic self-sufficiency, 'became the dynamo of economic expansion' (p.164). Bernard Waites repeats and develops a point made earlier, rebutting traditional Marxist arguments about Nazism as the tool of monopoly capitalism:

> . . . we have to distinguish between contingent benefits that capitalists enjoyed because of Nazi rule and the actual identity of interests between industry and the regime. There is very little evidence that capitalists dictated political and strategic aims to the Nazis and while certain sectors of industry identified with the regime's macro-economic objectives, others did not. Those traditionally reliant on exports did not generally support autarky, the chief beneficiary of which was the chemicals industry. (pp.169–70)

Hitler, we are told, 'rejected the totalitarian doctrines of Fascist Italy as setting the state above the race', but he admittedly did share 'the objective of re-using state and civil society in new political totalities with monopolistic claims to allegiance'. It is particularly important to note the criticisms made of Hannah Arendt's influential study *The Origins of Totalitarianism*, first published in 1951, in which

> she argued that the totalitarian movement sprang from the break up of the class structure of civil society, the decay of its social ties and the 'atomization' of individuals torn out of their customary roles and allegiances by World War I and the economic catastrophes of the inter-war period. In power, Arendt argued, the movement made this atomization a fundamental principle of its rule by tolerating no ties except those which bound the masses to the leader and his élite. (p.172)

The crucial flaw in this, Bernard Waites points out, is that it viewed the behaviour of the masses entirely from above.

> Only relatively recently have historians begun to look at Nazi Germany from 'the bottom up' by reconstructing everyday experiences and popular mentalities. Research into these social aspects of the Third Reich has revealed the incompleteness of the regime's hold on the hearts and minds

of the people and the existence of strong currents of popular dissent, amounting (in the opinion of some historians) to a massive challenge to the regime. Even if the challenge has been exaggerated, it is clear that German society is not simply the passive instrument of the Nazi state. (p.172)

The most controversial topic in this whole area is that of the relationship between the regime and the industrial workers. The neo-Marxist historian, T. W. Mason, has been the chief protagonist of the view that class conflict was the 'fundamental reality' of the Nazi system. Waites writes:

> Between 1933 and 1936 the restoration of employment and the threat of the Gestapo kept labour quiescent; many were grateful to the Nazis for providing jobs and shared the sense of national revival. But, after 1936, the discipline of the labour market was much less effective and, argues Mason, 'economic class conflict re-emerged in Germany on a broad front . . .' (Mason, 'Intention and explanation', 1981, p.210). It manifested itself with spontaneous strikes, defiance of work-place rules, absenteeism, going-slow, and such forms of collective pressure on employers as threatening to leave *en masse* unless wage demands were met. The last tactic was particularly successful in the building industry where smaller and medium-sized firms had to reckon with the solidarity of their whole labour force. (p.180)

Waites's own conclusion is clear and persuasive, if, as so often in such historical debates, inconclusive:

> The fact that there was more evidence for so-called 'Workers' Opposition' in British than in German coalfields in the early 1940s should have given pause for thought about what exactly the term means. For me the comparison underlines the fact that industrial militancy and labour-management conflict do not necessarily entail opposition to the political form of the state. The term 'Workers' Opposition' strikes me, therefore, as an interesting but unproven thesis. (p.181)

The remainder of this long and complex unit takes us into the question of the origins of World War II which has already been the subject of full discussion in Unit 29. For that reason, also, I shall not be entering into a discussion of Unit 20 *Origins of World War II* by Antony Lentin.

3.5   Unit 19 *Mass society 1918–1939* (by Tony Aldgate)

As one of the sections of the fifth overall course aim makes clear, we are concerned that you should be involved with the immense variety of source material available to the historian. Of all the units in the course, Unit 19 is the one that goes most fully into the potential of film, radio and gramophone records (remember, for instance, that the Margaret Bondfield talk was on record, not radio). I shall be recalling much of what Tony Aldgate has to say later when I turn to the topic of 'War and culture'; my consideration of the other aspects of this unit can, therefore, be fairly brief. You will already be familiar with the notion that one way of describing some of the most characteristic developments of the twentieth century is to talk about the emergence of mass society: questions then immediately arise about the place of war in the development of mass society. Let us just be sure that we are clear what we mean by mass society. Unit 19 starts by referring to a most important book, *The Age of the Masses. Ideas and Society in Europe since 1870*, by Michael Biddiss. According to Biddiss, 'mass socialization' must be recognized as

> the most fundamental fact confronting those in dialogue with the historical situation of the last hundred years . . . In the context of European history it is the emergence of mass society, and the associated developments of mass politics and culture, which most essentially and dramatically distinguishes this period from what has gone before. (1977, p.14)

'Mass society', Biddiss says, 'is differentiated from what precedes it by an enlargement in the scale of activities, institutions and loyalties'. As Tony Aldgate summarizes: '. . . it has been characterized by the presence of such features as widening electorates, mass markets, increasing educational provision and enhanced literacy, the spread of mass communications, material improvements, greater leisure, and rising expectations' (p.193).

It is important that you should be fully aware of all the different facets of mass society and, of course, the information on film and broadcasting provided by Tony Aldgate in this unit.

You are already familiar with the distinction between the one-party dictatorship of 'totalitarian' states, discussed by Bernard Waites and Geoffrey Warner, and the Western liberal democracies discussed by John Golby. 'Mass society', however, can serve as a description which embraces both democracies and dictatorships. But, as Tony Aldgate then points out, moving to a rather different point, 'mass socialization has given rise to a host of conflicting ideas and theories', and he then goes into some detail on the fears many intellectuals had about mass society. These fears pre-dated World War I, but war certainly played a part in reinforcing and extending them:

> For many of the crowd psychologists, indeed, World War I proved their worst fears about mass gullibility to be correct, not least because of the extensive use made of propaganda by the belligerent nations. 'To the social psychologists who had been warning the world of the terrors of propaganda for twenty years and more', Anthony Smith concludes, 'the wave of mass propaganda which accompanied the war operated exactly according to the old textbooks' (*The Shadow in the Cave*, 1976, p.26). (Unit 19, pp.197–8).

Note, particularly, this summing up by Tony Aldgate:

> For many such intellectuals, then, mass society was perceived as a grim reality. No matter that with hindsight one might query the validity of their perceptions – how, for instance, could Ortega y Gasset write in 1930 of 'hyperdemocracy' or fear 'the political domination of the masses' when women still did not have the vote in his native Spain (and only voted for the first time in the 1933 elections)? The point is that their perceptions held good as far as they were concerned and their perception of the masses was of a threatening entity. Just as valid for many among the political élites was the perception that the masses could be manipulated and that the media provided the means of manipulation. And it was the political leaders, of course, who had to contend with the effects of mass society. (p.201)

Many political leaders, particularly those on the Left, it must be stressed, welcomed the growth of mass society, and the growing participation of the many in the better things of life. Still, there can be little doubt that many British conservatives, and many in the civil service, had a rather low opinion of the general public. It is very relevant to our major concerns that the British people responded to the bombing in World War II rather differently from what many had forecast. Speaking specifically of the film director Alexander Korda, Tony Aldgate concludes his unit:

> What his film had demonstrated most of all was an élitist fear about the collapse of morale and the likelihood of social unrest as a consequence of the mass bombing of the civilian population. His film predicted panic, anarchy and the breakdown of civilization. This did not materialize, even under the testing conditions of the total war that followed. (pp.226–7)

4 THE DEBATE OVER THE SOCIAL CONSEQUENCES OF WORLD WAR II

As in the debate over the impact and consequences of World War I, the sort of questions being asked throughout Units 22–25 are: Why did certain developments come about in the way they did and when they did during World War II? What part did the experiences of war play in effecting these changes? Can war be singled out as a cause of change from all the other potential causes?

Arthur Marwick points out, in the introduction to these units, that although the questions may be similar, some of the debates cover quite different ground. For example, Marwick refers to Mark Roseman's article, printed in the Course Reader. In this article Roseman argues that in the case of Germany, it is essential to take into consideration not only the war years, but also the changes brought about by the Nazis in the six years before war broke out in 1939, and those wrought by the occupying powers in the years following 1945. Roseman argues that in Germany 'war and wartime measures' were essentially 'a continuation of the Nazis' pre-war policies' (Course Reader, p.300), and that the influence of the Soviet Union in East Germany and the United States in West Germany were crucial in the shaping of German post-war society. From this evidence Roseman concludes that, at least in the case of Germany, '"total war" is not an independent cause of social change. Its influence on German society was shaped decisively by the nature of the regime which waged it and that of the regime which followed it' (p.315).

Roseman's article pinpoints two major areas of debate in any discussion concerning World War II. First, by stressing the importance of the Russian and American occupations of Germany, he provides ammunition for those who argue that the major determinant of social change in Europe after 1945 was the division of Europe and the influence of these two major powers. Second, Roseman acknowledges that the experience of Germany was quite different from a country such as Britain, where 'the only changes in the political system were those brought about by the needs of war' (p.315). Consequently, although 'total war' may not have been an independent cause of social change in Germany, this does not exclude other countries, especially those which did not experience the sort of political discontinuities witnessed in Germany, from being substantially affected by the experiences of war.

This leads on to another area of debate, which relates in particular to World War II and which Tony Aldgate raises in Book IV, section 3 'Mass society 1939–45'. Aldgate quotes Michael Howard, who argues that World War II 'brought social involvement in belligerent activity to a new level of intensity by eliminating the distinction between "front line" and "base"'. Compared with previous wars, 'the pressures arising from a situation in which the Front was *everywhere*, whether because of air bombardment as in Britain, Germany and Japan, or because of invasion and occupation as in continental Europe and the Soviet Union, were of a different order of magnitude altogether' (quoted in Book IV, Units 22–25, p.136).

It is important to bear these two areas of debate in mind while examining the particular areas of change which Marwick, Purdue and Aldgate discuss in Units 22–25.

Social geography

In the medium-term the war had an enormous impact on the social geography of Europe. There was a greater loss of life than in World War I, with countries in East, Central and Southern Europe suffering most severely. In addition, there were vast movements of population within Europe, starting with the 'New Order' aims of Germany and the resettlement plans of the Soviet Union in the early years of the war, and culminating in the transfer of some 6 million Germans back to Germany in the aftermath of 1945. In all, the movements of population for ideological reasons and because of frontier changes involved some 25 million people during and immediately after the war.

Although there were higher marriage and fertility rates in Western Europe in the post-war period compared with the inter-war years, immigration (especially immigration into West Germany) was the major reason for the increase in the population of Western Europe.

Economic performance and theory

Again as in World War I, the economies of the European powers were diverted from traditional areas of production towards wartime economies. In this respect Britain and Russia, in Roberts's words, 'achieved the greatest subordination of economy and society to the war effort' (p.555). The Soviet Union had, so Purdue argues, a virtual war economy before 1939. State resources were already focused on heavy industrial production and armaments, so that by 1940 the state budget directed to armaments alone was 32.6 per cent. In Britain the politicians drew upon the experiences of central planning learned in World War I. Coal mines, shipping and railways were put under state control, and Purdue states that 'The government moved in a corporatist direction as Bevin attempted to enlist the support of trades union leaders for the direction and allocation of labour' (Units 22–25, p.67).

Compared with Britain the 'totalitarian' state of Germany did not achieve anything like this degree of economic mobilization until well towards the end of the war. The reasons why Germany did not undergo central planning to the extent of that experienced in Britain is well explained in Roberts, pages 557–8, and the Roseman article already mentioned above. (Note, however, that the article by Richard Overy in the Course Reader challenges some of these assumptions.)

In World War I, France, Belgium and Serbia in particular suffered devastation and a vast destruction of property. Between 1939 and 1945 the arena of war ranged far more widely and, consequently, devastation was more general. By the end of the war all the European countries faced, in varying degrees, formidable economic problems: food shortages, dislocation of industrial production, lost export markets, the liquidation of overseas investments and inflation.

Nevertheless, as Bill Purdue points out, 'the infrastructure of the European economy had been damaged but not destroyed by the war' (p.74), and the preconditions for industrial recovery in Europe were present. With financial assistance coming from the United States, within five years of the ending of the war, 'European output of almost everything was to be substantially above pre-war levels'. Although, partly as a result of the war, Europe's trading and financial position declined in importance relative to the world economy, 'in absolute terms it not only remained dynamic and sophisticated but had considerable potential for expansion' (p.63).

National cohesion

Clearly nationality and race were prominent issues in World War II. Nazi notions of racial purity, *Herrenvolk, Untermenschen* and anti-semitism, together with the aim to unite all Germans under one great empire, eventually involved not only a holocaust but vast movements of people throughout Central and Eastern Europe. This, together with Russia's territorial ambitions and other national rivalries within Czechoslovakia, Hungary and Yugoslavia in particular, meant that nationality was a significant issue before, during and after the war.

Arthur Marwick concludes that 'On the whole it could be said that the general movement which had accelerated earlier in the century towards each nationality having its own nation state was consolidated in the aftermath of World War II' (p.96). But as he states, this consolidation was achieved at a brutal human cost. As Bill Purdue points out,

> If the Versailles Settlement had sought to make frontiers fit people, the more ruthless and less civilized expedient at the end of World War II was to make peoples fit frontiers. Germans were pushed westwards and their place taken by Poles and Czechs; Poles and Czechs were in their turn pushed westwards and their place was taken by Russians. There were exchanges of population between Czechoslovakia and Hungary and between Hungary and Yugoslavia. Well over 200,000 Italians left territory gained by Yugoslavia, while 103,000 Hungarians were repatriated from Romania. (p.60)

Class

In section 2.3 of Units 22–25, Arthur Marwick considers, in considerable detail, whether the experiences of the war did or did not result in changes in social structures, and the relationships between and attitudes towards classes. In the case of Britain, he examines critically an important article, 'The "levelling of class"', by Penny Summerfield. In this article Summerfield argues that in Britain there was very little sign, if any, of social levelling during the period 1939–45. If you wish to refresh your memory, read the last four paragraphs of her article (pages 274–5 of the Course Reader) where she sets out her main conclusions.

Arthur Marwick contests these conclusions and, although he argues that 'social levelling' is an unsatisfactory phrase, he contends that it did occur to some extent.

'The working class in general gained in living conditions and in self-confidence; it was treated less contemptuously by members of other social classes' (p.85). Tony Aldgate, in his study of British cinema during the war years, supports this view. He points out that there was a new emphasis on the part played by working men and women within society. 'Working-class figures were given a fuller and more rounded characterization' and, in addition, 'subjects were broached in the cinema, as on radio, that had been barely touched upon before' (p.153).

Turning to France, Marwick explores the notion of whether 'participation' resulted in social gains and he relates this especially to those who participated in the Resistance. He concludes that the experiences of the Resistance did result in social mixing, although he admits that until the last year of the war, the Resistance only involved about 4 per cent of the population. Overall, he concludes that in the longer term the effects of World War II on the working class in France were similar to those in Britain. 'The working class did not change its position in the hierarchy, but it benefited from the social legislation introduced after the war' (p.88). Also, there were 'changes *within* the upper class, much greater recruitment from below, and perhaps quite far below compared with Britain, taking into consideration the strongly working-class composition of the Resistance' (p.89).

In the section on France, Arthur Marwick draws upon Stanley Hoffman's article on 'The effects of World War II on French society and politics'. He refers to Hoffman's contention that the French social system begins to change around 1934 (echoes of the Roseman article), but that the old system only disappears with the war itself. Again, it is worth referring back to the final pages of the article (Course Reader, pp.250–2), where Hoffman summarizes his arguments, one of which is that 'the two groups which gained most from the war years were business and the Catholic Church'.

With Italy, as with France, Marwick explores working-class participation. 'It is a moot point whether (mainly non-violent) resistance to Mussolini, or the military resistance to the German occupation which took over in the north of Italy in September 1943 . . . were more important in stimulating social change at the end of the war'. Overall he concludes that 'As elsewhere, then, the story is of general working-class gains (though intense privation after 1943) within a basically unaltered class structure. Wartime conditions were again favourable for the peasants who, as in France, could keep their food to themselves or put it on the black market' (p.90).

Mark Roseman's thesis outlined in his article, 'World War II and Social Change in Germany', has already been touched on. He argues that social changes and changes in class relationships were already taking place before the war in Nazi Germany. The war continued this social mobility, and after the war the Allies played a significant role in ensuring industrial harmony. While Marwick questions the extent of the influence of the Allies in this respect, he does agree with Roseman that what emerged 'was a hard-working, consumer-oriented, sceptical and unpolitical working class. A strong suspicion of the bosses coexisted with the feeling that labour's status had collectively improved' (Course Reader, p.314).

Less change took place in the social structure of Russia than in any of the other major powers, and Paul Dukes, cited by Marwick, has argued that any chances of change within Russian society were ended by the Cold War. (Duke's article is in *Total War and Social Change*, edited by Arthur Marwick, 1988.)

Social policy and social welfare

In the discussion of the impact of World War I on social change, Arthur Marwick drew up a league table of countries which benefited most from social legislation during and after the war. If he had done the same for the period of World War II, Britain again would have headed the list. A spate of social legislation towards the end of the war and during the period of the post-war Labour government affected all sections of British society. The 1944 Education Act, the 1945 Family Allowance Act, the 1946 Acts involving National Insurance, Industrial Injuries and the National Health Service, and the National Assistance Act of 1948, all played their part in establishing what came to be known as the British welfare state. Some of this legislation was based on and influenced by the Beveridge Report, which was first published in December 1942. Arthur Marwick concentrates much of his discussion on this Report with its 'comprehensive policy of social progress' in order to argue that a document produced during the early years of the war must form 'a vital link in any chain joining the war experience to the enactment of social legislation. It also had symbolic significance when resistance fighters and progressive elements in other countries discussed the kind of society there should be after the war' (p.102).

After Britain, it was France, ahead of Germany and Russia among the leading powers, which benefited most from new welfare legislation. A number of important ordinances relating to social security were established in 1944 and 1945, some of which were based on the proposals expounded in the Programme of the National Resistance Council and first published in 1944. If you turn back to Book 1, Unit 1, you will see that Marwick argues that the significance of this programme, drawn up by a body consisting of resistance groups of various political viewpoints, 'is that it shows the experience of war (specifically of Resistance) engendering ideas of consensus on behalf of progressive economic and social planning. Because of the prestige of the Resistance, and because of the feeling that defeated France had been a flop, many of these proposals were put into practice after the liberation' (p.30).

Material conditions

In considering material conditions, it is important to differentiate between the immediate and the long-term effects of the war. As Arthur Marwick and Bill Purdue both point out, recovery from the war came relatively quickly. However, as Arthur Marwick shows, in Poland, where 18 per cent of the population was killed, and Russia and Yugoslavia, where over 11 per cent of the population died in each country, material conditions during the war were dire in the extreme. In Germany and Italy conditions deteriorated rapidly from 1943 onwards. While the black market flourished in Italy, the amount of food available for most Italians was significantly reduced. Prices in 1945 were twenty-four times above those existing in 1938, and income per head of the population was lower than it had been in 1861.

Both Britain and France suffered fewer casualties in World War II than in World War I. Only 0.9 per cent of Britain's population was killed compared with 7.4 for that of Germany. Although food was comparatively scarce, the rationing system in Britain ensured a fairer distribution of food and 'for many families, higher nutrition standards than had obtained before the war' (p.108).

Customs and behaviour

Customs and behaviour might well have been influenced during the course of the war, so Arthur Marwick argues, in two major ways. Firstly as a result of the vast shifts of population and the changes in class relations. Secondly through the violence and disruption which accompanies wars and which affects civic morality. Marwick notes, in relation to the first point, that there was 'less formality, less sense of hierarchy in most countries', but with regard to the second, 'civic norms were in fact established remarkably quickly' (p.113).

As to whether American involvement in Europe during and immediately following the war led to a marked acceptance of American customs and patterns of behaviour, Marwick argues that some commentators have over-emphasized American influence. In making your own judgement on this matter it is worth referring again to the discussion of document II.43 in *Documents 2*, 'An average French town in 1950' in Unit 27 (pp.230–1).

The changes in customs and behaviour that occurred during World War II which Marwick regards as significant are:

1   developments in religion, especially the political role of Christian Democracy in West Germany and Italy, and the MRP (Popular Republican Movement) in France; and in Russia, the Russian Orthodox Church, by supporting the government during the war, was granted in return 'the right to exist as an institution in Soviet society' (p.115).

2   the popularizing of radio as a means of communication both in conveying news and entertainment.

Women and the family

Arthur Marwick argues that in Britain the war brought new employment opportunities for married women in particular, and it helped to break down the prejudices against married women taking jobs. 'The conclusion is inescapable that the Second World War offered women opportunities normally unavailable in peace time to improve their economic and social status, and to develop their own confidence and self-consciousness. In many cases these opportunities were firmly grasped; whether they would be extended depended very much on women themselves, for, without doubt, old attitudes, overpoweringly strong in 1941 [or 1939], were still influential in 1946' (p.116).

British films, such as *The Gentle Sex* and *Millions Like Us*, emphasized the important wartime roles that women were playing, and certainly there was a feeling, as Aldgate points out when he quotes Jack Beddington, the head of the film division of the Ministry of Information, that there had been a 'change in the status of women in recent years' (p.135).

Contrast this attitude with that of German film-makers who, so the leading authority (as cited by Aldgate), David Welch, contends, represented women only in submissive roles as wives and mothers. (Welch's book is called *Propaganda and the German Cinema 1933–1945*, 1983.) This fits in with the point that Roseman makes in his article that many Nazi leaders were reluctant to involve women in the wartime economy: '. . . the number of German women in the economy actually fell between 1939 and 1941 and in 1942 was still lower than in the pre-war period. Whereas in 1943 almost two-thirds of British women were in employment, the equivalent figure for Germany was only 46 per cent (Course Reader, p.304). (Paul

Overy, in a still more recent article, has challenged some of these views — see Marwick's discussion, pp.118–19.)

Whether women's work in the resistance movements led to social promotion is a moot point. Bédarida, although pointing out that French women finally were enfranchised in 1944, is doubtful whether they made any other gains. However, Marwick quotes Tannenbaum, who argues that in Italy 'the active role played by many women in the Resistance helped to change the status of women as a whole in the postwar period' (*The Fascist Experience*, 1972, quoted in Units 22–25, pp.117–18).

In Russia where, as Arthur Marwick points out, one would expect equal rights for women, the chances of reaching the upper echelons of political power were small indeed. In 1942, there were only two women representatives among the 125 full members of the Central Committee. But, quoting Dukes, Marwick indicates an improvement over the war period.

High culture and popular culture

In section 3 'Mass society 1939–45', Tony Aldgate stresses the importance of film and radio both as instruments of propaganda and as entertainment. After the war in France, as document II.43 in *Documents 2*, 'An average French town in 1950', points out, cinema-going was the favourite leisure activity and the public preferred French to American films. Arthur Marwick also argues that in France, Italy and Britain, film-makers developed their own traditions and that Americanization was not as powerful an influence as has often been suggested.

With regard to high culture, the

> . . . catastrophe of the First World War did have profound effects on the subject matter, beliefs and modes of expression of artists and thinkers. The Second World War came to a much less naïve world, and therefore did not have the same effect in transforming modes of thought and expression. It was, nonetheless, an experience of enormous intensity, and resulted in the production of a considerable body of work related directly to that experience. It can indeed be argued that while the trauma of World War I turned intellectuals in on themselves and towards the esoteric modes of modernism, World War II, as a war of peoples and partisans, induced a turning back towards realism. (p.121)

Political institutions and values

In sub-section 2.10, Arthur Marwick surveys each of the major powers in turn. He argues that in Britain during the war there was a growing desire for social change. Tony Aldgate adds to this view by stressing that this 'popular feeling' was one of resentment against vested interests and privileges and a wish for general improvements after the war, rather than a strong political expression. However, he does agree with Marwick that the return of a Labour government was directly connected with the war experience and the desire for social change.

In France, despite arguments that the spirit of change engendered by the Resistance soon disappeared, Marwick maintains that the reconstruction of the French civil service enabled the development of vigorous planning and economic initiatives in the post-war years.

Italy, so Marwick argues, underwent the most marked political changes of all the Western powers. The democratic system of government was vastly different in the post-war years from the Italy of pre-1914 or the years of Mussolini's rule. Although the Christian Democrats dominated the political scene, the Italian Communist Party was influential in many parts of Italy, and there 'was a new balance of political forces, committed to democracy, and tending towards community welfare' (p.131).

In Germany the occupying Allied powers played an important role in ensuring the eventual emergence of a German democratic system dominated by the Christian Democratic Party.

Conclusion

In discussing 'Mass society 1939–45', Tony Aldgate set out the problems confronting the European powers in a war which had no 'front line' or 'base'. Civilian populations faced

> conscription, evacuation, the increased likelihood of destruction and devastation, the enhanced threat of death – their leaders, too, were confronted with . . . the need to achieve widespread consensus for the waging of war, to maximize the people's participation in the war effort, to continue the mobilization, and to maintain morale among civilian and military populations alike. The war, in short, as Arthur Marwick has repeatedly stressed, posed a 'test' for society, not least of the relationship between the leaders and the led. (p.136)

After reading Units 22–25 it is up to you to decide whether there were signs of change in the relations between leaders and the led as a result of the war experience. The units have explored ten vital areas in which social change may or may not have occurred, and you must assess the often conflicting arguments of those historians like Arthur Marwick who contend that, in a variety of ways, World War II did bring social changes, and those like Angus Calder, whom Aldgate quotes, and who argues that in Britain, at least, 'The effect of the war was not to sweep society on to a new course, but to hasten its progress along the old grooves' (p.152).

Whatever your conclusions, Europe in 1945 was a vastly different place from the Europe we examined at the start of the course. As Roberts points out,

> Europe's self-inflicted wounds had all but destroyed her . . . At the moment, it was hard even to detect a glow in the ashes; the economic resurgence of the next quarter-century could no more be anticipated than the shape of new political structures which was to accompany it. All that was certain was that a dream which had haunted the interwar years had been blown to the winds; there could be no return to 1914. It was at last clearly impossible. (Roberts, pp.557–8)

5 *WAR AND CULTURE*

In revising this topic, two questions immediately arise: What are we talking about? What resources do we have in order to be able to talk about it? Let us first of all remember the distinction between, on one side, 'élite' or 'high' culture, and on the other, 'popular' or 'mass' culture. Obviously, on one side we have symphonies, poetry, painting, highbrow novels, and on the other side, films, radio, popular novels, popular music, and so on. Whether we also include sporting activities, or have a separate heading for 'leisure', is really simply a matter of definition and convenience. Whether science should be included in élite culture, and religion in culture in general, are issues which are again matters of definition. For the purposes of this discussion I am going to confine myself to the sorts of topics which, in our newspapers, would be defined under the heading 'The arts and entertainment'.

If you glance across the range of media, printed and audio-visual, you will see that we have supplied you with quite a rich collection of resources. Of course, if you are interested in the subject area you will probably have many more resources of your own to call upon, possibly including other Open University courses. It is in reading outside the course materials that you may find what I said about cultural theory in Unit 1 useful in relating the approaches other specialists adopt to those generally followed by the historians in this course.

Let me list, first, the primary sources we have supplied you with, and then the places where you will find secondary information.

Primary sources

These are: extracts from *Under Fire* and *All Quiet on the Western Front*, and the poem 'Strange meeting' by Wilfred Owen (in *Documents 1*); extracts from *Le silence de la Mer*, two poems by Louis Aragon, and an extract from *The Tin Drum* (in *Documents 2*); the extracts from *The Rite of Spring*, the *Inextinguishable* Symphony, *The Spirit of England*, Elgar's Cello Concerto, the *Leningrad* Symphony, and Britten's *War Requiem* (all on audio-cassette 1); the art pack – reproductions of twelve paintings accompanying audio-cassette 2; extracts from various films on the two video-cassettes; extracts from gramophone records and radio programmes on audio-cassette 3; posters printed on the covers of the eight books making up this course (a marvellous resource which you might easily have neglected).

There is also one primary source of a rather different character, that is the Resolution of the East German Socialist Unity Party, printed in *Documents 2*.

Secondary sources

These are: Josipovici's article in the Course Reader, and the comments on it in the Introduction; quotations from various literary critics towards the end of Book II, Units 8–10; brief references in Book III, Unit 16; substantial references in Book III, Unit 19 (I'll summarize these at the very end of my discussion of war and culture); the material towards the end of Book IV, Units 22–25.

Plan for revision

As a plan for revision I recommend that you start by reading the Josipovici article, together with the comments on it in the Course Reader Introduction. This should establish firmly in your mind the basic characteristics of modernism which, after all, is the central movement in the arts in the twentieth century. It is impossible to argue that World War I created modernism, but using what Josipovici says as a basis, one can begin to discuss where the experience of war emphasized, or made acceptable, particular facets of modernism; also perhaps where (this has been argued of World War II) there was actually a reaction against modernism towards a kind of realism felt to be more suitable to a 'people's war'. I would suggest that you then play side one of the music cassette (audio-cassette 1), and side one of the art cassette (audio-cassette 2) (both relating to World War I). Follow this up by reading the printed texts relating to World War I, in conjunction with what is said about them in Units 8–10. Then repeat the process, with the audio-cassettes and texts relating to World War II, together with the material in Units 22–25. That gives you a good basis for élite culture.

None of the radio or film excerpts is influenced by modernism (as an aesthetic movement) and, indeed, they can be seen as a kind of ultimate form of realism dependent, of course, upon the potential of modern technology. Be clear in your own mind about the distinction between news items, documentary items, and extracts from fictional and entertainment pieces. Your main secondary sources here are Unit 19, and the final sections of Units 22–25 and 27. Watching film and listening to radio are both good fun: I would suggest you use this activity both as a kind of relaxation, and also to provide you with an invaluable resource for coping with several different kinds of question.

In the remainder of this sub-section I am going to, first, say a little more about war and music, and then discuss each of the posters on the covers of the books, before finally picking up references in Units 16 and 19.

For music and war in particular you have, of course, been given only a very limited collection of sources. Basically what I have tried to do in the music and art audio-cassettes is to alert you to some of the problems involved in trying to discuss the relationship between war and high culture. One general distinction which I made towards the end of audio-cassette 2 is well worth bearing in mind: that is the difference between identifying the influence of war on one single piece of work (a *relatively* straightforward task), and deciding whether the whole development of a musician or artist, or of musical or artistic language as a whole, has been affected by war. But even where one concentrates on individual items (the best thing to do, I believe) the matter is not all that straightforward. I have tried to give you the views of some of the experts: their views are based on the detailed study of a particular artist's or musician's letters, diaries, and so on. But sometimes even the things artists or musicians say about their own works are not necessarily completely reliable, or, sometimes, completely clear (if that passage by Shostakovich did refer as much to Stalin as to Hitler, Shostakovich would never have dared say so openly).

Just to give you a little more material, and also to help in bringing various points together, I am going to discuss one other composer whose name sometimes arises when this sort of issue is discussed – the French musician Maurice Ravel, who was thirty-nine when the war broke out in 1914. Obviously it will help if you know something of Ravel's music (you probably know the *Bolero* of 1928 – 'a piece for orchestra without music', Ravel himself called it – perhaps the ultimate in the use of rhythm to which you were introduced through Stravinsky's *The Rite of Spring*; not something the Victorians would have approved of), but in any case, I think you'll find my few comments useful in helping you to gather your thoughts. The three pieces I am going to mention are *Le Tombeau de Couperin* (literally 'The Tomb of Couperin', meaning 'Memorial' or 'Tribute' to Couperin, the eighteenth-century French composer); *La Valse* ('The Waltz' of 1922–23); and the Piano Concerto for the Left Hand of 1929–30. Of *Le Tombeau de Couperin*, a piano suite in six movements (subsequently Ravel provided an orchestration of four of the movements), Ravel wrote, 'The tribute is directed not so much to the individual figure of Couperin as to the whole of French music of the eighteenth century'. In his book *Ravel*, Roger Nichols writes (1977, p.100): 'Each of the six movements is dedicated to the memory of a friend killed in the war and so the work is at least a double homage – to the civilization which Ravel most admired and to the friends who had tried to preserve some of its standards.' Despite being in poor health, Ravel had insisted on trying to enlist, and finally found employment in the dangerous job of lorry driver for the Artillery: he found the adventure of war highly exciting before, in 1916, ill-health temporarily discharged him. However, a major problem of relating the work to the war is that, as pointed out by Arbie Orenstein in *Ravel: Man and Musician* (1975, pp.70, 186), much of it had actually been written in July 1914. The individual dedications, and perhaps the final overall structure, are related to the war, but the overall intention and the musical language go back before the war. Beyond that, as so often, there was an intimate personal factor: while he was finishing the work in 1917, Ravel was very deeply affected by the recent death of his mother.

Ravel, remember, had been excited by the war. If we are to find deeper effects we must look to the aftermath of war (there is, perhaps, some parallel with Elgar here). Orenstein (p.189) writes of *La Valse*:

> . . . the concluding passages open up a fresh dimension in Ravel's art, that of tension bordering on breaking point. It is apparent that the disorientation of World War I and the composer's personal grief following his mother's death have been sublimated in this 'fantastic and fatal whirling'. This unprecedented tension will achieve its culmination in the Piano Concerto for the Left Hand.

This Concerto was specially commissioned by the pianist Paul Wittgenstein (brother of the famous philosopher), who had lost his right arm in the war. If it can be argued that the horrific catastrophe of war (more clearly apparent in the aftermath than during the excitements of war itself) brought tensions already existing in Ravel's personality to an ultimate culmination, then this Concerto (first performed on 5 January 1932 in Vienna), in its power and hopelessness, certainly sounds like impressive testimony to that argument. Since Orenstein has traced the development through *La Valse*, there is possibly a slight element of contradiction in his summing-up (or perhaps he is simply being faithful to the very complexities of this kind of issue:)

> The Piano Concerto for the Left Hand has given rise to a number of psychological interpretations, among them the composer's premonition of his oncoming mental affliction, or a commentary on the tragedy and uselessness of World War I. It seems to me to be rather a culmination of Ravel's longstanding preoccupation, one might say obsession, with the notion of death. (p.203)

Before offering you some guidance on how to relate all this to our twin concerns with modernism as a general development of the twentieth century, and with the particular influences of war, I want to turn to another issue to which, it happens, Ravel rather neatly relates. Please be clear, just in case I have left any confusion on this point, that German and Austrian music *never* was banned in France or Britain during World War I, though there were 'patriots' who said it should be (the difference in World War II is that nobody even tried to make the case; and that, indeed, the opening of Beethoven's Fifth Symphony, representing 'V' in the morse code, became a symbol for victory or, in effect, resistance). In France, in 1916, there was founded A National League for the Defence of French Music, which proposed what was in effect a ban on *contemporary* German and Austrian composers. Two celebrated composers, Saint-Saëns and d'Indy, did sign. Ravel, in a letter of 7 June 1916, which to me personally is one of the most interesting of all documents concerning war and culture, gave his reasons for refusing to sign:

> It is of little importance to me that M. Schoenberg, for example, is of Austrian nationality. This does not prevent him from being a very fine musician, whose very interesting discoveries have had a beneficial influence on certain allied composers, and even our own. Moreover, I am delighted that M. Bartók, Kodály and their disciples are Hungarian, and show it unmistakably in their music.
>
> In Germany, apart from M. Richard Strauss, there appear to be only composers of secondary rank, whose equivalent could easily be found within France. But it is possible that some young artists may soon be discovered, whom we would like to know more about here . . . (Quoted by Orenstein, 1975, p.74)

Saint-Saëns, of course, composed in the lush manner of the late nineteenth century. What I think we have here is French 'patriotism' being enlisted in opposition to what is seen as 'extreme' modernism: Ravel is defending the newest developments against this factitious patriotism.

Ravel, to come to my final formulation which I feel would, with appropriate alterations, apply to many artists and musicians, represents certain of the concerns characteristic of twentieth-century intellectuals. He has a deep sense of anxiety and of turmoil; he longs for the orderly world of the eighteenth century *before*, note, the upheavals of Romanticism (if necessary, remind yourself of what Josipovici says on Romanticism). To him, World War I was perhaps less of a completely unexpected shock than, after a period of excitement, confirmation of his deepest sense of foreboding and catastrophe. It can be stated without question that the most important works of the post-war years show a heightening of tension and disorientation not apparent in earlier works. I don't think one can go much further than that.

Posters

A trick, known to all professionals, and particularly useful to students, is to use every scrap of resource which is available to you. As already noted, the covers of the books in this course, each presenting a poster, are marvellous resources related to propaganda, mass society, and what I suppose comes towards the popular end of culture, though of course the posters were usually *produced* by those in power, or at least those with wealth and influence, for the *consumption* of the masses.

The poster on the cover of Book 1 advertising Peugeot bicycles differs from all the others in that it is a commercial poster. The interesting point for us, however, is the very strong military emphasis. The value of the bicycle is that it has enabled a soldier to bring a message to the mounted officer; the juxtaposition of two modes of transport, the traditional horse and the recently invented bicycle, is in itself illuminating. With regard to where exactly the poster should be placed in the spectrum embracing high art and popular art, it is significant that the poster is signed by the artist E. Vulliemin, who was a well-regarded professional artist of the time.

There is also a name under the illustration used in the poster on the cover of Book II (M. Lenz). This is an Austrian poster and the words read 'Subscribe to the Sixth War Loan'. So we have straightforward evidence here of the government's attempts to raise cash for the war effort. St George and the Dragon was a very conventional symbol for the good nation destroying the wicked enemy (no matter that St George was the patron saint of England, the symbol was used by both sides, though probably the first usage in World War I was in an earlier British recruiting poster). However, as Joseph Darracott comments in his catalogue *Imperial War Museum War Posters*, this Austrian poster, as art, was much superior to the British one, 'showing a peculiarly Austrian feeling for heraldic design'. One might note that the general tone is reminiscent of nineteenth-century medievalism, little of the devices of modernism being apparent.

As an historical document, the poster on the cover of the Course Reader is, perhaps, the most fruitful and complex. The quotation from the great French nineteenth-century novelist, Victor Hugo, reads:

> This sky is our purest blue, this field is our land! This Lorraine and this Alsace are ours!

Alsace and Lorraine, whose inhabitants speak a form of German inter-mixed with many French phrases, had been captured for France in the seventeenth century by Louis XIV; there was, of course, no unified German state until 1870, the year in which the Germans conquered Alsace and Lorraine. The recovery of Alsace-Lorraine is often listed among the reasons for French readiness to go to war in 1914. Professor Paul Smith, who is writing a large book on the subject, has stated (in a lecture I heard him give in 1989 at the German Historical Institute, London) that the matter was scarcely an issue either to the people of Alsace-Lorraine or to the majority of people in France. It was the war itself, he says, which turned Alsace-Lorraine into a major issue (and France, of course, regained these territories in the Treaty of Versailles). What is fascinating is that the artist who produced this poster was himself born in Colmar in Alsace. His name is in itself interesting, with a French first name, Jean Jacques, always, however, shortened to the German sounding Hansi, and the German-sounding surname, Waltz. Yet well before the war, Hansi Waltz was notorious for his pro-French sentiments. He studied art in the French town of Lyon, and on his return to Alsace specialized in producing satires of his German rulers, to the extent that he was actually condemned for high treason. So he fled to Switzerland; and when war broke out in 1914 he joined the French army as a private, soon being transferred (note this very important point) to propaganda work. This war poster presents a vision of Alsace as restored to French rule, signalled by the French flag on top of the church, a very typical combination of religion and patriotism. The imagery is that of a fairy-tale land. War is represented by the aeroplane and the barrage balloon – significant symbols of twentieth-century war. In the foreground are three French soldiers, and the message is very clearly, 'this is what we are fighting for'.

There is some uncertainty as to exactly what the poster on *Documents 1* signifies. The German words can be translated either as 'U-boats out!' or 'The U-boats are out!' Darracott speculates that the poster may be advertising a book or a film. The design is striking, perhaps owing something to the innovations of modernism: note particularly the large areas of flat colour. We have credits for both the artist, H. R. Erdt, and the printers Hollerdaum and Schmidt. Whatever the uncertainties, the general historical significance is not in doubt. The Germans realized that their only hope of defeating the British navy lay with their submarines; German submarine warfare eventually played an important part in bringing the United States into the war. In the background there is the outline of a battleship; in front of it we can see a smaller ship. It would be fair to say that there is a certain element of gloating brutality in the image, though this isn't a specifically German feature, since one can find the same sort of thing in Allied propaganda posters as well.

The German World War II poster on the cover of Book IV is an extremely potent comment on bombing: the German reads, 'The enemy [portrayed, as death with a bomb in his hand] can see a light. Put it out!' A rather different aspect of the domestic front is illuminated in the poster printed on the cover of this book (V). It is from *Purnell's History of the Second World War*, in which this British poster is contrasted with a German one (which we have not reproduced) featuring the slogan 'Victory follows our banners!'. The author comments: 'Germany's propaganda apparatus was well-geared to the nation's war machine, but Britain's early efforts tended to be naive, amateurish.' Personally, I think this is a grossly unfair comment on, as I see it, the beautifully executed British poster, with its neat adoption of modernist cartoon techniques. I would surmise that this poster was extremely effective in persuading women to turn to war work (the subject, of course, featured in two of our films, *The Gentle Sex* and *Millions Like Us*).

The poster on the cover of Book III, by Vladimir Lyushin, and dated 1931, declares in Russian, 'The Young Communist League is the shock battalion of the Five-Year Plan': you should have no difficulty in relating this to what you have learned in Units 16 and 19. The poster on the cover of *Documents 2*, by Albert Aslyan (1958), is a clear statement on nuclear war. The word 'No' is in Armenian characters, so we have here a graphic representation of the ethnic diversity of the Soviet Union.

Points made in Unit 16

With regard to culture in the Soviet Union, I want to draw your attention to section 1.4 'Intellectual and cultural life under NEP'.

> The Soviet state under NEP was a relatively liberal dictatorship which tolerated considerable cultural and social pluralism. The Communist Party monopolized political power but was itself a forum of lively debate, not only about industrialization, but over cultural and intellectual matters as well. Radical literary critics, grouped in the All-Russian Association of Proletarian Writers, wanted a complete break with existing literary traditions and the censorship of 'fellow-travelling' writers. Trotsky, in 1923, argued (against the radicals): 'It is fundamentally incorrect to set in opposition to bourgeois culture and bourgeois art a proletarian culture and proletarian art' (*Literature and Revolution*, quoted in Carr, 1959, p.89). At that time, mere association with Trotsky's name did not yet suffice to damn any policy and his ideas on culture carried great weight in the party. Lenin and most of the Old Bolsheviks shared Trotsky's position; Bukharin was a particularly notable patron of the non-party intelligentsia.
> This openness to cultural and intellectual diversity made the 1920s a

decade of memorable variety and achievement, both in the party's own intellectual life and outside. The combination of the revolutionary experience and freedom from official cultural dogma created a context in which artistic and cultural experiment thrived: '. . . the modernism of the cultural avant-garde flourished spectacularly if briefly under the lenient reign of the political avant-garde' (Cohen, *Bukharin and the Bolshevik Revolution*, 1974, p.272). Novelists and poets, such as Pasternak, Mandelstam and Akhmatova, produced their major works; Eisenstein, Pudovkin and others pioneered the modern cinema; experimental producers like Meyerhold and Tariov revolutionized the theatre; artists like Tatlin, Rodchenko and Lissitzky placed the Soviet Union at the forefront of modernist painting, architecture and design (Cohen, 1974). (Unit 16, pp.81–2)

Then, of course, came the Stalinist cultural ice age, aspects of which I refer to in Units 22–25.

Points made in Unit 19

Now let me just remind you of some of the main points relating to the topic of culture made by Tony Aldgate in Unit 19. He tells us that *La Grande Illusion* was the top box-office success in France in 1937, as well as winning major French prizes and considerable international success. Its director, Jean Renoir, who had been a cavalry officer and aviator in World War I, wanted 'to express all my deep feelings for the cause of peace'. Tony Aldgate compares this film with its broadly pacifist message with three similarly pacifist German films of the period: *All Quiet on the Western Front* (1930), *Westfront 1918* (1930), and *Kameradschaft* (1931). Even before coming to power, the Nazis had been influential enough, or had had enough support for their militaristic and nationalistic ideas, to secure the banning of *All Quiet on the Western Front*: once in power they banned *La Grande Illusion* because of its plea for greater Franco-German unity and its sympathetic portrayal of a Jewish character.

While the dating of *La Grande Illusion* naturally turns our thoughts towards the origins of World War II, it is important to note that it is firmly set in World War I. Renoir, Tony Aldgate says, wanted to convey something precise about the effects of World War I. 'The plot concerns three very different French officers – Captain de Boeldieu, Lieutenants Maréchal and Rosenthal – who are incarcerated in a German prisoner-of-war camp, under the command of Major Von Rauffenstein, until Boeldieu loses his life in helping his two comrades to escape to Switzerland' (p.196). Discussing the relationships between the three principal French officers and Rauffenstein, Tony Aldgate says:

> It is not harmonious, that is for sure, and for reasons beyond the fact that the French officers and Rauffenstein are wartime enemies, and they are his captives. There is an obvious divide between the two aristocratic career officers, Boeldieu and Rauffenstein, who have much in common, and 'the rest'. Not that the rest, mind you, easily equate with the masses. The French are all officers and there is not a private soldier in sight. They include a Greek scholar and an artist among the ranks, as well as the *nouveau riche* Jewish businessman, Rosenthal, and Maréchal who is, incidentally, an engineer. Still, Rauffenstein plainly sees them, with the exception of Boeldieu, as the lower classes, and to him they are the masses.

He is contemptuous of them and racist as well – notice his scrutiny of the
scholar's features and his scorn of Rosenthal.
    As Roberts comments, the film admirably dramatizes the shared
aristocratic assumptions of Rauffenstein and Boeldieu. (p.196)

A little later in the same unit Tony Aldgate turns to the 'wave of cultural critics'
who 'identify what they saw as the threat to society emanating from below',
writers whose work is evidence of 'The alienation of the writer from society'. You
might reflect on whether this alienation has anything to do with the war, or
whether its source goes much deeper. You should carefully revise this section,
reading again the extracts quoted from the poetry of T. S. Eliot and D. H.
Lawrence, and also the comments of the literary critic Valentine Cunningham,
and the historian Geoffrey Barraclough (pp.198–9).

    Turning to cinema, Tony Aldgate places considerable emphasis on Soviet
cinema, quoting Lenin – 'of all the arts for us the cinema is the most important' –
and Stalin – cinema is 'the greatest means of mass agitation'. The 'revolutionary
epics' of the 1920s, made by Eisenstein, Dovzhenko and Pudovkin, Aldgate says,
'served, essentially, to legitimize the revolution and the Bolshevik regime by
highlighting the plight of the masses in the Tsarist era'.

> Eisenstein's *Strike* (1925), for instance, dealt with the subject of industrial
> conflict in Tsarist society. In this film, the workers at a factory go on strike
> and thereafter suffer hardship, intimidation and finally death at the hands
> of the police and army authorities. Throughout the factory owners are
> presented as fat, cigar-smoking capitalists, intent only on their own
> gratification and profits, who care nothing for the grievances and misery of
> the downtrodden workers and their children. Its emotional message was
> enhanced by skilful and innovative editing – 'intellectual montage' – which
> juxtaposed disparate images so as to bring out the point being made. Thus,
> at a moment when police spies are introduced to the viewer, each spy is
> given the characteristics of an animal, such as an owl or a fox, and visually
> contrasted with the same, in order to emphasize the base and furtive
> nature of their roles. Similarly, at the climax of the film, the scenes of
> massacre of the workers are compared with gruesome images of bulls
> being slaughtered. [Note the elements of modernism here.] (p.202)

As Aldgate points out, the concept of intellectual montage was put to even greater
effect in Eisenstein's next film, *Battleship Potemkin* (1926). The Soviet epics were
banned by the British and French censorship authorities, though they could be
exhibited at private film societies. Of course, the direct relationship of these films
is to the revolution and developing Soviet society, rather than to the war itself.
Any connections that might be made would have to tease out the relationship
between the revolution and the war.

    Though propagandist in intent, these Soviet films are genuinely feature films.
Leni Riefenstahl's glorification of Hitler, *Triumph of the Will*, brilliantly done, was
pure documentary. Whether documentaries, newsreels, and 'straight' radio
broadcasts should be accounted part of popular culture, or treated separately as
mass communications, is merely a matter of definition. You should re-read what
Tony Aldgate says about newsreel coverage of Guernica in connection with my
comments on audio-cassette 2 about Picasso's painting.

    Censorship, basically to protect 'public morality', had been introduced for
British films *before* World War I. Tony Aldgate refers to one of the better

documented examples of censorship from the 1930s. On 15 March 1936 the British Board of Film Censors suggested to the Gaumont British Company that it would not be a good idea to proceed with the filming of Walter Greenwood's bestselling novel about the tragedies of unemployment, *Love on the Dole* (1933). The BBFC commented that the novel contained 'too much of the tragic and sordid side of poverty' and so 'it would be very undesirable as a film'. What is really significant about this with regard to the main concerns of this course is that *Love on the Dole*, the film, was not made until after the outbreak of war. It ended with a message, delivered by a Labour minister in the Churchill coalition government, saying that unemployment was part of the bad old days and would not exist in the new world to be built after the war. I don't want you to strain for connections between cultural artefacts and war. We study cultural artefacts because they are an important aspect of society; we are interested in their relationships with society, but if our analysis shows that war is an irrelevant factor, then saying so will all be part of our general exploration of historical causation.

6   CONCLUSION

On page 41 of Book II, Units 8–10 (dealing with World War I), I wrote:

> . . . the main fashion in writing about war in the last ten years or so has been to argue that neither World War I nor World War II had any significant or long-lasting effects in the realms of social change . . . Recent writers have tended to stress long-term structural and ideological trends, seeing the war as of little real significance compared with them, but rather as, perhaps, a temporary distortion, or even an interruption to long-term change.

The writers of Book V of our course have given slightly different weightings to, on the one side, the effects of war and, on the other, structural, ideological and other factors, including different assessments of the importance to be attributed to the concept of Americanization. The arguments that can be used in support of the significance of structural trends, for instance, have been most effectively rehearsed in the section on 'Continuity' by Bernard Waites in Unit 29.

Let me now make two final points:

1   Any attempt to provide an explanation in history (as, say, in an examination answer) must establish a balance between different causes (for example, 'war', 'structural factors').

2   Much depends on the precise questions being addressed: in some areas war may be very important; in other areas not at all important.

References

Addison, P. (1975) *The Road to 1945: British Politics and the Second World War*, Jonathan Cape.

Aldcroft, D. H. (1970) *From Versailles to Wall Street, 1919–1929*, Allen Lane.

Arendt, H. (1951) *The Origins of Totalitarianism*, André Deutsch.

Arendt, H. (1963) *On Revolution*, Penguin.

Bartov, O. (1985) *The Eastern Front 1941–1945: German Troops and the Barbarisation of*

Warfare, Macmillan in association with St Anthony's College, Oxford.

Bernard, P. and Dubief, H. (1988) *The Decline of the Third Republic 1914–1938*, Cambridge University Press.

Biddiss, M. (1977) *The Age of the Masses. Ideas and Society in Europe since 1870*, Penguin.

Calder, A. (1971) *The People's War: Britain 1939–1945*, Granada.

Carr, E. H. (1959) *Socialism in One Country, 1924–1926*, vol.2, Penguin.

Clark, M. (1984) *Modern Italy 1871–1982*, Longman.

Cohen, S. (1974) *Bukharin and the Bolshevik Revolution*, Wildwood House, Oxford University Press paperback edition, 1980.

Dyer, C. (1978) *Population and Society in Twentieth Century France*, Holmes and Meier.

Fussell, P. (1975) *The Great War and Modern Memory*, Oxford University Press.

Kitchen, M. (1988) *Europe between the Wars: A Political History*, Longman.

Kravchenko, V. (1947) *I Chose Freedom*, Hale.

McKibbin, R. (1974) *The Evolution of the Labour Party, 1910–1924*, Oxford University Press.

Maier, C. S. (1975) *Recasting Bourgeois Europe: Stabilization in France, Germany and Italy in the Decade after World War I*, Princeton University Press.

Marwick, A. (1968) *Britain in the Century of Total War: War, Peace and Social Change 1900–1966*, Bodley Head.

Marwick, A. (1974) *War and Social Change in the Twentieth Century*, Macmillan.

Marwick, A. (ed.) (1988) *Total War and Social Change*, Macmillan.

Mason, T. W. (ed.) (1981) 'Intention and explanation: a current controversy about the interpretation of National Socialism' in Hirschfeld, G. and Kettenacker, L. (eds) (1981) *Der Fuehrerstaat: Mythos und Realitat*, Klett-Cota.

Mayer, A. J. (1981) *The Persistence of the Old Regime*, Croom Helm.

Millar, J. and Nove, A. (1976) 'Was Stalin really necessary?' *Problems of Communism*, xxv, no.iv.

Mommsen, W. J. (1981) 'The German Revolution 1918–1920: political revolution and social protest movement' in Bessel, R. and Feuchtwanger, E. J. (eds) *Social Change and Political Development in Weimar Germany*, Croom Helm.

Nichols, R. (1977) *Ravel*, Dent.

Open University (1987) A323 *Weimar Germany: The Crisis of Industrial Society, 1918–1933*, Study Guide, Milton Keynes, The Open University.

Orenstein, A. (1975) *Ravel: Man and Musician*, Columbia University Press.

Roberts, J. M. (1989) *Europe 1880–1945*, Longman (first published in 1967).

Smith, A. (1976) *The Shadow in the Cave. The Broadcaster, the Audience and the State*, Quartet.

Stevenson, J. and Cook, C. (1979) *The Slump*, Quartet.

Tannenbaum, E. R. (1972) *The Fascist Experience: Italian Society and Culture 1922–1945*, Basic Books.

Welch, D. (1983) *Propaganda and the German Cinema 1933–1945*, Clarendon Press.

INDEX